SPIDER EATERS

SPIDER EATERS

A MEMOIR

Rae Yang

University of California Press
Berkeley · Los Angeles · London

University of California Press
Berkeley and Los Angeles, California

University of California Press, Ltd.
London, England

Library of Congress Cataloging-in-Publication Data

Yang, Rae, 1950– .
   Spider eaters : a memoir / Rae Yang.
      p.   cm.
   ISBN 0-520-20480-8 (alk. paper)
      1. China—History—Cultural Revolution, 1966–1969—
Personal narratives.   2. Yang family.   3. Peking (China)—
Biography.   4. Yang, Rae, 1950–   .   I. Title.
   DS778.7.Y42 1997
   951.05'092—dc 20
   [B]   96-31622
                                                              CIP

Printed in the United States of America
9   8   7   6   5   4   3   2   1

*To my dear Aunty, Tian Xi Zhen,
my grandmother, Zhang Hui Zhen,
and my parents*

Many historic lessons were obtained through tremendous sacrifice. Such as eating food—if something is poisonous, we all seem to know it. It is common sense. But in the past many people must have eaten this food and died so that now we know better. Therefore I think the first person who ate crabs was admirable. If not a hero, who would dare eat such creatures? Since someone ate crabs, others must have eaten spiders as well. However, they were not tasty. So afterwards people stopped eating them. These people also deserve our heartfelt gratitude.

—Lu Xun (1881–1936)

Contents

Illustrations follow page 114

Author's Note

In this book the italicized parts are meant to show what I thought and how I felt when the events were unfolding, in contrast with my understanding of such events afterwards.

The names of my family members are real. Other names are simplified or disguised.

I

A Strange Gift from the Pig Farm

Fifteen years ago when I left China for the United States, I wanted to forget the dreams my peers and I used to have. These we had inherited from our parents. Some of them had long since turned into nightmares for me. I wanted to open a new chapter in my life. Let the old fear, anger, and guilt melt away and the barriers between myself and others slide into the melting pot. But by and by I realized that this was just another dream.

I could not leave my past behind, as I could not help waking up at three o'clock in the morning. I acquired this habit in China in the early seventies. When I woke up, for a moment I did not know where I was. The chill in the air reminded me of Manchuria. Then as light slowly filtered into my bedroom, worries began to flood back into my mind.

The J-1 visa I was forced to take when I left China, a handicap in my hopes to compete with others in the United States.

The agents the CIA sent to the door of my university to check on me.

The liberal professor who told the agents to get out of his sight (while I had hoped that he might answer some of their questions in my favor).

The sense that I was an outsider, socially and culturally, then and thereafter, no matter how hard I tried to fit in.

The doubt that I was as competent as others . . .

Such thoughts told me that I was in America. My new life was not easy. What the future held for me I was not sure. So the old memories, though painful at times, had become quite reassuring.

So I turned my thoughts back, to China, to the pig farm where I worked on the night shift and acquired the habit of waking up at three o'clock. For a seventeen-year-old girl who had grown up in big cities—Bern, Geneva, and Beijing—the night shift was a tough job. The day before I had to work for more than ten hours like everybody else, racing after the pigs on the grazing land, feeding them, and cleaning the sties. At dusk others would finish their work and go back to the village to eat and sleep. After the last person was gone, I alone had the company of several hundred pigs. My duty was to protect them from whatever danger might arise during the night and to drive them out three times (at midnight, three o'clock, and dawn) to relieve themselves so they wouldn't mess up the sties.

On such nights the light of my oil lantern was small, a faint, shivering, yellow ring against the immense darkness that reigned over the huge swamp called the Great Northern Wilderness. Here the night wind flew high and the moon was as pale as a ghost. The grass around the pig farm grew to the height of a person in summer. Wolves, hungry for piglets, lurked in it. Outside my window, my dogs howled in the middle of the night like wolves, echoed by other dogs in the village; or maybe it was the wolves running across the plain who answered them. I really couldn't tell which was which.

When winter came the nights became endless. At four o'clock I lit my oil lamps, which I kept burning until after nine the next morning. Outside, all was covered with snow, two to three feet deep on the plain. On the southern side of the shacks, the snow formed a slope after the first blizzard. The tip of it nearly touched the eaves. Throughout winter the snow would not melt. After midnight the temperature dropped to forty degrees below zero, centigrade or Fahrenheit, it made no difference. The heavy old sheepskin coat Mother sent me felt like a piece of paper once I stepped out into the wind.

Sometimes when the region was pounded by a snowstorm, I remembered the stories the villagers told: some people lost their sense of direction in it. Scared to death, they kept running until they dropped to the ground. Afterwards they were frozen in the snow. The next April, if the wolves did not get there first, people would find their remains.

Even more unfortunate were those who perished within a stone's throw of their own homes. Blindfolded by the storm, they walked in endless circles, hour after hour. Being "walled up by ghosts," the local people called it. In such cases, people were doomed unless timely help reached them from the outside.

With such stories lurking at the back of my mind and the snoring of the pigs rising and falling all around me, I moved from sty to sty to carry out my duties. A lantern and a whip, I held in my two hands. A pair of sharp scissors was hidden in a pocket next to my heart; I would use the scissors as a last resort to defend myself.

Of course even at the age of seventeen, I was not so naive as to really believe that the scissors would save my life or my reputation if I were attacked. But what alternatives did I have? I once thought fire-crackers might work better. Yet how to keep them dry and light them in an emergency, I never quite figured out.

On the wall of our shack, somebody had left a gong. With a smile I stood in front of it and contemplated the idea. After a while I decided that a gong was no good either. The nearest house in the village was a good half-mile away from the pig farm. The weather was so cold in this region that people slept with their windows shut even in summer. During winter, sawdust was packed between windowpanes, the houses were lit-erally sealed up. If something happened on the pig farm during the night, no one would hear me no matter what I did. I'd better face the fact.

Actually I wouldn't need to work on the night shift and worry about such things if I had not volunteered to do so in the first place. Before I came to the pig farm, no one had ever imagined that a woman would work on the night shift. It had always been strictly a job for men. Then in 1969, somehow there was a temporary shortage of manpower on the pig farm. So I told Chen, the head of the farm, that he could count me in to work at night. When he realized that I meant what I said, he looked at me as if I were from another planet.

This was, however, not the first time that I volunteered myself. In the summer of 1968 I had volunteered to leave Beijing for the coun-tryside. I did this out of a conviction that it was not fair for some young people like my schoolmates and me to enjoy all the privileges China could offer, which included living in big cities, having access to top schools, good libraries, large bookstores, museums, parks, and theaters, while others had to stay in their native villages and never had a chance to prove themselves. In new China everybody should be equal. If we wanted to reform society, we ought to have the courage to let the change start from us. By giving up our privileges, we would make room for the children of the peasants. Let the hardship in the countryside temper us as revolutionary wars did our parents. Eventually we would eliminate the gap between cities and rural areas in China. This idea soon carried me to a small village in Manchuria called Cold Spring, a thousand miles northeast of Beijing.

In Cold Spring, before three months was over, I volunteered again. This time I went to the pig farm where the work was the dirtiest. I wanted the challenge. Ever since my childhood I had lived in clean houses with clean toilets. My worst nightmares had always been that squashy, smelly excrement surrounded and suffocated me. My feet got stuck in it. I could not move. The hot excrement seeped through my shoes. I was so disgusted that I woke up with goose bumps all over my body.

In my mind, such an ordeal would be a hundred times worse than all the tortures the revolutionary martyrs had gone through. Yet I knew that this way of thinking was wrong. It belonged to the exploiting classes. No doubt about it. Peasants in China loved excrement, using it as manure. So working on the pig farm, I reckoned, would be the most effective way to correct my thinking as well as my feelings.

The night shift was the third entry in my history of volunteering. It was also the last. After that, I discovered some unpleasant truth about volunteering: in China it always turned out this way. When you first volunteered, the leaders would be agreeably surprised and would praise you. Pretty soon, however, it became an obligation. They expected you to do it. But that was not the worst. The leaders would also use your example to put pressure on others and make everybody "volunteer." So a few months later when all the women on the pig farm had "volunteered" to work on the night shift and some of them, I knew, were quite uncomfortable doing this, I began to feel sorry about what I did.

The truth is, I did not feel too bad about my volunteering until the summer of 1971, when the night shift got Laomizi into trouble. Laomizi, which means Sleepy, was the nickname the villagers gave to a girl from Harbin, the capital city of Heilongjiang province. Like many others from the north, she was tall and plump, well developed physically at the age of eighteen. One night she worked on the night shift and something happened. The next morning Laomizi told people in the village that Chen had come during the night and raped her.

The incident occurred when I was on my first home leave. By the time I got back from Beijing, Laomizi was gone, transferred to another farm that was remote. It was usual practice in those days. Supposedly it would protect her. Thus I never had a chance to talk to her.

I heard, however, a great deal of gossip that was still spinning around in the village. The young women on the pig farm told me that before Laomizi left, she cried and said repeatedly, "What am I to do? How can I face people after today? I lost face for my parents. I lost face for my whole family. They will disown me. I don't want to live!"

Many of the villagers, however, men and women, believed that Laomizi was not raped but merely seduced by Chen. "She must have been willing at the time and regretted it only afterwards." Why? Because Chen was not a stranger. As the head of the pig farm, he had worked with her side by side and taught her many skills. In the evenings she was often seen at Chen's home, having a meal or using their sewing machine to mend her clothes.

While this was true, Laomizi was not the only one who did this. In fact, all the young women on the pig farm had worked with Chen, learned from him, and visited him at home in the evenings. Such activities were encouraged by the leaders as parts of our reeducation by the poor peasants. Chen was a poor peasant and a veteran of the Korean War. The exact type for us to "unite" with.

A few days later another argument prevailed in the village, which said that Laomizi was a fool. First she let herself be taken by a married man who was probably older than her father. Then she went around telling everybody that he had raped her. As a result, it would be useless to transfer her, for gossip would surely find its way to her new work unit. In the future who would want to marry such a woman? So if her reputation was ruined and her future was in jeopardy, she had no one else but herself to blame for it.

As for Chen, after he was questioned by Zhao, the political instructor who was the number-one leader of our village, he packed up his belongings, left the pig farm, and reported to work at the construction site. Seeing this, some people said Zhao was partial to Chen, because they were both from Yangzhou of Anhui province. Yet others said that Chen was hardly punished because it was not easy to punish a peasant in China. You could not strip him of his Party membership if he did not have one in the first place. You could not demote him, as he was already at the bottom of the society. Take away his city residency? That was out of the question. Expel him from the country? Where could we send him? So as the saying goes, "A dead pig is not afraid of boiling water." A peasant in China was a dead pig.

So this was how the Laomizi incident ended. Gradually people ran out of things to say about her and she was forgotten. Perhaps that was what she wanted. After she left the village, she never came back to visit us. Nor did she send letters to anyone. She simply vanished from our lives. Yet she comes back, in my dreams, and she stays, in my memory. Always a grown-up teenage girl, with rosy cheeks, big hands, and big feet. She is blushing and smiling. She is happy. I have never seen her cry.

Besides this incident, something else made me regret that I had worked on the night shift. In the beginning it was a small problem: the pig farm did not have an alarm clock, which did not seem to bother others. But without it, for a while I found it extremely hard to wake up at three o'clock.

To this day I remember vividly the panic I felt, when I opened my eyes in broad daylight, knowing that I had overslept. As a result, the pigsties were an awful mess and others had to toil for hours under the low roof, attacked by mosquitoes from all sides, to clean them. This unpleasant truth I would soon have to reveal to my fellow workers, and their eyes would shame me to death even if they said nothing. It would be useless to try to explain or apologize.

Yet buying an alarm clock was out of the question. In those years my wages were thirty-two yuan a month. Everything had to come out of this budget: food was twelve yuan a month; the rest had to cover my clothes, shoes, working gloves, postage stamps, toothpaste, tooth-brush, soap, shampoo, toilet paper, feminine napkins, candles, batter-ies, plus a few cans of fruit that I could not resist. On top of this, I needed to save thirty yuan in two years for a train ticket to Beijing or else I wouldn't be able to have a home visit. Taking these into consideration, I decided that an alarm clock at more than ten yuan was beyond my means and I would have to cope without it, like everybody else.

Gradually I trained myself into waking up at exactly three o'clock, as if I had a magic clock ticking in my head. At first I was thrilled by what I had accomplished. Later, however, it became a scourge. The alarm went off every night at three o'clock, on the nights I worked and the ones I didn't. Three years later I left the pig farm and began to work in the fields, and the invisible clock kept waking me up.

Another two years passed, I left the Great Northern Wilderness and began to study with my parents. The old habit followed me back home like a ghost. Even the Pacific Ocean could not stop it from chasing me. Therefore the pig farm gave me a souvenir I was unable to forsake.

Many times when I woke up in the middle of the night and could not find my way back to what the Chinese call *heitianxiang* (the black and sweet homeland), I was so annoyed that I found myself in tears. When I took up my studies again in 1973, seven years had elapsed with-out my hand ever touching a textbook. At the age of twenty-two, it wasn't easy for me to start all over. I hated to lose sleep at night, know-ing the next day my head would be a big jar of paste, thick and heavy; nothing would register there. At such times I wished I could make a deal with a deity or even the devil himself. I was willing to give up ten years of my life if only he could rid me of this cursed habit.

Despite the bitter regrets, now when I look back on it, I must say that waking up at three did me some good as well. For instance, it made me remember and think about my dreams. The ones I had while I was awake and those I had in my sleep. Most of them would have been forgotten, if I had not suddenly waked up in the middle of the night.

On the farm I hardly had time to think about dreams or anything. By day the work was very hard. At night I shared a room with nine other women. Five slept side by side on one big bed on the southern side of the room; the other five on the northern side. Between the two beds there was a passage some five or six feet wide. In such a room I had privacy only when I woke up at three o'clock.

Knowing that no one was watching me, I felt safe enough to ask myself: what kind of person am I? A die-hard Manchu aristocrat like Nainai, my grandmother, or an educated new peasant in a new society? Am I a true believer of communism or a hidden counterrevolutionary with many dangerous thoughts? Is my life meaningful only because I can serve the people or work for the revolution? What is the purpose of my life? What things am I willing to sacrifice for the sake of my dreams? And what are those, I know by now, I won't give up despite the dreams my parents and I have cherished? In trying to make our dreams come true, what foolish things have we done? What crimes have we committed? If the crimes were committed out of good intentions for the world, would heaven punish us for them or pardon us? If there is no retribution from heaven, should there be no indictment from the court of my own conscience?

2

Old Monkey Monster

Speaking of dreams, I recall a famous Chinese dream in which Chuang Tzu, an ancient philosopher, became a butterfly. In the spring wind he fluttered his wings; he danced among flowers. He drank dew and rested under a green leaf. His heart was ever so happy and serene. When he woke up, he was Chuang Tzu again. Wearing a scholar's hat and a long robe, he sat in his study meditating on the nature of all beings including himself. "Am I really Chuang Chou who dreamed that I was a butterfly, or am I a butterfly who is dreaming that I am Chuang Chou?"*

When I look back on what I have been, sometimes I, too, am perplexed. The pictures that remain vivid in my memory don't seem to fit together.

—In the fifties there was a black-eyed and black-haired Chinese girl on Lake Geneva. A precious pearl on the palms of her parents, followed everywhere by her devoted Chinese nanny. Pink satin dress. White leather shoes. Colorful hairpins. She was proud. She was nice to people. Tourists were charmed by her. They asked to take her picture.

—In 1966 there was a Red Guard who jumped on a train and traveled over a thousand miles to Guangzhou to spread the fire of the Cultural Revolution. She criticized First Party Secretary Zhao Ziyang to his face for his tolerance of capitalism and saw drops of sweat as large as soybeans roll down his face. An order issued by her and her comrades shook the city like a hurricane. In its wake, thousands of privately owned shops were devastated.

—In the early seventies there was a peasant on a pig farm. Her face was dark brown and weather-beaten. Her hair was as dry and brittle as straw in late fall. She had strong muscles and a loud voice. She loved to eat dog meat with raw garlic. Her face did not change color after she gulped down several cups of Chinese liquor, which was more than

Chou is the personal name of Chuang Tzu, which means "Master Chuang."

8

60 percent alcohol. Although her clothes and boots carried a lot of stinking mud, the work she did was neat and she took great pride in it.

—In the nineties there is a Chinese professor in an American college. She has a Ph.D in comparative literature. She teaches Chinese language and a variety of courses on Chinese culture and literature. To her American colleagues and students, she is very Chinese. Yet her Chinese friends say that she is westernized. Some suspect that she is a feminist, because she is too independent. She has a son, whom she chose to raise by herself after a divorce. It seems unthinkable that she is doing quite all right without a husband.

Can these be the same person? Can this person be me? Among these, which is the real me and which are the roles I have played? Once in a while I even doubt my memory. But I am sure of one thing: since I was a child, I had a feeling that the materials of which I was made were ill at ease with one another.

My parents brought me into this world on December 1, 1950. My father, people said, was an old revolutionary. He joined the Chinese Communist Party in the early 1940s. My mother, who graduated from Yanjing University (now called Beijing University) the year before I was born, was a new enthusiast for the Maoist revolution. She, like many of her peers, believed that only the Chinese Communist Party could save China. It would provide secure jobs for intellectuals and liberate workers and peasants from slavery. It would root out corruption that had plagued all the previous governments and revive China's economy that had collapsed in the 1940s.

One thing the adults liked to tell my generation when we were young was that we were the most fortunate, because we were born in new China and grew up under the red flag. In my case only part of this was true. I was born in new China. But when I was one year old, my parents took me to Switzerland. There I grew up under a red flag, not one with five golden stars symbolizing the Communist Party and four hundred million Chinese, but one with a large white cross on it. That must have messed things up for me from very early on.

In Switzerland we lived in Bern and Geneva, in quiet and comfortable surroundings. At that time there were four of us in our family: Father, Mother, Aunty, and I. From Monday to Saturday, I hardly saw my parents. They were both busy working at the Chinese consulate. In the morning they always left in a great hurry; in the evening unfinished work, meetings, or banquets kept them away. By the time they got home,

I was already fast asleep. On Sunday, Mother usually slept until noon and Father until two o'clock in the afternoon. So in those years Aunty was about the only one who was always there for me.

Aunty, I later found out, was no relative of ours. She was my nanny. My paternal grandmother, whom I called Nainai, hired her in Beijing shortly before I was born. Five days after Mother gave birth to me, that is, as soon as we left the hospital, Aunty took over the work from Mother. Henceforth day and night, it was she who fed me, washed me, and rocked me in her arms. I fell asleep to her soft wordless songs. It was her smile and her voice that I remembered when I was a baby. My own mother, on the other hand, left me when I was barely one month old. She flew to Switzerland to resume her work. As for my father, I did not meet him until I was one year old. At that time he came back to report on work. While he was in Beijing, he celebrated my birthday with me. Afterwards he took Aunty and me to Switzerland.

On arrival at our new home, Father said: "Now in China it is a new society. Everybody is equal. There are no more masters and servants. People are of one big family. So let Rae, our little girl, call her Aunty instead of nanny from the start."

Thus I learned to call her Aunty. For me, the word Aunty was dearer than Mother and Father put together, and over the years I became more important to Aunty than her own daughter, whom she had tried hard to forget. I do not know when my parents found out how I felt or how they took it when they found it out. Were they sad or glad of the fact that because of their dedication to the revolutionary work, they let a nanny steal the heart of their only daughter whom they insisted they loved very much?

When I say this, I do not mean that I did not love my parents. Of course I did. Yet that love was different. It was rational, unlike the mysterious tie that bound Aunty and me together, body and soul. By this, I mean if a misfortune was about to befall Aunty a thousand miles away, I would feel it in my blood. I would have bad dreams at night. Such premonitions were hard to explain; yet they turned out to be right when I had them in 1978. In contrast, when my mother died suddenly in 1976, I did not feel anything. I learned the bad news the next day from Father's telegram.

In the late 1950s, when I came back to attend elementary school in Beijing, I discovered that my attachment to Aunty was not unique. Many of my classmates, who were children of high-ranking cadres, were just like me. They loved their nannies, aunties, or grandmothers more than their own parents. Sometimes the parents became so jealous that they told the nannies to go home. Others let the nannies stay for the children's sake. Of these parents, many were richly rewarded a few years later. That is, when the Cultural Revolution broke out and the parents got into trouble, the nannies took the children into their own homes and brought them up as if they were their own.

Aunty's love for me made her blind to my shortcomings. To her I was the best child in the whole world. My younger brothers were extraordinary kids too. But I was undoubtedly the smartest and prettiest. She was proud of me at all times.

According to her, I could remember things that occurred very early in my life. Such memories were of isolated scenes. The sight, the sound, the smell, and the touch stayed with me. Some of them were quite vivid in my mind. But the context was lost. She and my parents often had to supply the where and when.

In Cold Spring village, the scene that came most often to my mind was of our second-floor apartment in Bern. In the morning bright sunshine poured through the large windows and glass doors. I opened my eyes in the warmth. I saw Aunty's face break into a gentle smile; tiny wrinkles appeared at the corners of her eyes. I knew soon she'd go to the nearby bakery to buy my favorite pastry. "Little mice bread" was the nickname Aunty and I gave it.

The short while she was away was the most exciting time of my day. I tried to hide myself in the closets, on the balcony, or behind a piece of furniture, knowing Aunty would soon be back and would seek me out. The rest of the day I did not have many games to play. I had a room filled with toys: dolls, stuffed animals, music boxes, little houses, kitchen and tea sets, a train that ran around the room . . . but the problem was: I had no one to play with me.

For five years I was the only child. Although we had neighbors, my parents never tried to socialize with them. Was it because of rules that forbade them to make friends among the local people? Or was it the neighbors who were afraid of being tainted by us, knowing that we were from red China? Whatever the reason, I hardly had a friend in my childhood. So in those years the seed of loneliness dropped into my heart. Later, when it grew into a monstrous tree, I tried very hard to cut it down but I failed. Now I am an adult, I realize loneliness is my fate and I might as well enjoy it: I can sit in the shade of this gigantic tree, far away from the comings and goings of the world. Breathing a deep sigh of sadness and relief, I forget the intricate network of relationships in China and elsewhere.

Despite the loneliness, my childhood was not unhappy. Father, Mother, and Aunty all loved me. I loved them too, Aunty especially. By then, Aunty was in her early fifties. Her long hair was still mostly black, but silver threads were beginning to show around her temples. Each morning she would spend some time combing and oiling her hair. The hair oil sent out a mild sweetness to my nose. Afterwards she'd coil her hair up and pin it into a bun, which looked so elegant behind her head. This, Aunty told me, was the traditional hairstyle for a married woman in China. She had been dressing her hair like this for more than thirty years.

Aside from her hair, her clothes were also traditional. In my memory Aunty was always wearing a slender cotton dress called *qipao*, which was either silver gray or indigo blue. It fitted her perfectly because she made it herself. European fashion did not affect her. In Switzerland, the only Western garment she had was a fur coat, and even that was a gift from my parents.

Like most women who grew up in old China, Aunty had never been to school. When she came into our family, she did not know how to write her own name. Her mind, however, was a treasure box, filled with stories. Some she learned from Peking operas to which she loved to "listen" (as people in old Beijing put it, rather than see). Others were folktales told to her by her own grandmother. It was from these stories that I came to know China, my native country, which was thousands of miles away: the peasants, the water buffalo, the rice fields, the forbidden city in Beijing, the emperor and his concubines, scholars and the imperial examinations, ancestors who protected their descendants and depended on them for food and money in the nether world, and the various animal spirits that obtained Tao and magic power through meditation.

The old monkey monster in my favorite story was such an animal spirit. To this day I remember vividly how Aunty told it to me.

"Once upon a time there was an old monkey monster who lived in the deep mountains. One day he saw a little girl in the village who was very pretty. He started a whirlwind that darkened the sky and put dust into everybody's eyes. In the wind, the old monkey monster grabbed the girl. Carrying her under his arm, he flew over many mountains and took her to his home, which was a dark, smelly cave.

"He asked the little girl to be his wife; but she said no. The old monkey monster was very angry. But he did not eat the girl. He shut her up in the cave.

"One morning when the old monkey monster went out to gather wild fruit, the girl's mother arrived. She had followed the whirlwind all the way to the cave. When she found her daughter there, she took her into her arms and the two of them cried. Afterwards she taught the girl what to say and went into hiding.

"Soon the old monkey monster came back, in a gust of wind. He came into the cave and sniffed around, saying: 'The smell of a stranger person! The smell of a stranger person! If I catch her, I will eat her up!'

"The girl said: 'Nonsense! There is no stranger person here. Only my mother came to visit us. She has a secret remedy that can cure your festering eyes.'

"When the old monkey monster heard this, he was very glad. For many years his eyes had been red and watery. They bothered him a lot. So he asked eagerly: 'Where is your mother? Quickly bring her in. I want to see her. I will not eat her!'

"Hearing this, the mother came forward. She had gathered a lot of tree gum on her way, which she melted in a big wok and spread on a long piece of foot-binding cloth. She told the old monkey monster to sit still and shut his eyes while she put the medicine on. She wrapped the cloth round his head many times.

"'You must keep your eyes shut and do not move for three days. If you move or open your eyes before that, the medicine will not work and your eyes will never be cured!' After she said this, she took her daughter by the hand and the two of them sneaked out of the cave. They returned home safe and sound. Three days later when the old monkey monster tried to open his eyes, he couldn't. For the glue had dried up. The cloth stuck to the old monkey monster's hair and skin. He could never get it off and open his eyes. After that, the mother and the girl lived together for many, many happy years."

I loved this story. Each time I listened to it, Aunty's voice made me sense the danger and I was a little scared. I imagined myself to be the little girl who was snatched away by an old monkey monster. Yet I knew that I was safe, for Aunty was holding me with both her arms. Aunty, I believed, loved me as much as the little girl's mother did, and she was every bit as smart and brave. In the future she could and she would save me from the grip of any monsters.

Another scene I remembered was the pavement in Bern. In the spring when it rained, the pavement was covered with earthworms; I did not dare let my feet touch it. On such days Father would carry me to places on his shoulders, and I loved it there! My father by then was just over thirty. He was tall and handsome, always well dressed. I was very proud of him. He walked with long, springy steps on the sidewalk, overtaking other pedestrians. From time to time he rocked me a little. One step toward the left; one step toward the right. I was scared, so I held on tighter to his neck.

Besides earthworms, I was afraid of numerous other things. For instance, at home people had to warn me before they flushed the toilet; Aunty had to make sure I was out of the kitchen before she put vegetables into a hot wok. On the playground I was afraid of the swing and nobody could make me climb to the top of the slide. The seesaw was better, but when my end went up, it had to move very slowly and never go any higher than Aunty's waist. The sandbox was the only place where I felt safe. As a result, each day I made more cakes than the baker from across the street.

In winter after snow had fallen, sometimes Mother would take me to a small slope behind our house for sledding. I wore a little white fur coat and Mother a long green woolen overcoat. The new snow was soft. My footsteps were small and Mother's big. On our way we stopped beneath a leafless tree on which crimson apples hung. Pretty little birds were picking at them. Mother whistled to the birds and the little birds answered her. Then we were at the slope and the sled began to move. The wind blew into my face. I had to shut my mouth and hold my breath. Involuntary tears of fear fell down my cheeks like a little stream.

Once our lives were really in danger, Aunty said. By then I was four. "One day," she said, "it was in May; your parents took us boating on a mountain lake. It was a nice day. Warm and sunny. Your father was half asleep. The boat drifted by itself. Suddenly he saw a sign—there was a waterfall downstream. Alarmed, he jumped up and tried to row the boat back. But he couldn't. At that place the lake narrowed. It was like a big river. The water was swift. Your mother tried to help. After a while, the sun was setting and no other people were in sight. We were all terribly frightened.

"I held you tightly in my arms. I thought if we were to go down that waterfall, I would die with you. At that moment I was really sorry I had come all the way to this foreign country to die. It was so far away from home. Our spirits would be lost. We'd be hungry ghosts for eternity.

"All this while your mother was furious; she scolded your father non-stop. Your father was furious too after a while. So he started to yell back. The two of them quarreled as if heaven and earth had been turned upside down. Yet in the meantime they rowed together as fast as they could."

"What happened next? Did we go down the waterfall?" I asked.

"Of course not, you silly child! We were rescued by a steamboat."

"Aunty! Was I afraid at the time?"

"No," she said, "you were asleep in my arms. I did not wake you up."

So on the day when our lives were really in danger, I was the only one who was not afraid. I was glad to hear that. By then my parents took me out more often, to parks, restaurants, and theaters. This I liked very much, not because I was sophisticated enough to appreciate the food and the performances. It was because I had a feeling that the people I met liked me. Mother agreed with me a few years later when we talked about this.

"People liked you because you were nice and sweet!" she said with a great deal of annoyance in her voice. "What has gotten into you and made you change so much after we returned to China that I can hardly recognize you?"

I had no answer to her question. It was true that my temper changed for the worse when I reached the age of seven. Somehow I lost the desire to be a sweet little girl.

My family went back to China when I was five. We traveled by train, on which we had a compartment to ourselves. Father, Mother, Aunty, and I each had a bed. My little brother, Lian, who was a baby, slept in a basket under Aunty's bed. Day after day I sat in front of the window to watch the scenery. The great cities of Europe were left behind. Vast wilderness of Siberia, Mongolia, and Manchuria rushed forward to welcome me back. Snow flakes in summer, tall grass to the end of the sky, yellow flowers, and blue lakes. Half a month later our train pulled into Yongding Gate Station in Beijing.

From there we went to Nainai's house, which was situated to the east of the forbidden city in a place known as Wangfujing. When we were in Switzerland, my paternal grandfather died of lung cancer. So by now Nainai was the head of the household. In fact, many said she was in charge even when her husband was alive.

3

Nainai's Story Turned into a Nightmare

In my memory, Nainai's house is always what it looked like in 1956, when Nainai, her two sons, their wives and children, as well as her daughter, whom I called Third Aunt, lived together in it. In the real world, however, the beauty and elegance of this old Beijing residence was destroyed. In 1966, when the Cultural Revolution broke out, six families who called themselves "revolutionary masses" moved in without the consent of Nainai or anybody else. They put Nainai, who was then bedridden with diabetes, into a small storage room that had no windows. Not even servants of the family in the old society had lived in this room. For more than five years Nainai lived there by herself. In the end, she died in it alone.

The six families, on the other hand, divided the house up among themselves. Soon they dug out Nainai's tree peonies, leveled Third Aunt's roses, turned the covered corridors into storage rooms, and built makeshift kitchens in the courtyards, using whatever material they could get hold of: concrete, broken bricks, plywood, and felt. The place was so ugly that I did not want to set eyes on it anymore.

Back in 1956 when we first came back from Switzerland, Nainai's house had its ancient beauty intact. In the compound four rows of bungalows, made of gray bricks and wooden pillars, paralleled one another. Along the front of each bungalow there was a rain veranda. The verandas were linked up at both ends by covered corridors, which had wooden pillars, balustrades, and tiled roofs. On the beams were paintings of birds, flowers, and landscapes, the color of which had long since grown faint, while the tops of the balustrades were made shiny by those who sat on them. Beyond the corridors, gray brick walls enclosed the entire compound. In old Beijing many houses were built in this style. People call them *siheyuar* (yards enclosed on four sides).

In Nainai's *siheyuar,* the first row of bungalows that had its back against the street was the *xiafang* (the lower houses). This row was slightly lower than other houses and the windows faced north, which meant the rooms would not get sunshine in the winter, nor much of the cool breeze in the summer. When my great-grandfather and grandfather were alive, I was told, many servants used to live there. Among them were the family's driver, tailor, gardener, and a chef who came from Yangzhou. This chef was the envy of other servants, because he earned one hundred silver dollars a month, a large sum in old Beijing in the twenties.

The fancy food he cooked, however, my father did not like to eat. Father, when he was a college student, preferred to eat *wowotou* (steamed corn-flour bread) and salted vegetables in the lower houses. From the servants whom he befriended, Father learned what the university did not teach him. He came to know how hard the lives of the working people were in old China and how unfair the society was: the rich lived in luxury and extravagance. The poor worked like horses and oxen from childhood to old age. Yet they could hardly fill their bellies and support their families. When the blood and sweat were wrung out of them at old age, they'd die in the street like cockroaches. . . .

For two years Father ate *wowotou* in the lower houses and thought about the social injustice he witnessed. Afterwards he decided that mere thoughts were not enough, he ought to put his thoughts into action. So he left home and joined the Eighth Route Army led by the Chinese Communist Party in their fight to drive out the Japanese invaders and to build a new China. In this new China, Father thought, everybody would be equal and all would be free. No more exploitation and oppression. No more masters and servants.

When new China was established in 1949, all the servants in Nainai's house left except two old women. One was Third Aunt's wet nurse. Everybody called her Old Nanny. The other was bought by Nainai's father from the south and came into this family as part of Nainai's dowry. They insisted that they belonged to Nainai and refused to leave. So Nainai let them stay. When I saw them, they were both in their seventies. A lot of white hair, walnut faces, backs bent down, quick tiny feet, which were bound ever since they were five or six. Though no one asked them to work, they were always busy, dusting furniture with chicken feather dusters, sweeping the floor with bare brooms, sprinkling the yard, washing, and picking vegetables . . . Their help was actually much needed, for at that time Nainai hired only one person who would come during the day to do grocery shopping and cook for the entire family.

The other three rows of bungalows in Nainai's house were the upper houses. Taller and facing south, they were naturally warm in winter and cool in summer. The first row of the upper houses was the guest house. Being nearest to the street and closer to the servants' quarters, it gave the guests convenience and the host family privacy. Despite the fact that in the past the word privacy could not be found in the Chinese vocabulary, the layout of Nainai's house convinces me that this nameless thing did matter. For many people, however, it was a luxury they could not afford.

In 1956 the guest house was soon taken by my maternal grandparents, who moved from Shanghai to Beijing to be near to their two children: my mother and her younger brother. This uncle of mine whom I called Jiujiu was studying Russian at Beijing Foreign Language Institute. Russian was a hot subject in China in the fifties. Everybody wanted to learn it, including my parents. But their studies did not go very far. For in just a few years, Russian Big Brothers became Russian Revisionists. Trade and exchange with them were cut off. The foreign experts went home. Russian became a useless language. Nobody wanted to study it anymore. While Jiujiu and his colleagues lost their jobs, English became popular again.

Nainai herself and Third Aunt occupied the second row of the upper houses. Third Aunt was a medical doctor. She worked at Beijing Union Hospital, a prestigious hospital in Beijing. People told me that she had studied in a medical school for eight years before she became a doctor. It seemed such a long time that I couldn't even imagine it. In 1956 Third Aunt was in her early thirties. She was still single and she had many friends. On Sundays they came to visit her. Some were doctors like her, others were patients she had cured. They would have tea on the veranda and talk. From a distance I could hear their voices, which were loud and clear. Nobody had learned to speak under his or her breath behind closed doors yet.

When no one came to visit, Third Aunt would put on her blue cotton jacket and work among the flower beds. Both she and Nainai loved flowers. The two of them turned the second courtyard, which was the most spacious, into a fabulous garden where winter jasmines, lilacs, purple swallow orchids, tree peonies, roses, and chrysanthemums bloomed one after another from early spring to late autumn.

The family's dining room was also in this row, a big room with windows facing south. Along its northern wall a small room was partitioned out; because it had no window, it was dark day and night. Before 1949 the family used it to store food, which was sometimes in short supply, and then the prices would shoot up. So all big families in Beijing laid away rice, flour, cooking oil, and other stuff to cope with such emergencies. In the fifties people no longer worried about sudden food shortages. So the storage room was quite forgotten. If it had not been for what happened to Nainai during the Cultural Revolution, I doubt if I would remember there was such a room at all.

The last row of houses was occupied by our family and the family of my uncle. I called him Second Uncle, because he was Father's younger brother. We lived in the east end and they in the west, sharing a rather dark hallway in the middle.

Little Ox and Little Dragon were my cousins. Little Ox was one year older and Little Dragon one year younger than me. Little Ox I admired because he was such a good climber of Tai Lake rocks, which were shaped by the wind and waves of Tai Lake in the south over thousands of years. Because of their unique beauty, in the olden days people moved them several hundred miles up north along the Grand Canal to decorate the emperor's palaces and rich men's courtyards. In Nainai's house there were about ten of them. The three best-looking ones stood outside the corridors in the second yard. The rest were piled in the middle of the third yard under a huge locust tree. The rocks had many round holes in them; some large and some small, which made the climbing easier and the hide-and-seek more fun. After I learned from Little Ox how to climb the rocks, I was no longer the timid girl in the sandbox.

Inside the rooms, all the furniture was made of hardwood. Wardrobes were so tall that they almost touched the ceilings. Tables and chairs had pieces of marble inlaid in them, the natural shapes of the black and white in these slabs made them look like traditional landscape paintings. Around the marble the wood was carved, showing designs of clouds, waves, pines, or bats. Also carved was the wall on the western side of Nainai's room. I used to stand in front of it to make out shapes of vases, fans, incense burners, old style books, and scrolls. People told me that this wall was designed by the previous owner of this house named Pu Xuezhai. He was the emperor's relative and a well-known artist. The wood he used was faintly fragrant. At nightfall, however, the fragrance of the wall was drowned out by that which came from Nainai's snow-white tuberoses. People in Beijing called them Fragrant Jade of the Night, which Nainai always kept in a large antique porcelain vase on a long hardwood table.

The sweet scent of tuberoses always reminds me of Nainai's stories, which she tended to tell when the sun began to cast long shadows over the western corridor. Unlike Aunty, Nainai had studied with tutors when she was young. On her nightstand I saw books such as *Three Hundred Poems of the Tang Dynasty* and *Dream of the Red Chamber*. But the stories she told me were not from books. They were true stories.

From her I learned that our ancestors were Manchus who originally lived in Mongolia. For generations they had been herdsmen, hunters, and warriors who were born, raised, and died in the saddle. On the boundless grassland their horses ran as fast as the wind. The hoofs drummed the ground. When they fought, their bows opened like the full moon and arrows flew across the sky like shooting stars. For one word of promise, they'd lay down their lives for a friend. Because of an insult, they'd plunge a white blade in a man's body and pull out a steamy red one.

In the seventeenth century the Manchus fought their way down south. The Great Wall was unable to stop them. Soon they watered their horses in the southern sea. Nainai's ancestors must have distinguished themselves in the war, for in the years to come their descendants were given high official positions by the emperors of the Qing dynasty. After two centuries, however, their fiery temper cooled down. Their blood grew thinner and their faces turned pale. They acquired polite language and good manners. Warriors were no longer born into this family. The sons became civil officials and the daughters gentle ladies.

Nainai told me that her grandfather once served as *xingbu shangshu*, minister of punishment. The position was very prominent, similar to that of a justice in the supreme court. Yet the old man was miserable day and night, according to Nainai, because he was superstitious. He believed that people would all become ghosts after they died. Those who died of natural causes would become peaceful ghosts, while those who died by violence turned into ferocious ones. The peaceful ghosts would stay in the world of yin and not bother human beings. But the ferocious ones would sooner or later come back to this world to avenge themselves.

This belief made the old man especially uneasy in the fall when the *qiushen* (autumn trials) came round. This was an old practice in the Qing dynasty. Each year when the bleak autumn wind rose, the important convicts of the entire country would be sent under escort to Beijing for a final trial. After this, the condemned men and women would be dragged out to Caishikou, a marketplace in Beijing, to be executed. Nainai's grandfather had to preside over the trials and the beheading.

On the execution ground, he sat behind a huge desk in his official robe, surrounded by many bodyguards. His words, every one of them, were echoed loudly by soldiers and executioners. In his hand he held a writing brush dipped in red ink. One after another, the executioners presented the convicts to him. His job was to put a red dot on the labels that bore their names to indicate the final approval of the verdict. Once his brush fell, the person's fate was sealed. All hopes were lost. Executioners as fierce as wolves and tigers would grab the person by the arms and drag him or her out. The head was chopped off on the spot. Blood poured out from the headless body. A scream of intolerable pain and terror was cut short.

The beheading went on. The executioners' eyes turned red. A large crowd, hundreds of men and women, gathered to watch the event. Some cheered at the top of their voices; others grew pale and were made sick by the sight. The yellow earth drank the blood like red wine. Finally even the earth couldn't take it anymore. Dark puddles formed on the ground. A fishy smell permeated the air.

While this was going on, Nainai's grandfather, an awe-inspiring figure representing the great empire and the law, was in despair. This hateful position was a "favor" bestowed on him by the dowager empress and the emperor. He did not dare refuse it. Thinking it over and over, he could not come up with any feasible solution, except wishing that someday they'd bestow this "favor" on someone else. But on that occasion he could hardly think, because the doomed men and women's eyes were fastened on him. Some were pleading. Others were desperate. Some drowned in tears. Some were spurting fire. Amidst panic and pain, once in a while he would be startled by a pair of eyes that were unusually calm and lucid.

All these eyes were like sharp long needles that poked through his body and soul. Sitting up on high, he did not know how to escape them. He was paralyzed. His heart filled with terror. He knew that people who looked at him with such eyes would never forget him. They would remember him through life and death and three reincarnations. Sooner or later they would come back, seek him out, and make him pay the debt of blood.

Of the many stories Nainai told me about our ancestors, this one somehow sank deepest into my heart. In the sixties when class struggle was emphasized, for a few years I really wished that I had never heard any stories from Nainai so that thought reform would not be such a difficult task for me. In fact, in those years I even wished that I had never had such a Nainai and those ancestors of hers. They were bloodsuckers, parasites, smiling tigers, piles of garbage, cow ghosts, and snake demons . . . If I could erase them from my memory, I would become a reliable successor to the revolutionary cause like my schoolmates.

In 1966, just as I was secretly congratulating myself, for I believed that I had finally made a clear break with Nainai and her ancestors, I had a strange dream. It happened soon after the Cultural Revolution began, when I was a Red Guard. By day I was busy writing *dazibao* (criticism in big characters) and attending thousand-people mass rallies to criticize capitalist-roaders, reactionary academic authorities, foreign spies, and renegades. I was extremely serious about the Cultural Revolution. I believed that through this revolution the Chinese people, led by our great leader Chairman Mao, would wipe out bureaucracy, corruption, and privileges from among government officials. We would build an exemplary society for the entire world.

At night, however, I had no control over my dreams. In one dream there was a mass rally just like the ones I had attended in those days; but instead of the capitalist-roaders and reactionary academic authorities, I was the person the crowd struggled against. Around me, the frenzied revolutionary masses were yelling at the top of their voices. Everybody hated me. I was a tiny boat sinking in a vast raging ocean. I wanted to speak up, to debate with others and defend myself, but no one was willing to listen to me. They were all convinced that I was guilty. So they sentenced me to death. The sentence was to be carried out immediately . . .

Next I was on my way to the execution ground. Somehow my grass-green army uniform and Red Guard's armband disappeared. I was wearing a long white robe, which was the costume worn by innocent convicts in traditional Chinese operas. Around my wrists and ankles, iron chains were dangling and clanging. A bleak autumn wind was rising; my silk robe fluttered and my hairband flew up. People lined the street to watch me, thousands of them. When I looked them in the face, I could not tell whether they were glad or sad. They all seemed to be wearing masks.

As for myself, I remember that in my dream I felt very sick at heart because I was wronged and I had to die so young. But I said to myself: As the sentence could not be changed, I'd better meet my end heroically. There was no point in making a scene and disgracing myself at the last moment. I wanted to keep my memory intact. That much at least I could do.

Then I knew I was dead. My body was lying on the ground, but somehow I still had consciousness. I saw many people walk by my dead body. Perhaps it was a parade. This time they were not wearing masks, so I recognized my classmates, friends, neighbors, and relatives. Nobody stopped to look at me. Not a soft sigh was uttered; not a single tear. They all fixed their eyes on something high and glorious. I wanted to scream at them to attract their attention. But I found that I had lost my voice. It was a soundless world. Eventually they all passed me by and the light began to fade. I knew that I was really dead.

4

Nainai Failed Her Ancestors

Reflecting on the fact that I could not forget Nainai's stories no matter how hard I had tried, I realize that I am more attached to her than I once cared to admit. As I was her only granddaughter, she told me more stories about her life than she told my cousins.

To people who did not know her well, Nainai's life in the old society appeared carefree. Her forefathers had power and privileges, her father-in-law and husband had a great deal of money. Only I knew that Nainai's life was not as easy as others might have imagined. In a way it was extremely difficult, owing to the upheavals in China and the fact that she was a woman.

When Nainai was young, she had been to many places in China. Those were the good years in her life. At the beginning of the twentieth century the emperor granted her father an official position, not because the latter had any remarkable talent, but for the sake of his ancestors. At first Nainai's father was a local magistrate in Hunan, a province south of the Yangzi River. A few years later he was promoted to the position of *niesi,* also called *nietai* in Guizhou province. There he was the number-three official and, like his father, he was charged with the administration of justice.

His family, including his wife, Nainai, and a younger brother, went to these places with him. At first they traveled along the Grand Canal by official boats. Later they rode in covered wagons. On the way Nainai was deeply impressed by the beautiful spring on the Yuan River, the various dialects that Nainai's family could not understand, the distinct flavors of the local food (some were so spicy that they set fire to people's mouths, others were as cool and smooth as water from an ancient well), the minorities with their fantastic costumes and festivals, the hard life of the peasants, especially the women who in the south had to do the hardest physical labor as well as take care of the kids and housework . . .

Such experiences in her youth made Nainai different from her peers who were confined to the inner quarters of their fathers' residences.

"Never to come out the front gate, nor to walk across the second gate"—the Chinese saying testifies how far such young ladies were permitted to go in those days. The theory behind this was that if a young lady never sets eyes on strangers, her virtues and chastity would be preserved. To make sure that women would not go out and meet strangers, their feet were bound at the young age of five or six. From then on they would have to live like birds with broken wings.

Nainai was lucky, for she was spared this ordeal. The Manchus, though they had adopted many conventions of the Han people (the major nationality making up more than 90 percent of the Chinese population), were never crazy about "three-inch golden lilies." Perhaps that was why many old Beijing residents said that Manchu women were on the whole much more sagacious than the men in their families. The most outstanding example of this was Dowager Empress Cixi, who for fifty years held the entire country under her thumb, along with two emperors who were her son and her nephew. During her reign, however, the Great Empire of Qing was like the setting sun. Quickly it dropped beyond the western hills.

In 1911 the revolution broke out. The Qing dynasty was overthrown. Nainai's father lost his official position, but the family made it back to Beijing unharmed. Once they settled down in the old capital, they found that nothing was the same. The great Qing dynasty was history. Gone with it were the power and privileges of the Manchus. For two hundred and sixty-seven years they had been the ruling class in China. Then almost overnight, they became a small, isolated minority, surrounded and hated by tens of millions of Han Chinese.

So in the years after the revolution, many Manchu families lived in fear and grief. Their money, now like a river without a source, quickly dried up. Many of them dared not think about the future, for the future was like a bottomless pit, waiting to engulf them. It was in those years that Nainai was married to my grandfather. As far as I know, Nainai had never told anyone about her feelings toward this marriage. People of her generation did not talk about such things. But the facts were obvious. First of all, my grandfather was a merchant and merchants were considered despicable throughout China. Second, he was not a Manchu. None of his ancestors had been members of the aristocracy. Instead he was born into a poor peasant's family in Zhucheng county, Shandong province. Both his parents died in a famine when he was in his teens. Unable to feed his mouth in his native village, he went away with others to Manchuria where there were more opportunities for a desperate young man like him.

In the northeast, the lucky star shone on him. First he got to know my great-grandfather, who was not his real father. He was not even a relative, but just another desperate man trying to make it in a frontier town. Next the two of them started a business together. In about ten years they made a fortune. What was the nature of their business? In my family this has been a riddle for more than seventy years. The two old men forbade people to talk about it. This made my father's generation even more curious, so they speculated and argued about it behind the old men's backs. But until my grandfather died in 1953, he never gave them a single clue.

Sometimes I even went so far as to imagine a bloody murder scene at midnight or an armed robbery of a gold mine, for otherwise why should the two old men refuse to let their own descendants know about their success story? But Third Aunt disagreed. She said it was probably nothing but a restaurant or a tailor shop, for she had noticed that my great-grandfather knew a great deal about cooking and making clothes. "Maybe they kept it a secret because in China these trades were considered low and degrading. If the servants, for example, knew that their masters had taken such jobs, they'd gossip about them behind their backs. Officials and other rich merchants in Beijing might refuse to associate with them."

Whatever their business was originally, the fact remained that Nainai and my grandfather were not a match. The former was a well educated gentle lady, the latter a rough peasant who was illiterate. It could not be for anything but his money that Nainai was married to him.

In the years after 1911, during the golden age for Peking opera, my great-grandfather and grandfather owned a well-known theater in Beijing, named Jixiang (auspicious) that normally pulled in nine hundred silver dollars for them each month. Besides the theater, they also owned a large silk store in Wangfujing and some other businesses. Their property amounted to well over a million silver dollars.

Nainai's own family, in the meantime, had fallen into straitened circumstances. After the revolution her father no longer had any income. Yet old habits were difficult to kick. He still had to smoke opium. In fact now he had an even greater need for it. Besides he liked fine food, good wine, and operas. If he did not celebrate his birthday properly, he'd feel that he had lost face in front of his old friends. If there weren't a couple of servants in the house, it would be very inconvenient . . . Thus in a few years he had pledged all the properties his ancestors had left, and the valuables of the family all found their way into pawnshops. At last he had nothing left except his only daughter.

So he initiated Nainai into this loveless marriage. But perhaps I should not say so, for don't a lot of Chinese say, "Unlike the Westerners who first fall in love and then get married, we Chinese get married first and then fall in love"? This theory was to some extent true, especially in cases of old-time marriages. As the saying goes, "Married to a rooster, follow the rooster; married to a dog, follow the dog." Many women learned to get along with their husbands because they had no alternative.

In Nainai's case, she had to put her filial duty before her personal feelings, for she knew that her father, mother, and younger brother depended on her. If she should fail to help them, soon they'd be in the street begging for food. Yet this must have made life doubly difficult for Nainai; for in her husband's home, everybody lived under the tyranny of my great-grandfather.

According to Father, Second Uncle, and Third Aunt, my great-grandfather was a real despot in the family. All decisions, big or small, were made by him. He never consulted anybody when he made decisions about them. All the others had to ask his permission if they wanted to do anything.

"He thought everybody was indebted to him, because he was the one who made the money!" Years later, when Father said this to me, his voice still betrayed a great deal of anger. "The employees were all indebted to him, because he gave them jobs. Nainai was indebted to him, because if he hadn't sent her parents gifts of money, they'd have been drinking northwest wind for meals. I was indebted to him too, for I was his oldest grandson who would someday inherit his money and his business. I could never make him understand that I did not want his money and had no interest in taking over his business. I'd rather work to earn my own living and be free. Actually, I pitied him because he was such a slave of his money! Money possessed him and obsessed him! It ruined his life!"

Father also told me that because the old man thought he was everybody's creditor but no one was paying their debts back with due love and respect, he resented everyone in the family.

"His biggest hobby was to curse people. He had a large stock of poisonous words which, when he was in a bad mood, he would deal out to people around him generously. It was only when he was cursing others that he looked happy and satisfied!"

Nainai must have suffered a lot at his hands, or perhaps I should say, at his tongue. Being a daughter-in-law, tradition required her to obey the old tyrant completely and be respectful all the time. Her filial duty said that she should never talk back to him or complain about him to anyone. So she put up with all the insults from her father-in-law. In the meantime, while the old man was feared, shunned, and hated more and more by members of his own family, Nainai quietly won everybody's heart.

She was not only loved and admired by her husband and children, but also by other relatives and even servants because of her kindness and generosity. Although she was the mistress of the house, she rarely voiced her opinions. She always listened to others with patience and sympathy. Yet sooner or later, people realized that she was not a fool or a person who could be manipulated. She knew her mind as well as what was going on around her. There is an old saying: "Great wisdom appears dull-witted." It is similar to "Still waters run deep." Nainai seemed to exemplify such sayings.

My opinion of Nainai was actually not my own. It reflected Aunty's opinion of her, which in its turn was influenced by the opinion of her aunt. Aunty's aunt was an old servant in my grandfather's house, who knew a great deal about her masters and mistresses. In 1950 she recommended Aunty to Nainai to take care of me. For that I am very grateful to her, although I cannot recall what she looked like.

Seven years after Nainai married, her father died. Her mother soon followed him into the nether world. Now it was Nainai's responsibility to help her younger brother. Her brother in his youth had also studied with tutors. So he could read and write. Some said he was pretty good at calligraphy and flower-and-bird painting. But as he grew up, the idea that someday he would have to work to make a living had never crossed his mind. He wouldn't have needed to work, if the emperor had continued in power. The latter would have granted him an official position as the previous emperors did his forefathers.

With or without an official position, he wouldn't have needed to worry about his livelihood. During the Qing dynasty all Manchu men received monthly *qianliang* (money and grain). Theoretically they were all in the army, so no one was supposed to have another job. This *qian-*

liang the Han people in Beijing jokingly called "crops that grow on iron stalks," because the "harvest" of such was always guaranteed. For many decades it had enabled its recipients to idle around teahouses, wine-shops, bird markets, antique stores, and opera theaters. Some of them became artists and writers. Others wasted their time. Nainai's brother grew up expecting such an easy life. After the revolution uprooted the magic crops, he was at a loss.

Nainai tried to help him out, and providing him with a job seemed to be the most fundamental way. Of course this was not easy. On the one hand, her younger brother was not fit for any of the existing jobs in the family business. On the other hand, her father-in-law had made it clear that he'd never put any relative on the payroll unless he was really needed. So what was Nainai to do?

Finally she came up with an idea. She persuaded my grandfather that the theater needed a reliable person to watch over it during the night and her brother was the right one to do it. All he needed to do was to sleep in the theater after the performance was over. By day he could still enjoy himself in the teahouses and wineshops. In the evening he could see as many operas as he liked. Each month he'd receive a salary, which of course would be called a gift. However, soon the brother proved that he could not deal with even a job like that. One night he caught a severe cold sleeping in the theater. A couple of months later, he joined his parents in the yellow earth.

His death made Nainai heartbroken, for she loved her little brother. In the past the two of them had traveled in the same wagon and played on the same boat. They had studied with the same tutors and Nainai had spent many hours writing characters and memorizing ancient poems with him. When the weather changed or when he was ill, she would help her mother take care of him and over the years he had become dependent on her.

Yet even this was not the real reason why Nainai was so sad when her brother died. The real reason was that he was the only male descendant in her family. When he died without issue, the once powerful and prominent Manchu family was extinct by Chinese standards. Nainai's children did not count in this case, for a daughter's children belonged to her husband's family.

Nainai's own ancestors had no more offspring. After a hundred years, who would offer them delicious meals when the festivals came around? Who would repair and sweep their graves at *qingming,* the special day in April on which dutiful descendants visit their ancestors? Who would burn paper money and send cash into the nether world for them to spend? Who would burn incense and chant Buddhist scriptures to expiate the sins they had committed and beseech blessings for them? . . .

Nainai's ancestors would be cold and hungry for eternity, hanging like dry leaves on a dead tree, shivering in the chilly wind of the Yin. They'd be weeping and their tears would flow out like a bitter river. But river or rain, nothing could revive this family. It was too late. Henceforth sunshine, full moon, spring wind, peaceful years, and bumper harvest, all good things belonged to other families. Nainai's ancestors were beyond help. Their relation with the human world was cut off once and for all. People would soon forget them. Their memorial tablets would be thrown out by strangers.

That was why in China families had to have sons. The more sons the better, for the ancestors would feel safer and happier. If a man failed to produce sons, he did his ancestors a great wrong. That was why Mencius said, "There are three ways in which one fails his filial duties. Not having a son is the biggest among them." The ancestors, I guess, could not care less about daughters whose children would take the husbands' surnames and carry on the family lines for other families.

5

Why Did Father Join the Revolution?

After Nainai married my grandfather, she gave birth to ten babies in ten years. Father and Second Uncle weighed more than seven pounds at birth. Third Aunt was less than six pounds. After her, the babies continued to come. One each year. Smaller and smaller. Nainai did not know how to stop them. Nor did she know how to save them. So the babies died in a few days or just a few hours, before they could open their eyes and see their mother's face, which was as pale as the moon.

The heavy loss made Nainai love even more dearly the three children whom heaven allowed her to keep. She hired the best wet nurse she could find for Third Aunt, because she herself was too weak to nurse her. As for her two sons, they each had a nanny too. Yet Nainai's heart was with her children day and night to make sure that they got the tender love and proper care they needed. As a result, the three of them all grew up healthy and strong.

The Chinese had a saying, "At the age of three, one's personality begins to show." Father and Third Aunt turned out to be more like Nainai herself, quiet and sensitive. Second Uncle, on the other hand, inherited my grandfather's fiery temper. If he was happy, he would laugh out loud. If he was mad at someone, he would tell the person to his face how he felt. After he spoke up, he did not bear the person grudges. Soon he would forget what had happened between them and be the person's good friend once again.

Despite the differences in their temperament, Nainai's three children had one thing in common: their love and devotion to their mother. When she was cursed by her father-in-law, the children knew how to comfort her to bring a trace of smile back onto her sad face. When she was distressed by the deaths of her parents and younger brother, the children turned her thoughts from the past to the future. Because of the children, new hopes began to sprout up in Nainai's heart. She said to herself that in the future she would send all her children to universities. Her daughter as well as her sons. Especially her daughter! Her daugh-

31

ter would not be a housewife and a dependent like herself. She would have a profession so she could support herself. That way she would not need to put up with the insults she herself had swallowed with bitter tears for so many years.

After her children graduated from universities and got jobs, of course, they would all get married and have children. The more children the better. Boys and girls. All were welcome. They'd fill her house with laughing, crying, crawling, climbing, running, and jumping. She'd hire wet nurses and nannies for each of them, and she herself would tell them stories. Of course, all her children and grandchildren would live with her in her house. A big family. She could not imagine that things could be otherwise.

When the year 1942 came round, Nainai's dreams seemed to be coming true. Father, Second Uncle, and Third Aunt were all in universities. Father was a junior majoring in Western literature in Furen University, Second Uncle a sophomore studying economics in Yanjing University, and Third Aunt had just started medical school. Nainai was ever so proud of each of them.

What she did not know at this juncture was that her children were planning to leave home. They made the decision because of the Japanese invasion. In the thirties, first the northeast was lost. Then big cities like Shanghai, Nanjing, Tianjin, and Beijing fell one after another. Throughout the country people were outraged, by the Japanese as well as by the Nationalist government, which they felt was ineffective in its resistance. Many students agreed with the slogan "Although China is vast, there is no longer enough room for a peaceful desk."

Being "slaves without a country" day in and day out was more than Father, Second Uncle, and Third Aunt could bear. Everyday in the street the students could see Chinese civilians bullied by Japanese soldiers. Western professors were made to quit one after another. Patriotic Chinese were arrested, tortured, and killed. The hated "plaster flag," as the Chinese nicknamed it, flew haughtily above everybody's head, making it hard for a Chinese to breathe. Father, Second Uncle, and Third Aunt thought it was time for them to leave Beijing.

Father was the one who had the connections. So he first arranged for his brother and sister to leave. With the assistance of underground workers, they went through Japanese blockade lines and headed for the southwest. Their destination was more than a thousand miles away. With the war going on, the expedition was a journey of danger and chaos. On the way they witnessed bombing, looting, accidents, and all kinds of extortions. Sometimes they rode on trains and buses; sometimes they walked or ran. It took them several months to reach Sichuan, where they eventually resumed their studies in universities.

As for Father, instead of going to the southwest where he could join Second Uncle and Third Aunt, he joined the Communists at Jinchaji anti-Japanese base, a mountainous area between Hebei and Shanxi provinces. Why did he do this? This is another riddle, which unlike the previous one I have a hard time figuring out, for over the years Father has given me too many answers.

For instance, he told me that he joined the Communists because he believed only they could create a new society in China where everyone would enjoy freedom, equality, and happiness.

But then he also told me that he hated the Japanese invaders and wanted to fight them as a guerrilla in the front. When his country was in danger, a young man should not stay in the rear and let others shed their blood and win the war for him. This was what the rich people had been doing in China and elsewhere. "If you have money, donate your money. If you have strength, put forth your strength." Even the slogan seemed to say this was all right. But Father disagreed and he was serious.

So he went to Jinchaji, which by then was repeatedly attacked by the Japanese troops. *Saodang* (sweep it up) was what the Japanese called it. When the invaders came, they burned down houses, destroyed crops, took away all the food they could find, and killed people whom they suspected. Meanwhile the Eighth Route Army and guerrillas led by the Chinese Communist Party and supported by local peasants were fighting back. Many people lost their lives in the war. Yet more were coming of their own accord to keep up the resistance. Among them many were college students like Father.

Father arrived at Jinchaji when things were at their worst. By the end of 1942, Father told me, most of the houses in the region were without doors and windows. During the night, when the temperature dropped to ten and sometimes twenty degrees below zero, they had no coal, no firewood, no warm clothes to fend off the severe cold. Cotton-padded jackets and shoes were very hard to come by. Food was in such short supply that soldiers and peasants were all eating bran and wild herbs. The best food in the region was corn flour bread. White flour and green vegetables were never seen. Even salt was scarce.

On top of all this, the region was in dire need of medicine. The shortage was caused by the Japanese blockade. As a result wounded soldiers were sometimes operated on without anesthetic. Thousands of people in the area suffered from epidemic diseases: typhoid fever, smallpox, flu, . . . Many died because no medicine was available.

Father was aware of this situation when he was in Beijing. He heard it from a friend who later turned out to be an underground Communist. So before Father set off, he secretly purchased a fairly large amount of medicine that was urgently needed at the anti-Japanese base. The medicine was tightly controlled in Beijing. Yet as the Chinese saying goes, "With money, one can make the devil turn the millstone." Father soon obtained what he had put down on the list, with the money and through the business connections of his hated grandfather.

Later Father brought the medicine through Japanese blockade lines. This was a dangerous task. Several times Japanese soldiers searched passengers on the train. If they should find the medicine in Father's suitcases, they would arrest him and the consequences would be dire.

To make matters even more complicated, later one of the guides along the line was caught by the Japanese. This happened shortly before Father's group arrived. As a result, everything they had achieved thus far came to naught. For without the guide they did not know how to get in touch with the next underground worker, so they could not go on. They could not stay in the region either, where they were a group of strangers. The collaborators would soon notice and report them. So they had no other choice but to return to Beijing and start all over again.

Eventually Father arrived at Jinchaji with all the medicine he had purchased. He immediately donated all of it to the local government. The medicine saved many lives. Father was praised by the leaders. A medal was awarded to him, his very first during the wars.

Later Father was sent to study at Huabei Lianda, a branch of the Chinese People's Anti-Japanese Military and Political College. A few months down the road Father got typhoid fever, which nearly killed him.

By that time, the medicine Father had brought to Jinchaji was already used up. Father had to fight the disease with his own strength. For days he lay in bed, running a high fever. A horrible pain turned his stomach and bowels upside down. He could not eat anything. It was almost a miracle that he survived. When finally he was able to leave bed and sit in the sun, he felt that he had become as light as a straw. A gust of mountain wind could make him lose his balance.

One day he borrowed a mirror from a comrade and looked at himself in it. He was shocked by what he saw. While he was sick, he had lost so much hair that he was almost bald. His eyes were frighteningly large, sitting in two dark pits. His skin was dry and sallow. His face was wrinkled, like that of an old peasant. Seeing him like this, who would believe that only a couple of months before, he was considered the most handsome man among the students who came to this region to fight the Japanese.

A director told him he was when he asked Father to play Mr. Darcy in his spoken drama *Pride and Prejudice*. Father was amused by the proposal, but he told the director he had never been on the stage before. The latter said it was all right. So he became Mr. Darcy, the Pride.

According to Father, the play they staged was a hit, despite his inexperience. "The peasants loved it. Everybody came to see it," Father said, "even though they did not understand it. None of them had seen spoken drama before. So they thought the play was a lot of fun. They found the English gentlemen and ladies we played awfully weird."

After Father recovered, he was transferred to Yan'an where Mao Zedong, Zhou Enlai, and the central committee of the Chinese Communist Party stayed during the war of resistance against Japan and the civil war that followed. In the early 1940s few people there spoke foreign languages. Thus when the leaders at Jinchaji found out that Father could speak English and some French, they immediately sent him to Yan'an as an interpreter. Consequently throughout the wars Father was in the army only in name. He never fired a single shot at an enemy.

As for his fellow students, later some of them were sent back to Beijing to do underground work; others stayed in the countryside and became guerrilla fighters. It was the organization—the Party—that decided who went where and did what. Father and his comrades obeyed willingly, for they had vowed that they would "sacrifice the individual and obey the organization" when they joined the Party.

In addition to joining the Party, Father also abandoned his old name Zhichang, "blazing prosperity," chosen by his grandfather together with the old man's surname. He created a new name for himself: Yu Shan, which means "at the mountains."

For many years I thought Father did this because he was determined to make a clean break with his upper-class family and live as a new person after he joined the revolution. Only years later when my zeal for the revolution died down did it occur to me that by changing his name

Father had also protected Nainai and others in the family who remained in Beijing. Or else he'd have gotten them into trouble with the Japanese and the Nationalists, for both considered the Communists their deadly enemies.

Actually, Father told me, it was really because of Nainai and my great-grandfather that he joined the revolution. The old man taught him to hate oppression. Day in and day out, he was the oppression incarnate in the family. When he bullied Nainai and others, it made Father's blood boil. Father vowed secretly that someday he would avenge the wrongs the tyrant did to everybody by tearing down his evil world and establishing a new one on its ruins. In this new world, no human being would be allowed to oppress other human beings. Nainai's life, Father thought, would be much easier and happier in it.

With such a dream, Father left home and went to the mountains. When he sneaked out, he did not tell Nainai where he was going. So for years Nainai thought that he was studying in the southwest just like Second Uncle and Third Aunt. This was a blessing for her. For had she known Father's real whereabouts, the raids made by the Japanese troops, the disease, and the hardships, she would have worried to death.

As for her life in Beijing in those years, I heard a story from her two old servants who refused to be liberated after Liberation.

Before Father left home, one day he planted a Chinese yam, called *shanyao,* in the courtyard. It was only a passing whim. Afterwards he forgot about it. Soon he left Beijing. A couple of weeks later, however, the yam sprouted. Nainai put an exquisite fence around it as soon as she saw it.

The Chinese yam was a perennial plant, usually grown by the peasants around their cottages. Nainai kept this yam in her garden among beautiful tree peonies and roses. Gradually, the tender vine of the yam crawled all over a Tai Lake rock.

In those years, Nainai must have been awfully lonely. She missed her children. Because of the war, no news came from any of them. When she became too anxious, she would go and talk to the yam.

Sometimes the plant listened to her in silence as if it understood her feelings but could find no word to comfort her. Sometimes there was a gentle breeze and the numerous heart-shaped green leaves fluttered. Nainai thought that the yam was whispering to her, telling her something about her children in a secret language, which with the love she had inside of her she could almost understand. It soothed Nainai's burning heart. She felt that as long as the yam thrived and she could hear it murmur, things could not go terribly wrong with her beloved children.

Nainai prayed day and night to heaven and to her ancestors, asking them to protect her children and to put an end to the war. In 1945 the Japanese surrendered. Second Uncle and Third Aunt came back to her. But it took Father another ten years to return home.

6

Second Uncle Was a Paper Tiger

When we returned from Switzerland in 1956, Nainai's dream came true. Finally the entire family was together, living in Nainai's big house. After my great-grandfather and grandfather died, Nainai was the head of the family.

Although I do not remember ever seeing Nainai read Lao Tzu, the way she ran our family was very much in keeping with the latter's teaching. According to the ancient philosopher, the best rulers ruled by nonaction. That is to say, they let ten thousand things take their own courses; they did not impose their will on any of them. As a result, all were perfectly happy and the world was in harmony. Nainai seemed to have a profound understanding of this world order called Tao.

For example, at the house of Laolao (my maternal grandmother) there were numerous rules. During dinner, the way I held chopsticks was always wrong. I could not rest my elbows on the table. Other bad manners included speaking with food in my mouth and clinking chopsticks. I was to hold up my rice bowl throughout the meal. Water and other drinks were not allowed to go with the food. I had to wait till the end of the meal to drink the soup.

Rules like these made me reluctant to have dinner at Laolao's place. As a child, I could not have cared less if I missed the southern delicacies Laolao made that the adults said were so great. After all, didn't they say that freedom should be cherished above all things—food included, of course?

By contrast, freedom was in abundance at Nainai's place. There I could climb Tai Lake rocks if I wanted to or use a ladder to climb onto the walls to beat down red dates from the tall date trees. On the evening of the National Day (October 1), Little Ox, Little Dragon, and I were permitted to climb onto the tiled roof of Nainai's house, the tallest in the compound, to watch fireworks at Tian'anmen Square.

In the backyard there was an old locust tree. The branches of it spread out like a huge umbrella. On that evening it caught several brightly colored parachutes, each as large as a square scarf, with a whistle attached to it. They were carried here by the southwest wind from Tian'anmen Square. To me, they were like gifts from heaven. I was so thrilled that I refused to come down from the roof long after the fireworks were over, hoping that more parachutes would come this way. Such behavior annoyed my parents, but Nainai just smiled and said that I could stay there a little longer.

In Nainai's house I was truly happy. I had never been so happy before. In the past I was very lonely. Now I could play with Little Ox, Little Dragon, and other kids who were our neighbors. The gates of their houses stayed open during the day, and so did ours. Kids were welcome anytime. We could just drop in. In this environment I felt safe, and the nameless fear I had in Switzerland went away.

Occasionally my parents would be angry at me because I was too wild. When this happened, there was always someone in the big family who was willing to intercede for me. Most of the time I would turn to Nainai, knowing that she would shelter me like a big tree. Soon the menacing thunderstorm would change into gentle breeze and fine rain. Before long, all clouds would dissipate and sunshine would return to my world.

Nainai, although she was an old woman, was not old-fashioned in her way of thinking. For one thing, she was not biased against girls like other grandparents. On the contrary, I somehow had a feeling that she indulged me more than the boys. Looking back, I wonder if Nainai was following the unique Manchu tradition that said girls must be treated well at home, for in the future (I should say in the past) they all had a chance to be chosen into the palace. There if they found favor in the emperor's eyes, they could become imperial consorts. That way they would honor their ancestors and gain power and prestige for their families. Or else maybe Nainai was sympathetic toward me? From her own experience, she knew that a woman's life would not be easy in China. Many dangers, pitfalls, and heartaches were in store for me.

Saying this I do not mean that others were not happy in Nainai's house. All seemed to enjoy life in their own ways. The adults all worked, women as well as men. In the new society, it was a shame not to work if one was young, healthy, and educated. Those who lived on the old money of the family were called parasites. They were despised by everybody in spite of their money. Times had changed.

From Monday to Saturday, every morning Shenshen (which means the wife of an uncle who is the father's younger brother) was the first to get up. She worked in a textile factory in the eastern suburb of Beijing. It took her an hour to get to her factory by bus. So she usually left home at about half past six.

After her footsteps died down, the house was quiet again. Father, Mother, and Second Uncle were not awake yet. They usually went to bed late and for them, the sweetest sleep came in the morning. When the clock struck seven, they reluctantly got out of bed. Next I heard them take brass basins from the washstands and go into the kitchen to wash their faces. Later they brushed their teeth in the yard, puffing the water out onto the ground with a great noise. After this, they would say it was too late, no time for breakfast, and rush out of the house like a gust of wind.

During this time I often lay awake. I could hear everything, because in Nainai's house the walls between rooms were made of wooden boards and the ceiling was just a few layers of rice paper. This was typical of all the old houses in Beijing. The theory must have been that among family members there ought to be no secrets. Brick walls were used only to keep away outsiders.

The old women and the children were the last ones to get up and have breakfast. No need to hurry. We had plenty of time to play and tell one another stories. In those days, no one had heard of the thing called "electric view," so of course we did not miss it. We were busy enough without television.

In the yards, there were cicadas singing in the trees, and we tried to catch them with melted rubber bands put on the tips of long bamboo poles. At the foot of brick walls were crickets, which we captured by pouring water into the crevices in which they hid. In the second yard there were two big earthen vats in which goldfish swam leisurely among water lilies. Under the eaves, swallows made nests to raise their young. Sometimes we picked flowers from the locust trees and sucked the honey from them. Sometimes we waged miniature tugs-of-war with the leaf-stalks of poplar trees.

Occasionally we would go treasure hunting in Nainai's old trunks. Among the things we found were a shiny peach seed that was carved into a tree and five babies—Nainai said this was called "five sons excel in the imperial examinations"—a silver spoon with a spray of plum blossoms engraved on the handle, a jade pendant in the shape of a calabash, coral beads, ink sticks, silk flower hairpins, embroidered handkerchiefs, old coins overgrown with green rust, mah-jongg pieces . . . Many of these had a little history. While Nainai was telling us about them, time flew away. Soon the adults began to come back from work one after another.

At six thirty, the whole family sat down at a big round table. The food on it was steaming hot and delicious. All the dishes were placed at the center of the table. People used their chopsticks to pick whatever they liked into their own rice bowls. No one was forced to eat anything because it was good for her. No one was told not to talk. Now the family was together, naturally people wanted to tell one another the interesting things they saw or heard during the day. If someone wanted to laugh, it was all right. "One good laugh makes a person ten years younger," as the Chinese saying goes. If someone was late—Third Aunt sometimes had to stay at the hospital and Shenshen might miss a bus— no problem. Others would go ahead and eat. Enough food would be set aside and kept warm in the kitchen for her. At Nainai's dinner table, there was neither hierarchy nor formality. Everybody had a good appetite.

After dinner, sometimes Second Uncle would take Little Ox, Little Dragon, and me to the nearby Dong'an Market to go window-shopping. Dong'an in Chinese means peace in the east. During the Cultural Revolution the name was changed to Dong Feng, which means east wind. It was from Chairman Mao's quotation, "the east wind will prevail over the west wind," meaning China and other socialist countries in the East will triumph over the capitalist countries in the West.

In 1956 the market was still Peace in the East and had numerous privately owned small shops in it. Occasionally, Second Uncle would buy something for us: clay dolls, masks, tiny glass animals, and pagodas of porcelain . . . None of them was worth much money; yet each gave us a lot of joy.

On other evenings we would ask Second Uncle to show us martial arts. At such a request, he would unlock a big wooden chest painted red on the outside and take out his weapons: a shiny blunt sword, a pair of wooden daggers, a red-tasselled spear, and a shield with the design of a laughing tiger. Next he would run around the yard fighting with invisible enemies, jumping, kicking, yelling, dodging blows, and striking back. I watched him with awe and admiration, thinking that he was a great kung fu master like the ones I had heard about in stories. Only after I grew up did I realize that Second Uncle's martial art was just a show. Being an opera fan, he learned it from the stage and performed it at home to amuse us children. It was no good in real combat.

On hot summer evenings his audience included almost the entire family who stayed out in the yard "to ride the cool," as people in Beijing put it. All the adults were waving big, round palm-leaf fans to cool themselves and drive away mosquitoes. Shenshen was the only one who stayed inside, for her hobby was to make clothes. At that time, she had just bought a new sewing machine. As soon as dinner was over, it would start to hum like a honeybee. When the evening grew old, I fell asleep to its soothing sound, as so many generations of Chinese before me had found sweet dreams in the hum of spinning wheels.

To me, Shenshen was the prettiest woman in Beijing at the time. Her figure was slender and her dresses were beautiful. Her face was the shape of a duck's egg, very smooth, and her eyes were always smiling. To this day her childlike smile remains vivid in my mind, but in the real world it vanished once and for all in 1957 when Second Uncle was labeled a Rightist.

That year, a million scholars and cadres fell prey to the Anti-Rightist Movement. Their downfall came from their naïveté in politics and their trust in the Chinese Communist Party. At the beginning of the movement, the Party urged people to criticize their leaders so as to help them discover and correct mistakes. Later, however, the political wind shifted and those who did what the Party told them to do became class enemies. Their criticism was turned into evidence against them, "evil attacks on the leadership of the Communist Party." But Second Uncle did not even criticize his leaders. So how did he become a Rightist?

According to Third Aunt, who told me the following behind closed doors in 1975, before the Anti-Rightist Movement, Second Uncle had made enemies at CAAC, the Chinese airline, where he worked as an accountant. There some of his superiors, taking advantage of their positions, traveled to places for private reasons. When they came back, they wanted Second Uncle to reimburse them for the costs of such trips. The latter turned them down, saying it was against the rules that the leaders themselves had made.

This, of course, offended people. He made them lose money. He made them lose face too. For he turned them down bluntly, in front of other people. So the leaders hated him, but they said nothing. "When a gentleman wants to avenge himself, waiting for ten years is not too long."

Second Uncle, on the other hand, was totally unaware of what was going on in these people's minds. He came back home with a clear conscience, thinking that he had done the right thing. He slept well at night and forgot the whole thing the next morning.

The leaders waited till the Anti-Rightist Movement to avenge themselves. When the campaign started, they were the ones to decide who would get the "cap" in their work unit. That was very convenient. They put the "cap" on Second Uncle, even though he had not criticized the Party. The theory was since Second Uncle was from a capitalist family, he must bear some conscious or unconscious grudges against the Party and the socialist system.

Nobody dared challenge this theory, knowing the leaders had more "caps" in their hands ready to deal out. Throughout the movement, Second Uncle never had a chance to defend himself. Nor could he find any place to appeal against the decision made by those leaders. Thus Second Uncle, despite my childish belief that he was a great fighter, was defeated and eliminated in the very first round of the merciless political struggle that would entangle every Chinese in the decades to come.

Father and Third Aunt survived the campaign. Father, being an old revolutionary, had more political experience than others. When he was at Jinchaji, he had heard a great deal about the Yan'an Rectification Campaign that took place in 1942. During that campaign, intellectuals had been the targets. So he would always think twice before he said anything. As for Third Aunt, she was lucky because she inherited Nainai's good temper. Considerate and introverted, she never hurt others' feelings. She had no enemies in her work unit.

In 1957 I knew nothing about the troubles Second Uncle had until one day I saw him packing. Mother told me that he was going to a salt farm to "reform himself through labor." I had no idea what that meant except that after Second Uncle left, there was no more window-shopping in Dong'an Market, and no one to perform martial arts for us. The evenings became much longer, the courtyard a lot emptier. I missed Second Uncle!

As for my maternal grandparents, they were as distressed as Nainai, because my other uncle, whom I called Jiujiu, was also labeled a Rightist. He got into trouble because one of his friends reported him. Once he had said to three of his best friends that he did not think it was fair that the leaders of his college always sent students with revolutionary family backgrounds to study abroad. The students' academic accomplishments were never taken into consideration. During the Anti-Rightist

Movement, this remark became evidence of his dissatisfaction with the Party leadership. So he became one of the youngest Rightists in China, only nineteen at the time.

Twenty-two years later when we met again, I asked him if he knew which friend of his had betrayed him. He said he did not know and he did not want to know. The most important thing was the fact that he had been rehabilitated, he said. "Let's look forward. Why be so obsessed by the past? It won't do anyone any good! Believe me!"

I wanted to believe him. Yet I could not help wondering about such things. Perhaps it is my nature that I like to "dig up the roots and get to the bottom of things." Or maybe it is merely a reaction against the adults in my family who were always trying to hide things from us children.

The Anti-Rightist Movement was certainly a big lesson for Chinese *zhishi fenzi*—those with a college education and beyond—who had been rather outspoken and rebellious since the turn of the century. After the campaign, people began to watch what they said, even among close friends and family members.

病从口入
祸从口出!

In olden days there was a saying, "Diseases go in by the mouth and disasters come out of the mouth." Now all of a sudden people discovered that it held a great deal of wisdom. Words wrongly said or said to the wrong people were time bombs, hanging over one's head, quietly ticking away. When they exploded, they'd blow one's hopes, happiness, career, and family all to pieces.

Was this why after the Anti-Right Movement, fewer friends came to visit Third Aunt on weekends? When they came, the veranda was no longer such a comfortable place for them. They much preferred to have tea inside Third Aunt's room. Third Aunt was a quiet person even before the campaign. Afterwards she was a silent person, who devoted herself to her work and her flowers. By and by, handsome young men no longer came to visit her. She did not seem to mind it. For instead of going out to meet new people, she just stayed home and remained single.

After the campaign was over, we moved out of Nainai's house. Father told Nainai his work unit had given him an apartment right next to where he and Mother worked. While this was true, it probably was not the whole truth. Today as I look back on it, it seems obvious that after the Anti-Right Movement, the political atmosphere had changed. It was no longer appropriate for Father and Mother, who were both Communist Party members, to live in Nainai's house.

The political pressure was invisible, but if someone were foolish enough to ignore it, the consequences could be very serious. As Confucius put it, "A person without foresight will have to deal with emergencies." My parents were wise. They knew what they had to do, yet they did not want to hurt Nainai's feelings. So Father came up with such an excuse.

Nainai accepted the excuse, saying now winter was coming, it would indeed be more convenient if we lived at my parents' work unit. She did not press us to stay. On the contrary, she made it easy for Father to leave. Years later when I reflected on this, it occurred to me that Nainai probably knew quite well why my parents had to move out. For unlike the other old women, she read newspapers everyday. Though she never talked about politics, she was not ignorant about the larger world. Yet she seemed unaware of it. That was my Nainai, who never embarrassed anyone.

After we moved out, though Father took us back to visit Nainai on weekends, Nainai's perfectly happy days were over. On the one hand, she missed us. On the other hand, she worried about Second Uncle. In a few years, the news that came from him went from bad to worse.

When Second Uncle first arrived at the salt farm that was a labor camp on the bank of Bohai Sea, he worked extremely hard, as if he were not a scholar but someone who had been doing physical labor all his life. He hoped that in this way he would convince the leaders that he had reformed himself, so they would allow him to go back to his family in Beijing. But in those years it was not easy for a Rightist to make a good impression on anyone, least of all the leaders at the labor camp. Thus four years passed and his unremitting efforts met with little success.

Then in 1962, one morning suddenly all Chinese newspapers reported on the front page that the Nationalists in Taiwan declared that they were going to fight their way back to the mainland. The editorials even warned people against a third world war, because if in China the Communists and the Nationalists were to fight, the Russians and the Americans would get involved. A world war could be triggered and atom bombs used. Quickly the whole country was mobilized. Old people and children were sent away from big cities. The army and young people were ready to fight.

Such preparation for war upset Second Uncle. He became extremely anxious. All the horrid scenes he had witnessed and the dreadful stories he had heard in the early forties when he traveled from Beijing to the southwest came to life in front of his eyes.

Bombs rained down from the sky. Fire shot up and engulfed homes. People burned to death in it, their bodies as black as charcoal. Those who escaped from the ocean of fire ran away, in a human torrent. Suddenly a hail of bullets came from nowhere, cutting people down like reeds. The wounded were robbed and left there to die. Women were raped, children abandoned . . .

If a war broke out while he was so far away from Beijing, how would Nainai, Shenshen, and the boys cope with all this? Second Uncle dared not think any further. For several nights he couldn't close his eyes. Too much apprehension made him forget that he should be cautious. He wrote a letter to Shenshen, discussing what they should do in case there was a war.

The letter never reached Shenshen. It was intercepted by the political workers at the labor camp. They opened it and read it, as if they had never heard of the 1954 Constitution of the People's Republic of China, which stipulated that the secrecy of private letters of Chinese citizens was protected by law. Or maybe they thought Second Uncle, being a Rightist, was not a citizen anymore. The letter became evidence of Second Uncle's yearning for the Nationalists to come back. Thus the conclusion: he was a hidden counterrevolutionary.

When the verdict was read to Second Uncle, he did not know whether he should laugh or wail. He wanted to shout at the top of his voice that the war was exactly what he had dreaded and if he could, he would do anything on earth to prevent it. But he knew it would be in vain. Who would believe his words now? He, a counterrevolutionary as well as a Rightist!

"Of course he tells lies! Of course he wants the Nationalists to come back! In his sleep, he must be dreaming of his lost paradise. When he is awake, he is secretly planning crimes: putting poison into food at a cafeteria, blowing up a crowded department store, setting fire to a hospital . . . A counterrevolutionary is a monster who enjoys killing innocent people!" This was what people everywhere in China thought of a counterrevolutionary in the early sixties. How could he convince people that he was different? Not if he had a hundred mouths all over his body. Even if he jumped into the Yellow River, he could not wash himself clean.

Life's logic sometimes is absurd. Second Uncle's concern for his family soon made him a man without a family. When the bad news reached Beijing, Shenshen shut herself in her room and cried. But the next day when she came out, she was calm. She went straight to the district court and asked for a divorce. As this was considered a revolutionary act, the court soon approved it and gave her the custody of her two children. She did this of her own free will. Nobody put pressure on her. Yet everybody knew that if she did not divorce her counterrevolutionary husband, she and her children would have no future. By then, she had given up all hope that someday Second Uncle would come back to Beijing as an innocent man.

But Second Uncle did come back to Beijing an innocent man in 1980. In his file, the official conclusion said it was a mistake to label him a Rightist in 1957 and likewise it was another mistake to label him a counterrevolutionary in 1962. Just a couple of mistakes. In 1980, all seemed so simple. Yet in the past, it was so hopelessly complicated. It took the Party twenty-two years to declare that it had made a couple of mistakes about Second Uncle. How many twenty-two years does one have in life?

When Second Uncle returned to Beijing, he remarried Shenshen, who had never moved out of Nainai's house. Throughout all the years, she had remained true to him. Moreover, she had brought up the two boys all by herself. If this happened in old China, people would build a chastity gateway for her and the entire neighborhood would be honored. Nowadays chastity gateways are out of the question. Yet anyone who knew about Second Uncle and Shenshen felt very happy for them.

Traditionally, we Chinese loved *da tuan yuan*, grand happy endings, to our stories. Tragedy was not to our taste. Thus I would like to say that the reunion of Second Uncle and Shenshen after twenty-two years was blissful. So blissful that it would move a stony statue to tears.

Little Ox and Little Dragon rushed forward to embrace their father. With tears in their eyes they told the old man that they had loved him secretly through all these years. Now the whole family was together, it felt like a dream. Second Uncle reached out a trembling hand and touched Shenshen's gray hair. He felt love and gratitude overflowing his heart. Holding Second Uncle's hand in her own, Shenshen could not help crying. But this time her tears were happy ones. When she saw that Second Uncle's hair had turned as white as snow at the age of fifty-nine and the lines on his forehead were as deep as if carved by a knife, she knew what he had gone through all these years and her heart melted with love and pity. In short, they lived happily ever after.

But that is a fairy tale. In the real world, the reunion of Shenshen and Second Uncle turned out quite a disaster. Maybe too many years' separation had killed Shenshen's love for Second Uncle? The old man who came back in the end was so different from the young man she remembered that he was a stranger. No! Worse than a stranger! He was the cause of all her suffering for so many years. She couldn't forget it! She couldn't forgive him!

On the other hand, I don't know if there was any love left in Second Uncle's heart for Shenshen. Perhaps this time it was merely a marriage of convenience for him, and he still bore her grudges because she had betrayed him when things were the most difficult for him. She had put salt on his bleeding wound, adding frost on top of snow. Maybe his love for her died on the salt farm where he was abandoned by the whole world for more than two decades.

Anyway, after they remarried, quarrels broke out day and night. The husband was irritable. The wife was explosive. Both were like smoldering volcanoes ready to erupt. As for the children, who were not children anymore, Little Ox grew up as stubborn as an ox. He had remained loyal to his father all these years. For this, he got himself into trouble and was criticized at his work unit. Once he almost became a counter-revolutionary himself. But nothing could shake his devotion to his old man. While he stuck to his choice as an act of defiance, did he really know his father as a person?

Little Dragon, on the other hand, could not help it that he hated his father. Perhaps because he was too young, he did not remember the evenings his father took us window-shopping or showed us martial arts? All he remembered were Second Uncle's faults and failures.

When he grew up he was bullied by other kids and his father was never there to protect him. Later he was not allowed to join the Communist Youth League, nor could he wear a Red Guard's armband, all because his father was a counterrevolutionary. Shenshen's divorce did not help much. Little Dragon was still called "son of a dog" by his fellow students. Later when he tried to find a job, he did not have a father who could open a "back door" for him. Instead, he was rejected on account of his father's political problems.

So how could he love him? It was all the old man's fault that his life had been miserable! Even though years later Little Dragon found out that it was not his father's fault and that the old man had loved him, it was no use. The resentment had taken root in his heart. The anger in his blood would not listen to reason. It exploded each time a small disagreement occurred between them. Then others in the family would take sides. Words were hurled back and forth like lances. Old wounds were opened up. New cuts were made. It was fortunate that Nainai did not live till the eighties to witness all this.

Seeing this made me wonder about the age-old Chinese metaphor: broken mirror be joined. How could it describe a happy reunion? A broken mirror is broken. When its pieces are joined together, the cracks will still show and the rough edges can cut like razor blades. But for some reason Second Uncle and Shenshen's marriage went on. Maybe there is still hope that someday they will run out of animosity and the whole family will be at peace once again.

7

The Chinese CIA

After we moved into our new home in the western suburb of Beijing in 1957, I soon forgot the troubles Nainai and Second Uncle were having. My life at my parents' work unit was filled with new thrills as well as new difficulties.

Our new home was located in a huge yard, many times larger than Nainai's compound. People called this place *jiguan*, which means mechanism. Later I learned that the *jiguan* we lived in was the Ministry of Investigation under the Central Committee of the Chinese Communist Party. In other words, it was the Chinese CIA.

So of course everything in this big yard was a state secret. I remember once Father called me into his room and warned me that I should never tell a stranger the names of anyone who worked in the big yard or anything else. "For those are all state secrets," he said with a seriousness in his voice.

That was exciting! That made me proud of my parents! In my imagination I compared them to those brave underground workers whom I saw in movies and heard about in stories. They all had important secrets to keep from the enemies. These secrets they would not reveal even though they were tortured and executed. Only hateful traitors would be afraid and sell out their comrades. As I grew up, I admired those unyielding revolutionary heroes and despised the traitors.

Yet the big yard did not look like the places I saw in the movies: dark, dangerous, filled with instruments of torture and stained by blood. If my memory is reliable, it was quite beautiful. When we first moved in, a few old barracks dating back to the warlord period still existed, testifying to the history of this place. Ancient weeping willows combed the sunshine. Large rose bushes covered with pink flowers stood among evergreen bushes. Cream-colored office buildings were of Russian styles. People called them by nicknames such as Airplane Building and Horseshoe Buildings. Beyond them, the western hills looked almost unreal, just a touch of blue against the blue sky.

Outside the yard were acres and acres of rice and lotus fields. "The red lotus is for seedpod; the white lotus is for roots." Aunty used to tell me this. As for the lotus leaves, she used them to cover the rice porridge that she cooked over low heat. The porridge she made was light green with a fragrance.

Although it was serene, the big yard was no Peach Blossom Spring, where the people lived in nature without the knowledge of any kind of government. The big yard was guarded by fully armed People's Liberation Army soldiers twenty-four hours a day, seven days a week. Anyone who wanted to come in or go out had to show a pass with their photo. Even children were no exception.

Only we often forgot to bring the passes. When this happened, we would try to slip through the gate, among a crowd, or behind the guards' backs. Sometimes we succeeded. If we got caught, the soldiers would send us into the reception room, a brick house behind their sentry box. The old man there was very kind. He knew everybody's parents. When we came in, he would ask us how our parents were lately and then ring the bell. This time the soldiers would have to let us go in.

In those days we children were a lot of trouble for the soldiers. If somewhere there was an opening in the fence or a way to climb over the wall, soon the secret information spread out and we all took advantage of it without scruples. Usually these were shortcuts leading to the nearby Summer Palace where we went swimming in summer and ice-skating in winter.

The rest of the year I was in school. In 1957 I became a student in West Garden Elementary School, located just outside the big yard. Most of the students there were from inside the yard. Their parents were government officials who were called revolutionary cadres in China. Others were from a nearby hospital named Chinese Medicine Research Institute. Of the fifty students in my class, few were from workers' families.

Looking back on it, I think a sense of superiority already existed among students who were from the big yard. But it was vague. Most of us were not as conscious of our parents' positions as cadres' children are today. Maybe it was because in the fifties people in China still believed Chairman Mao's teachings: "All our cadres, regardless of their ranks, are servants of the people." "The people are the masters of the country." "We should serve the people wholeheartedly."

I remember once a girl in our class was ridiculed because her father was an ambassador. In Chinese, the word "ambassador" (*dashi*) had the same pronunciation as the word "big shit." When the boys realized this, they were thrilled by it. They chased the poor girl all over the classroom, chanting in a chorus: "Oh, oh! Her father is a big shit!" The emphasis each time fell on the last two words. Soon the girl started to cry while she tried to deny that her father was an ambassador, or a big shit. It made quite a scene. Finally the teacher had to intervene. The boys were rebuked for their bad behavior and the girl was consoled.

If this incident was funny, another had more serious consequences. This time the girl who was jeered at by the boys was a manual worker's daughter. Perhaps her parents' income was low. During the winter, her family did not have enough money to buy coal briquettes that most people in Beijing used at that time for cooking and heating. So each morning she had to go to the dump near our school to look for coal.

The work must have been hard. In winter at six thirty, it was still pitch-black outside and the northwest wind cut people's faces like sharp blades. At the dump, she had to dig out from the garbage the coal briquettes others had used the day before, knock them open one by one with an iron poker, and gather those that were still black in the middle. From time to time, the wind blew ashes into her eyes. As she wiped her eyes with the back of her hand, her face grew stained. Her nose was running from the cold. Her hands were chapped. She was wearing shabby clothes to save the better ones for school. It took her a long time to collect enough coal for her family. While she was doing this, her classmates were sleeping in their warm beds. Their apartments had central heating.

One morning a boy in our class saw her at the dump. Later he couldn't refrain from telling others about his discovery. Pretty soon everyone in our class heard about this. The boys chanted: "Yo! Yo! Cinderella! Picking coal stones!" The girl's face turned red, but she did not cry or try to deny it, as the other girl did. She merely sat there with her lips tightened. After that, she shunned her classmates during the day and went home as soon as class was over. The next year she disappeared from our class. Maybe she transferred; maybe she dropped out. She probably dropped out, since other schools were all quite far away. Nobody cared enough to find out about what happened to her. She had no friend in our class.

This small episode was soon forgotten. In 1958 people's minds were occupied by great things, such as the realization of communism in China. What was communism to me at that time? Well, my parents explained to me that communism was the ideal society for humankind, in which everybody was selfless and therefore everybody could take whatever he or she wanted. And no matter how much he or she took, there would always be an abundance of everything. So no one would need to worry about it. That was wonderful! I liked communism, for there were a few things that I definitely wanted to get: candies, popsicles, and above all, little person's books!

Little person's books in China were not only popular among children, even adults enjoyed reading them. They were half the size of a paperback book, from one to two hundred pages long. On each page was a black and white picture in a frame and underneath it a brief description of what was going on. The stories were of a wide variety: some were classical; others were foreign. Many were about revolutionary heroes.

Little person's books were not expensive. In those days, they cost about twenty Chinese cents apiece. Yet Father would give me only one for each week. That always happened on Saturday evenings, the beginning of our weekend when everyone was the happiest. As soon as dinner was over, I would follow him into his room and watch him unlock his big wooden bookcase. There a stack of new little person's books would appear in front of my eyes. All had been carefully selected by Father himself to make sure that the pictures were well drawn and the stories interesting. I loved reading these books! It was from them that I first got to know Monkey and Pigsy in *Journey to the West,* Zhuge Liang and his generals in *Three Kingdoms,* the one hundred and eight heroes in *Water Margin* as well as *Hamlet, King Lear,* and *Othello.* I really wished that I could have all the books in Father's bookcase at once plus some others I saw at the bookstore. So I really looked forward to the realization of communism in China!

Perhaps the adults wanted something for themselves from communism as well. For they worked for it with such zeal that they forgot their meals, took no nap in the middle of the day, and often "spun round the axle," a phrase invented at the time to mean working through the night into the day and then through the day into the night. Their slogan was "Make one day equal twenty years."

That was the spirit of the Great Leap Forward, during which campaigns came and went like ocean waves. Everybody was involved. Everybody was a bit dizzy in the head. Once there was a campaign to raise the output of iron and steel, during which people all over China built small furnaces in their work units. Traditional methods were used to produce iron. We primary school students helped by going all over the big yard, collecting anything that we thought was iron. We dug up a lot of rusty nails, found a few bottomless basins and a broken chamber pot. Some students, fearing that their team might fall behind in the competition, stole iron woks and kettles from their own homes. I did not do such a thing, for I knew it would upset Aunty. Despite all the efforts, the iron produced in the big yard was no good.

The campaign to eliminate the four pests (flies, mosquitoes, rats, and sparrows) was much more effective. For three days in a row, there was no class at school. What we did was to sit on top of our two-storied classroom buildings, beating drums and gongs, banging on the bottoms of iron basins and cooking pots, waving banners, and shouting at the top of our voices. This was a unified action. The idea was to have people all over Beijing make a great noise so that sparrows would have nowhere to land. In three days all of them would die of exhaustion. So we had a great time making noise on the roof. By the end of the third day, splendid results were reported from the battlefields. Thousands of sparrows had fallen from the sky, and so had numerous other birds, beneficial ones as well as harmful ones. Well, that was the necessary sacrifice sometimes one had to make for the revolution. Compared with communism, our paradise on earth, the death of some birds was a small price to pay.

Later Aunty got involved in this campaign too. In the summer of fifty-eight, instead of a nap, every day after lunch she would go out with a fly mat under her arm, a small stool, and a matchbox. Only she and I knew that she had a secret spot behind a man-made hill in the recreation area of the big yard. In the past kids must have urinated there, so the place smelled. The smell attracted flies, and the flies attracted Aunty. So for a whole summer there she was, sitting in the hot sun, waiting patiently for the flies to land. After she killed one, she would pick up the body carefully and put it in the matchbox. She did this not for communism though. She did this for my sake, knowing there was a competition going on in my school. Each day we were required to bring the flies we killed to school. The teachers would count them and write down the numbers on a chart. Needless to say, I never fell behind in this match.

Aunty was always willing to help me in any way she could, especially in 1958, for in that year all of a sudden she found that she hardly had anything to do. In order to prepare for the oncoming communism, various work units hurriedly set up dining commons, laundries, and kindergartens. My parents insisted that we all eat at the dining common, together with others, so as to practice living and thinking collectively. Meantime all our clothes went to a newly opened laundry co-op where the inexperienced workers, Aunty complained, ruined our silk and woolen clothes. My parents had a hard time convincing her that these were the negligible shortcomings of a new phenomenon, which we should continue to support.

In addition, my parents decided to send Lian, my younger brother, to kindergarten so as to plant the spirit of collectivism in him at the age of two. The kindergarten he went to was open to kids from the big yard only. People said it was excellent, because it was modeled on Russian kindergartens. It had a large playground, a sizable wading pool with a mushroom-shaped fountain in the middle, flush toilets, new bathtubs, and many expensive toys.

Besides the modern facilities, the teachers there were young and educated. Everyone had a diploma of some kind. This was indeed different from the old grandmas in neighborhood day care centers who would let the kids do almost anything they wanted to do. Lian's teachers, on the other hand, emphasized rules and discipline. For example, in this kindergarten the children went to the toilet according to a fixed schedule, which was scientifically designed. When the time came, everybody had to sit on a toilet and afterwards no one was allowed to go back again. He or she had to wait until the next time.

In this kindergarten, Lian was to stay six days and five nights a week. That made him miserable. Every Monday morning before he left home, he would stall for time and then he would start to cry. He looked pitiable indeed, like a little lamb on its way to the wolf's big mouth. My parents and Aunty had to promise him candies and toys so as to coax him into leaving home.

Then each Saturday afternoon when Aunty and I went to pick him up, we always saw him standing behind the iron fence watching the road. As soon as he saw Aunty, he waved his little hands and jumped with joy. As soon as we were out of the teachers' earshot, he would start begging Aunty again: "Please let me stay home next week. I will be very good! I will help you do small things." To this, Aunty had to say No many times.

On Lian's third birthday, Aunty got up early, boiled some eggs, and painted them red. In Beijing it was an old custom to give young "longevity stars" red eggs so that they would be healthy and have good luck during the year. The eggs Aunty made were very pretty. So pretty that I wanted all of them. But Aunty gave me only two. The rest she put in a basket and took to the kindergarten. Before long, however, she came back with tears in her eyes. It turned out that she was stopped at the gate, where she was told that family members were not allowed to see the kids during the week. Moreover they were not supposed to send food either. Birthday or no birthday. The rule was the rule. Aunty was so disappointed that she almost burst into tears in front of the teacher. So in the end, I had all the eggs.

Because Aunty felt uneasy getting paid by my parents without doing much work, when the next campaign came and Mother suggested that she learn to read and write, she eagerly said yes. This time the campaign was to wipe out illiteracy in China. From then on, each evening Mother and Aunty would sit down at a desk. Mother would teach Aunty several characters and the latter would spend hours the next day copying and trying to memorize them.

In 1958 Aunty was already fifty-six, an old woman by traditional standards, who did not even know how to write her own name. To start learning those complicated Chinese characters as elementary school students did—that was hard for Aunty, ten times harder than the household chores. Nonetheless she persisted. I never heard her complain that the lessons were too difficult or that Mother went too fast. Soon she was advanced enough to go to the night school that was set up during the campaign. There she got small red flags and paper satellites from her teachers after each quiz as a reward for her good work. When Aunty showed these to me, her face was beaming and she was as proud as a little girl. She would surely have continued, had the campaign not suddenly come to an end in less than a year. By that time, Aunty had learned over a thousand characters, which enabled her to read newspapers and write simple letters.

Years later this turned out a true blessing for me. In fact, it was the only good thing I could think of that came out of the Great Leap Forward. Why was this a blessing? In the seventies, after I worked on the pig farm for a few years, I began to feel very lonely. It seemed that the whole world had passed me by and I was stuck. A toad sitting in a deep well, watching the sky. No one understood me. No one cared to know about the predicament I had. My parents were as bad as others. Their letters echoed the newspaper editorials, saying that educated youths had a great future in the countryside. On top of that, I was very angry at myself, for volunteering and other things I had done. For a while it seemed there was no way out.

But Aunty kept writing to me. Her letters were short and simple, telling me how much she had missed me and how she longed day and night for me to come back so that we could live together once again. These letters warmed my heart and gave me courage to go on living. I don't know what would have happened to me if Aunty had not learned to read and write during the Great Leap Forward. Loneliness and despair might have engulfed me.

8

When Famine Hit

The large-scale famine that set in around 1959 brought the Great Leap Forward to an end. Actually today many people say it was the Great Leap Forward that brought about the famine. Either way, toward the end of 1959 suddenly food became very scarce. Pork, chicken, fish, cookies, candies, nuts, canned goods, fruit, vegetables—in short, all edible things—vanished from the store shelves. Afterwards ration coupons were invented, all kinds of them: grain coupons, cooking oil coupons, meat coupons, fish coupons, egg coupons, tofu coupons, pastry coupons, sugar coupons, cigarette coupons, cotton coupons, cloth coupons, and many more. All of them were of vital importance for people living in cities.

These coupons caused changes. Suddenly money lost its magic power. My great-grandfather would have been heartbroken, if he was indeed like what his grandchildren had described. Without ration coupons, one could hardly buy anything with money. And where did ration coupons come from? Each month, the coupons were distributed by city governments to their legal residents according to their *hukou*. Consequently those small white cards, which in the past were merely registration of people's legal residency, became of vital importance. One had to have a city *hukou* to get ration coupons. Peasants were supposed to grow their own food and, beyond that, to deliver tax grain and sell surplus grain to the government. They got no ration coupons.

The coupons, moreover, differed from one place to another. Those who got coupons in Hebei province, for instance, could not use them in Beijing even though Beijing was right in the middle of Hebei province. After this system was established, it became increasingly difficult for people to move. Actually moving from a big city to a small town or to the countryside was still rather easy; but to go the other way, especially to get into Beijing and Shanghai, was harder than walking up into the blue sky. Thus the coupons took away much freedom from ordinary people and put power into the hands of some officials.

However, during the "Three-Year Natural Calamity" (1959–1962), as it was officially called in China, freedom was not the issue on people's minds. Food was the concern. Food became an obsession. When famine hit, everybody's stomach suddenly became a bottomless cave. The more food you put in it, the emptier it seemed to be. With such a rumbling stomach, the dream of communism was forgotten.

With ration coupons, an adult in Beijing was allowed to buy around thirty pounds of grain each month at a subsidized price. Children's rations varied according to their age. In addition, each person got up to a half-pound of meat, half a dozen eggs, four ounces of cooking oil, and some tofu. In fact, the rations varied depending on the supply.

Once in a while fish or animal offal came to the local store and was sold without coupons, on a first come first served basis. The news spread like wildfire in the big yard. Neighbors told neighbors. Friends called friends. People raced one another to the store. Long lines formed within minutes, winding round and round and creeping slowly like a huge serpent. Aunty and I used to take turns standing in the lines. Sometimes it would take two or three hours, sometimes even longer for us to reach the counter. When we were within a hundred feet, both of us were in the line so that we could buy twice the amount a person was allowed to buy.

I did not mind waiting in the line, under the hot sun, or in the chilly northwest wind. What I hated most was to see the food sold out to the person right in front of Aunty and me. At that moment, everybody cried, "Aiya! Meila!" in great disappointment and came to the front to see with their own eyes that all the boxes were indeed empty. But at least such disappointment never came as a surprise. The shop clerks usually warned people when the supply was running low. After that, Aunty and I would take turns going up to the counter to investigate the supply and count how many heads were ahead of us. As long as there was still a trace of hope, we would persist. Holding our breath and watching out for those who might attempt to jump the queue, we yelled, "Be conscientious! Stop squeezing in!" When I did this, no one blamed me for being impolite, and I felt it was exactly the right thing to do.

By this time, our family had stopped going to the dining common. When food was in such short supply, it was far better to keep it at home, in Aunty's careful hands. Others were probably thinking along the same lines. So the once crowded dining common was deserted. When friends and neighbors met in the big yard, they exchanged information about restaurants in Beijing: which one put more meat and oil in its stir-fry dishes, in which the rice was cooked with less water so that it would last longer.

"Go to Moscow Restaurant! They sell high-price pastry you can buy without grain coupons!"

"Go to Purple Bamboo! They have live fish these days!"

"Moslem restaurants are better! They have beef and mutton. They put more meat in their dishes!"

"The snack bar outside the Summer Palace serves imitation coffee. It tastes sort of like the real thing. Go and try it!"

So the next weekend we would be at one of these places. The party usually included only Father, Lian, and me. Mother and Aunty always insisted that they needed to stay home to take care of the baby. In those years, everywhere we went the prices were sky high and the quality of the food had never been so poor. A stir-fry dish with a few pieces of meat used to cost less than one yuan. Now it would sell for more than ten yuan and people were still buying it like crazy. To Father, money was not important. It came easily. It went easily. If a meal cost a hundred yuan, it was worth it. Some food in our stomachs was always better than a few cold bank notes. Under this guiding principle, the money my parents saved in Switzerland, four or five thousand yuan, which was a considerable sum in China at the time, was quickly used up. In a couple of years they closed their savings account.

After that, my parents often had to borrow ten or fifteen yuan from Aunty at the end of each month. This amount was paid back in a few days but before the month was over, they borrowed it back again. Aunty, on the other hand, had kept her savings of some fifteen hundred yuan that she brought back from Switzerland. When the famine was over, its purchasing power increased dramatically. But looking back on it, Father was not sorry for having bought so little with so much money. "You and Lian were both growing. I could not let you go hungry. And your mother was nursing a baby. She should not go hungry either."

But Mother went hungry anyway, voluntarily. Born in the year of the ox, she liked to say, "I am an ox. I am strong. I can eat grass and work in the fields from morning till night. Don't you worry about me." Thus saying, she took food out of her own bowl and put it into mine and Lian's. Thinking of this, now I am sure that she loved us very much. Yet when she was alive I did not understand this.

Sometimes I wonder why my mother never held me in her arms or called me by those funny "little names," as Aunty and other people's mothers did. And she never kissed me or Lian or said, "I love you." Maybe she was ashamed of doing so because she was a professional woman and a cadre? Or were there other reasons that dated back to her childhood? Could it be that my memory deceived me? For lately I have realized how unreliable one's memory can be. Anyway, in 1960, when Mother gave birth to a third child, her ration grew to include some extra eggs, fish, and meat. Most of these she quietly and resolutely pushed out of her bowl into ours. In the meantime, she was breast-feeding the baby. (She did not breast-feed Lian and me, for fear that breast-feeding might ruin the figure of which she was very proud.)

A few months later, however, her body began to show signs of "water swelling," a symptom of serious malnutrition, and her blood pressure shot up to over two hundred. Her face lost its rosy color. It looked as if it were made of yellow wax. Press a finger on her forehead, a hole would appear and stay there for quite a while. Everybody who saw her like that was alarmed, especially Father and Aunty. After that, Mother was taken better care of. But her blood pressure never returned to normal despite remedies such as Sea Treasure Soup and Chicken Blood Shots. Her health was ruined once and for all.

The baby, my little brother, Mother and Father named Yue, which means Leap, to commemorate the Great Leap Forward. This name seems really ironic today. But back in 1960, most people who lived in cities were unaware of the link between the Great Leap Forward and the famine. Those who knew what happened in the countryside during the campaign—local cadres lied about the yield; at many places crops rotted in the fields, because peasants were too busy building reservoirs and making iron and steel in their backyards; unscientific methods such as deep plowing damaged the soil—did not dare tell the truth to others. A few people who had the courage to speak up, like General Peng Dehuai, met the wrath of Chairman Mao and lost their positions.

As a result, in the sixties people in Beijing believed what the official newspapers told them: the famine was caused by natural calamities made worse later by the perfidy of the Russian Revisionists. However, our difficulties were only temporary. With a combined effort of the leaders and the common people, they would soon be overcome. And what else? Despite the severe natural calamities, not even one person in China had starved to death. If the situation had unfolded in the past, millions would have perished. This fact itself was another great victory! . . .

It was easy to convince people who lived in Beijing of the above, because their rations were higher than elsewhere. As for the big yard, it had stations out in the northwest. The soldiers there, I heard, were given orders to hunt deer in late fall. Subsequently the meat was brought to Beijing in trucks and divided up among the cadres. Nevertheless, when I looked at the albums, I was surprised to see how thin I suddenly became in 1961. I said "surprised" because I don't remember being hungry. Aside from Mother's sacrifice, Father had "tightened his belt" for us too. As a high-ranking cadre, he was taken special care of by the government. His privilege at the time was two pounds of meat each month, while Mother got only two pounds of soybeans as a low-ranking cadre. Nearly all of these, like the nutritious food Mother got, ended up taking care of Lian and me.

If the utmost my parents could do in a famine was to spend money, Aunty, who had been a poverty-stricken widow in the old society, was a lot more resourceful. With her, I had quite a few exciting adventures. I remember Aunty and I used to sneak out of the big yard at dusk with cotton sacks hidden in a handbag. We were going to buy illegal rice from the local peasants.

When we arrived at the village, it was already dark. Aunty knocked on a door. Somebody opened it from the inside. Quickly we slid into the yard. No greetings were exchanged at the door. No questions asked either. Once inside, the peasant would take out a sack of rice for Aunty to look at. Aunty reached her hand way down into the sack, took out some rice, spread it on her palm, and tried hard to find fault with it. Then they started bargaining in a low voice. After a while a price was agreed on and money changed hands; the peasant filled our sacks with rice. Finally the peasant would throw some green beans or other vegetables from his garden into the bargain to show goodwill and tell us to come back again.

I watched this process in the dark. Nobody paid any attention to me. This way of buying things was utterly unfamiliar to me. Unlike the state-owned shops where the price of everything was fixed and written on a tag, here everything was negotiable and they expected people to bargain. "Ask a sky-high price. Give an earth-low one in return." The more Aunty found fault with the peasant's rice, the happier he seemed to look. Sometimes when she said, "Forget it! The price you ask is ridiculous! I'm leaving," the deal was made. No ill feelings on either side. No real friendship either. It was strictly business.

On our way back, the sacks were heavy. Aunty carried the big one. I carried the small one. It was quite a walk. After a while I was sweaty. Yet I walked as fast as I could. Seeing this, Aunty would say that she was truly glad that I had grown up and was now such a big help. Meanwhile she also warned me not to tell anybody what we had done. Her words made me feel that I was trusted. "Of course I won't tell on her and get her into trouble! I know it is for our sake that she takes the risk. I am ten years old now. I understand such things!"

My parents understood this too, I think, in their hearts and bellies. But to save face or for whatever reason, they had to tell her that in their opinion buying illegal rice was wrong; as Party members and cadres, they could not endorse such activities.

"But I'm not a Party member and I'm not a cadre," Aunty protested. "I am not afraid of making mistakes. I cannot let Rae and Lian go hungry anyway! Besides, these days many families in the big yard are buying rice from the peasants. The leaders have not said anything about it."

That was true. So afterwards my parents dropped the subject once and for all. Aunty and I continued to visit the peasants at dusk, when our rations were about to run out. My parents gave Aunty more money for groceries and asked no questions. Neither did the latter report how she spent the money. She was completely trusted.

On other days Aunty got up at sunrise and went out with a bamboo basket. I knew she was going to the big stony bridge to buy frog legs, which people in Beijing called "field chicken" legs. In the sixties, the big yard was surrounded by large stretches of rice fields and lotus ponds, home for numerous frogs. In early spring I liked to watch tadpoles swim in the sparkling stream. For days they would remain the same. Then one morning, suddenly, little legs spread out from the sides of their bodies. Their color changed from black to grass green. They had become frogs, jumping, diving, swimming, and singing.

On starlit summer nights, they turned the rice paddies into an enormous open-air opera house. The fragrant breeze of rice and lotus flowers wafted their songs. The whole world seemed to be listening. By and by the moon came out from behind the willow trees. The grass was moved to tears. Night after night, I fell asleep to such noisy and peaceful lullabies.

If after 1958 there were hardly any birds twittering among trees in Beijing, during the famine the frogs were nearly wiped out. The peasant boys were out catching them every night with fishing rods. Before sunrise, the little singers were taken out of their bamboo prisons. First they were skinned alive. After that, their organs were torn out. Their bodies were washed in the stream and pieced together on sharp bamboo sticks. Soon the customers would arrive. Most of them were old women like Aunty. A string of five frogs would sell for around two yuan, a day's salary for a skilled worker in Beijing.

Since the trade was so profitable, the opera house was quickly emptied out. At night, a few scattered croaks reminded people of a big void. But I must confess that in those years when I saw Aunty come back with a bloody lotus leaf package, I was more glad than sad. For I knew that we would have a delicious dish at dinner, a meat dish! In fact, I not only ate the meat, I even chewed and devoured the smaller bones.

During the famine, Aunty not only bought food from various places, she produced food as well. That made her very busy once again. So busy that she no longer had time to study. With the help of Father and me, she reclaimed two pieces of land in the big yard. Each was a little over a hundred square feet large. Next she set up fences to separate our land from the sacred territories of our neighbors. Then we debated about what to plant. Eventually Aunty put in corn because it was high-yielding and sturdy. When the corn sprouted, she sowed beans among them to utilize the land to the utmost. After the beans grew up, she was hardly home. The crops had to be watered and taken care of. But most of the time she was simply keeping an eye on them.

Not far from our garden plots were chicken coops made of broken bricks and asphalt felt. One of them belonged to us. Watching over those feathered creatures with wings and legs was even more difficult than guarding the crops. One day a hen named Phoenix Head was missing. Aunty and I went all over the big yard to look for it. "Gu-gu-daa! Gu-gu-daa—!" Aunty kept calling until her voice grew hoarse. But there was no answer. The hen seemed to have vanished into thin air.

This made Aunty very upset. After three hours, we came back home utterly exhausted. But in less than ten minutes, she jumped up and went out again. This time by herself she searched all the garden plots and peeped into other people's chicken coops as well. After dark she had to give the hen up for lost. When she returned home, she looked as if she had lost a child.

Perhaps the hen was like a child to her. She bought the chicks from a peasant when they were tiny, too small for anyone to tell if they would grow up to be hens or roosters. Raising them in a famine was no easy job. Aunty and I went all over the big yard to gather edible herbs. After we carried them back, she would wash the greens, chop them into fine pieces, cook them, and carefully mix in some tiny bits of corn flour. In addition, she tried to catch worms for the brood. Only four of the chicks turned out to be hens, and Aunty gave each one a pretty name. All were laying eggs for her faithfully. Now suddenly one of them was missing. Most likely it was cooking in someone else's wok, almost ready to be served as a delicious dish. This thought made Aunty so indignant that she lost her appetite and cursed the thief under her breath for a whole evening.

9

A Vicious Girl

If the Great Leap Forward and the famine were like tidal currents that swept over China, affecting the lives of tens of millions, my private life in those years was like an undercurrent. The anxiety and despair I kept to myself.

All my trouble started with Lian, my younger brother, who was such a perfect boy. At the age of three he had large brown eyes, plump rosy cheeks, and soft black hair. When he smiled, tiny dimples floated up. All adults loved kids with such "wine nests," which unfortunately I did not have. Lian's good looks must have given him confidence. Thus he was never shy and the one thing he enjoyed most was to socialize with people. On the bus, in the street, at home, in his kindergarten, at stores . . . everywhere he went, he was well liked.

When my parents' colleagues who were also our neighbors came to visit, they always asked him to sing a song, to recite a short Tang dynasty poem, or to dance. To these requests he would gladly consent, and I had to admit that his performances were quite impressive. So compliments flowed in toward him. He was at the center of the stage, beaming like a bright star. I was left out in the cold. That made me very angry.

"It's not fair! I can sing and dance better than he can! I know more ancient poems, long ones as well as short ones. I've learned several classical essays by heart too. How come nobody asks *me* to recite them? Maybe they think poetry is not for girls. Girls are only interested in mothering dolls and cooking in a toy kitchen. But Father should know better! He should know I'm not that kind of girl! For instead of buying me those stupid dolls, didn't he himself teach me those classical poems and prose? And Mother taught me so many songs. Why didn't she suggest I sing a few of them? At this moment even they've forgotten me. When Lian was applauded by those loathsome guests, their half-hidden smile showed they were so proud of him. In the past I was the one they'd been so proud of!"

At the time, of course, I was quite unaware of Chinese traditions:

how important it was for families to have sons and how little any daughters mattered. Nor did I have an inkling that our guests, who talked about communism so enthusiastically, were also complying with social conventions: a considerate guest should admire the host family's sons. Paying compliments to their daughters, on the other hand, was tricky. Sometimes it would make the host family suspect that the guest was making fun of them. What he or she really suggested was that the hosts had wasted time and money making investments for other families. So wise guests avoided the pitfall.

If someone had explained all this to me, even if I might not have understood it completely, I would have known that Lian's popularity had something to do with history. But instead what people told me was that in new China women were liberated; men and women were completely equal; women held up half the sky . . . So there must be something wrong with me that I was not as popular as Lian. Or maybe there was something wrong with Lian? Yes! It was he, not I, who was to blame!

From then on, endless fights broke out between the two of us. At first we yelled at each other. Later we used our hands and feet. In my opinion, Lian was vain and arrogant. And he had no respect for his older sister. For that, I wanted to teach him a lesson and make him behave himself. But my parents just wouldn't back me up.

My father in those days had a theory—if a sibling ever got into a fight against another who was five years younger, the older sibling was definitely in the wrong. She should humor and take care of her little brother or else she would be punished!—Lian soon found this out and he wasted no time taking advantage of it.

Behind my parents' backs, he provoked me constantly by pulling my hair, pushing me from behind, messing up my things, calling me names . . . When I retaliated, he fought back like a wildcat. Then, as soon as he heard that one of our parents was coming, he dissolved into tears instantly. What a born actor he was! (In 1972 he even got an offer from People's Art, the leading theatrical company in Beijing, after a single audition. It was a pity that Father intervened, not knowing that Lian had such talent for acting!) So he never failed to give my parents the impression that he was a helpless little lamb, about to be torn apart and devoured by a ferocious tiger, which of course was me. (And it so happened that I was born in the year of the tiger and Lian in the year of the lamb.)

Only I knew the truth. But I disdained explaining it to my parents who were arbitrary and biased against me anyway. I would rather let them punish me. I would never beg them for mercy or anything! I became stubborn. I became obnoxious. I knew I was obnoxious, and that was my choice! I despised the sweet little girl I used to be when I was in Switzerland. In fact I even hated the fact that I was a girl. I refused to play girl's games. Instead, I joined the boys in climbing trees and getting onto roofs. I could play the boy's games better and run faster than most of the boys. But still I was not one of them.

I remember once I played hide-and-seek with a group of boys in the big yard. When it was my turn to seek, for a long time I couldn't find anybody. At last I figured out that the boys were all hiding in a men's room. "Those treacherous and shameless boys! They are all my enemies! Trying to take advantage of me? I'll teach you a lesson!" With such angry thoughts churning in my head, I went home, found a lock, and locked up the men's room from the outside. Revenge! Revenge! After that I was happy and I went home to have dinner. Later I did not inquire how the boys managed to get out of that stinking place. Since they lost face, none of them wanted to mention it either.

But my real enemy was not among these boys. It was Lian. The hatred I had for him simmered in my heart day and night. He was a needle in my eye, a thorn in my flesh. I just had to do something about him!

Saturday came. Lian was back from the kindergarten. The whole family sat down to have dinner. The sight of Lian turned the delicious food Aunty made into mud in my mouth. Look at him! He was the star again, talking joyfully and endlessly to others at the dinner table and deliberately ignoring me. I ate my food in silence, let myself be forgotten for a while. Then I lifted my head and announced: "Lian will die before he is five years old!"

These words interrupted whatever small talk that was going on. There was a moment of dead silence. Then, bang! The bomb exploded! Mother jumped up and yelled.

"What? You cursed your own brother? You want him to die? How wicked you are! You vicious girl! . . . "

She was so angry that her voice shook and her features changed. In the past, people believed that bad words had the power to bring about misfortunes. Could it be true that Mother, who was a Communist Party member and believed in materialism, also believed in such things? As for Father, he hit the table with his fist so hard that all the bowls and dishes jumped up. He grabbed me by the arm and dragged me away from the dinner table. In another room, he forced open my hand with his strong fingers and beat me on the palm with his own hand.

Actually the beating was more scary than real. It did not hurt. But that was not important. The important thing was that for the first time Father had lifted his hand against me! In the past he and Mother had cherished me as a lustrous pearl on the palm of their hands. He had never touched me with a little finger. In this sense the beating marked a turning point in my life, a rather unfortunate one it was. But I asked for it anyway.

After that, I was beaten from time to time. Sometimes Mother and Father beat me because I did bad things or I was stubborn. Sometimes they did so out of the conviction that I was a bad girl and I was always up to some mischief.

I will never forget the wrongs they did me! For example, one evening my parents attended a political meeting that lasted till almost midnight. While they were away, I read a book in their room and then fell asleep. A gust of wind must have shut the door. It locked automatically. When my parents returned, they wanted to go straight to bed and sleep. But they found the door of their room was locked from the inside.

They must have knocked and shouted for a long time before they woke me up. After I opened the door but before I could open my mouth to explain, Father seized my hand. He beat me on the palm and shouted: "How come you have become so vicious? Do you intend to lock me and your mother out for the night? Let me tell you this is my home! The next time you try such tricks on us, I'll beat you even harder. You bear that in mind!"

Of course I knew that: this was his home, and Mother's home, and Lian's home! It was not my home! I hated the fact that I was still a child. I could not work to support myself. I had to depend on my parents. I had to eat their food, wear their clothes, and live under their roof. That was so humiliating!

But I must add that usually my anger for Father would not last very long. Each time after he punished me, he would come into my room to reason with me. By so doing he gave me a chance to defend myself. If I could convince him that he had punished me wrongly, he would apologize for his mistake and promise that in the future it would not happen again. Only then would I allow my tears to flow. The tears were burning hot, for I had held them back for so long. I was determined not to weep in front of my enemies.

If I could not convince Father that he was in the wrong, then it was his turn to try to convince me that I had done something wrong. However after he made his point he would always add that he had been too impatient; beating people was wrong and he did not mean to be so harsh; actually he and Mother both loved me very much.

Each time I heard Father say so I was moved. But I did not really believe what he said, that is, that both he and Mother loved me. Mother, I had given her up a long time before. I found that she seldom made up her own mind. Although she was better educated and had more talent than Father, she simply worshiped him and took his opinion to be her own. Thus when Father said that I was a wicked girl, she said I was indeed hopeless. When Father beat me, she said I deserved the punishment, every bit of it. Her opinion of me would never change as long as Father did not change his. In our family, Father was the boss. Mother was nothing! She was unable to help me out. Nor was she willing to do so!

Looking back on those years, I realize that I was like a paper tiger too. On the outside, I was tough and aggressive. I had teeth and claws all over me. Everybody said I was a tomboy. "Play crazy, run wild." "No heart, no lungs." (Insensitive and thoughtless.) What did they know about me? Inwardly I was full of doubts about myself. I was confused. I was scared. Nobody knew how miserable I had been.

Sometimes I would weep in my quilt at night. I imagined that I was poor Cinderella: In the past, my father and mother both loved me and I lived like a princess. Now I am under the authority of a cruel stepmother. I am made to live in the ashes, while my ugly stepsisters are wrapped in silk and satin. They are dancing in the royal palace; I am slaving away in the kitchen . . . All this is happening because my real parents are dead. People have buried them beneath the nine springs. They are watching me helplessly. They are weeping for me . . .

Rehearsing such sad stories in my mind, I found their taste both bitter and sweet. Having doubts about myself at the age of eight or nine, however, was like hell. What if my parents were right and I was indeed a vicious girl? Why did I hate Lian so much that I divided the whole world into two camps: those who liked him were my mortal enemies; those who did not admire him might be my allies? Besides, there was something else that was troubling me. What if I was stupid? For I was not doing well at school. The Chinese texts we studied in grades three and four did not interest me. The characters I wrote often had problems: a dot was missing here, a little line was misplaced there. I just could not remember them as well as others. Father used to joke about this, saying that I had a "flowerpot head." A flowerpot had a hole in the bottom. It could not hold things. Just like my brain.

As for my calligraphy, it was strange to think that in two years no matter how hard I tried to practice, I never got a single 5 (A) or even a 4 (B) from that old master. The best grade he gave me was a 3+ and the worst was a 3– thanks to his kindness, which would still allow me to pass. Eventually I realized 3 was what I would get from him. I accepted my fate and stopped trying.

If I did not do well in Chinese and calligraphy, I could at least laugh at myself. But when it came to arithmetic, the only thing I wanted to do was to hide myself and weep! At the time, we were learning the mixed four fundamental operations: addition, subtraction, multiplication, and division. My classmates seemed to have no problem comprehending them. After the teacher explained the new material, I saw many of them raise their hands, offering to solve the questions on the blackboard. I seemed to be the only one who was lost, unable to make head or tail of what the teacher said.

Class after class, it went on like this. Even today I remember vividly what I felt, the panic, the shame, the helplessness, the sudden urge to cry . . . I tried to hide behind my classmates' backs, my eyes avoiding the teacher's eyes. The mere thought that she might pick me to solve the next question set my heart fluttering and my cheeks burning. The fifty-minute class was as long as a hundred years. Perhaps I was indeed stupid and Lian was much smarter?

Aunty seemed the only one who never believed that I was bad and stupid. For that, instead of love and gratitude, I only gave her more trouble than I did others. It was almost as if I had lost my senses, and I was making a tremendous effort against myself. I tried everything to prove to her that I was indeed a wicked child. Day and night, I said harsh words to her. I made my clothes dirty as soon as I put them on. I refused to sit still when she washed my hair. (Before I went to the countryside I had never washed either my clothes or my hair.) I would not go to bed on time. I messed things up for her . . . Nothing seemed to work. Then I started to steal money from her.

Stealing, I knew, was really bad! But I did it anyway. Don't ask me why. The first time, I took one yuan. The next time, I took three yuan . . . It wasn't that I needed the money for anything. I didn't need the money at all. I wasted it. I remember once I bought lychee, which was an expensive southern delicacy. But I did not even like lychee. So I shared it with several classmates of mine who were not even my friends. Other things I bought were equally senseless.

In the meantime I waited day and night for the bomb to explode, as it did after I said that Lian would die before he reached the age of five. I wanted to hear Aunty say I was a wicked girl. Yet I dreaded it, knowing such a verdict from her would really be the end of me. But days went by. Nothing happened. Aunty loved me and trusted me just as before.

By and by I started to comprehend, even though by then I could not explain. Aunty's love for me was different from that of my parents. If I turned out a failure or a social outcast such as a Rightist or a counterrevolutionary, my parents would face the reality sooner or later. They would admit I was indeed no good, even though this was painful for them because they loved me. In short, their opinion of me depended on how good and successful I would be.

Aunty was not like that. I might be a complete failure, I might be found guilty by the judges, I might be rejected or condemned by the whole world, she would love me all the same. No! She would love me even more so as to make up for the "wrongs" I suffered at the hands of others. It was my side of the story that she would listen to and believe wholeheartedly. Nothing on earth could convince her that I was not the best and the smartest. Such love was blind and unreasonable. One should think that it would spoil a child. But in my case, somehow it saved me. She expected me to be the best. Shame on me if I should let her down!

When I realized this, I was like a drowning person in a stormy ocean whose feet suddenly touched a piece of solid ground. The nightmares receded. Peace slowly returned to my mind. I no longer envied others for their good fortune. They might possess gold mountains and silver mines; I had my darling little island that would never sink. In its green harbor, I could moor the boat of my heart. By its sweet springs, I would relax, rest, and regain my strength and confidence. In the past, I may have lost a home. But now I found one and it was the safest and the sweetest. I was content.

I confessed to Aunty about what I did. She took it calmly. (Father and Mother would have made a fuss, that was for sure, if they found out that I had stolen money from somebody.) Aunty merely said to me:

"If you need money, use mine. But remember this: in the future if you have to borrow money from others, make sure you do not forget and you pay them back as soon as possible. In the past, you know, I was very poor. I had to be very careful, for I did not want people to despise me. If a person has no money, that is her fate. No need to be ashamed of it. But if a person has no *zhiqi,* she is no good."

These words sank into my heart and stayed there, guiding my thinking and behavior ever since, even though she did not say them emphatically. Perhaps I remembered her words so well because they were illustrated by the story of her life. It was a story about *zhiqi.* The word is very hard to translate. It means self-respect, dignity, ambition, and the willpower not to beg others for anything. Aunty had all these and much more, such as sagacity, perseverance, and chastity.

IO

Aunty's Name Was Chastity

Aunty's name was Tian Xi Zhen. Zhen, her personal name, means chastity. She was born in 1904. Emperor Guangxu was still alive, but by then the power was in the hands of the dowager empress. Many generations of Aunty's family had been the emperor's craftsmen. Their hereditary handicraft was to put up mat sheds for the imperial family before summer and for special events. Such mat sheds were made of bamboo poles and reed mats, giving people shelter and shade wherever they might need them. But that was not all. In old Beijing, one mark of a family's status was whether it could afford fine mat sheds or had only cheap ones. People would notice them, compare them, and make comments. Those who lost the competition lost face.

The emperor's mat sheds, of course, were always the best, thanks to Aunty's forefathers. Her family was known among old Beijing residents by its surname, Xi, as "the Xi family of mat sheds." When the Manchu emperors were in power, the Xi family of mat sheds lived in a special quarter to the west of the forbidden city, along with other craftsmen's families.

When Aunty was a girl, the neighbors must have gossiped about her family behind their backs, saying that their ancestors did not do enough good deeds. Why? Because out of the six children Aunty's parents had, five were daughters. The daughters of the Xi family, however, were quite extraordinary. Good-looking and dexterous—qualities for which, according to Aunty, they had their mother to thank.

The mother herself was from a hereditary craftsman's family. Unlike Nainai's folk, the emperor's craftsmen were not Manchus. They had neither power nor wealth. All they had were skills. Skills were the roots of their life, the source of their pride. They were their "crops grown on iron stalks," that is, if the younger generations were able to learn them well. In such families, some skills were passed down from fathers to sons, some from mothers to daughters.

Aunty's mother had many skills, which were not the ones described in traditional Chinese fiction, such as playing the lute, painting, and making poetry. Her skills were practical, which she tried to teach her daughters. Yet as the Chinese saying puts it, "The five fingers are not of the same length." Over the years, the five daughters each became especially good at some of the mother's skills.

Aunty's older sister, for example, became an excellent cook. Aunty, who was the second, surpassed others in making clothes. The third sister died in her thirties, long before I was born, so I did not know much about her. The fourth sister excelled in embroidery, while the fifth specialized in making snacks.

Looking back on it, I felt that these skills were like invisible dowries Aunty's mother gave her daughters. If in the future, their husbands turned out to be decent as well as successful, the daughters would be traditional housewives, and the dowry would not be tapped. But in case something went wrong, as in Aunty's case, she would be able to survive on her own.

As for Aunty's brother, the only male child who was also the youngest, he was of course "the crane among chicks." At home he was pampered by his parents, waited on hand and foot by his five sisters. He was sent to school for a few years to learn to read and write. In the future he would carry on the family's surname as well as the hereditary handicraft. He would bear the ancestors many sons and grandsons. The daughters, on the other hand, would soon be married into other families.

When Aunty reached the age of seventeen, a marriage was arranged for her. She was to marry a man from the Tian family of pastry, another family in which the men had been the emperor's craftsmen for generations. Everybody thought this was a perfect match. The parents on both sides were happy and there was no dispute about the dowry. All was arranged through a matchmaker. Later the Tian family gave betrothal gifts to Aunty's family. When her parents accepted such gifts, Aunty's "lifelong big affair" was settled. The fact that Aunty had never set eyes on the man who was to become her husband did not bother anybody. Marriages in China had always been arranged this way. Aunty's duty was just to obey her parents. Meanwhile she still had a few months to pray to the gods in heaven that her husband be a decent man.

Then came "the day of her great happiness." According to an ancient custom, the bride must weep when she leaves her parents' home, so as to show that she is a filial daughter. Aunty had no difficulty complying with this. In fact, she told me that she almost cried her eyes out, when the red sedan chair carried her away from her own home to that of a total stranger.

Maybe the gods heard Aunty's prayers. Her husband turned out to be a decent man. He had a few years' education, not enough to make him a scholar, yet it was sufficient to convince him that pastry-making was not for him. "Ten thousand trades are lowdown, only study is sublime." Nonetheless, he was a prudent and law-abiding man. He did not drink, gamble, or beat his wife.

By the time he and Aunty got married, the last emperor had abdicated. The emperor's craftsmen lost their hereditary jobs. Aunty's husband found a position in the new government. Although he was just a small clerk earning a small salary in a small office under the ministry of education, many people envied him. For in those years jobs in the civil service were extremely hard to come by. It was much easier for a young man to become a soldier. The warlords were fighting for power and territory all over China. But Aunty's husband did not have the right stuff to be a soldier. So he was grateful that he had his small job, which enabled his family to live in peace for a few years.

Aunty, in those years, was a traditional housewife. First she had a son. Three years later, she had a daughter. The husband's income could not support a family of four, but Aunty made ends meet through hard work. She took care of the babies herself. In the meantime she cooked, shopped around for the least expensive groceries, washed everybody's clothes, and kept the house clean. On top of that, the family never needed to buy shoes and clothes. Aunty made them at home.

Years later, she made shoes and clothes for us too. That, of course, was after my parents used up their savings. I remember how she did this: the silver thimble she wore on her middle finger shone like a diamond ring. The needle she used moved so fast through the fabric that it seemed alive, a tiny whitebait swimming vigorously upstream in a creek. From time to time, she scratched the needle against the side of her head, to oil it. After that the needle moved even faster.

All her life, Aunty had never touched a sewing machine. In Switzerland Mother offered to buy her one.

"No! I don't want it!"

"It'll save you time. Try it. It's easy."

"Easy, save time, but ugly! Look at these stitches. My stitches are invisible on the outside. Can the machine do that?"

After Mother gave up the idea, Aunty continued to bear a grudge against the machine that could sew even faster than she. In the past, no woman in her neighborhood could boast that. Aunty used to be very proud of the fact. As for me, years later it turned out that somehow I too enjoy sewing with a needle. It is slow, but I like the feeling. Stitch by stitch. The needle follows the heart. The heart is filled with peace. Unlike Aunty, I do have a sewing machine though. Once in a while I lend it to a friend from China. Most of the time, it sits in my attic gathering dust.

The house Aunty and her husband lived in was plain: gray brick walls, a small courtyard, three rooms facing south, and a kitchen, tiled roof overgrown with grass that leaked from time to time, windows with no glass but rice paper on them . . . Nonetheless the house belonged to Aunty's husband, and that was a very big help. The young couple paid no rent. Moreover, Aunty could grow some vegetables and raise a few hens in the courtyard. Aunty managed her household affairs with success. Over the years, she saved a small amount of money for her children's education. Since others' children could go to school, hers would not stay home and be illiterate. That was Aunty's *zhiqi*.

When Aunty's son was six and her daughter three years old, suddenly news came that Nanjing would replace Beijing as the nation's capital. Governmental organizations, including the one in which Aunty's husband worked, were to move south. This brought Aunty and her husband face to face with a real dilemma: if they stayed in Beijing, Aunty's husband would lose his job. Where could he find another one? After the central government moved away, even fewer jobs would be available in the ancient city and more people would go after them.

On the other hand, if they moved to Nanjing, the husband's salary would not be sufficient. For in that case they would have to rent a house and rent was never cheap in a capital. Besides, neither Aunty nor her husband had ever been away from Beijing. It frightened them to imagine living in a city hundreds of miles away from their hometown. No relatives. No old neighbors. All the shops and streets would be unfamiliar, and every person a stranger. What if something happened and they needed help? In China if one had neither power nor a lot of money, such help from an acquaintance was indispensable. Who could they turn to? So either way it seemed the family would run into a lot of trouble.

Aunty's husband was deeply worried, he suddenly looked twenty years older and walked with a stoop. His wife was not much help; each time she thought about their dreadful dilemma, her mind went blank and she ended up weeping helplessly. At last, her husband decided to stay behind and try to find another job. He looked for a long time without success.

While he was looking for a job, the family's financial situation quickly deteriorated. First, they used up Aunty's small savings. Then they sold the furniture, piece by piece. Aunty's jewelry, which consisted of a few silver bracelets and jade earrings, went into the pawnshop together with the better clothes and were never redeemed. Then they had to borrow money from relatives and acquaintances, who after some time began to avoid them. These people were not affluent, they could not afford to throw their money into the river just to listen to the sound of it.

Then as the saying goes, "Good luck does not come by twos. Misfortunes never travel alone." Aunty's husband came down with an illness. By then the family was so impoverished that they had to skip meals. Where on earth could Aunty find the money to send for a doctor and buy medicine? So in a few weeks her husband died, leaving behind a young widow of twenty-five, two small children, and a literally empty house.

It was a great disaster for Aunty. Now heaven had taken away her man, in the future who would be there to support her and her children? Aunty cried day and night. The thought of suicide, the time-honored solution for so many Chinese widows before her, loomed large in her mind. But she decided against it. Her son and daughter were too small! They were so helpless! Now their father was gone, she was the only one in the world they could turn to. She should be there for them. She would bring them up, no matter how hard it was.

To bring her children up, one option Aunty had was to remarry. Not a glorious option, of course, but feasible. Aunty was still young and good-looking. Neither her parents nor his family would object to the idea, since they were unable to give her financial support. So Aunty had a choice. Eventually she chose to stay as her late husband's "not-yet-dead-person." Until she died at the age of seventy-four, she never had another man.

"Aunty, do you love your husband?" Once after I read a romantic novel, I couldn't help asking her.

"What? No!" she said. Then she added, "I don't even remember him."

"Then why didn't you marry someone else?"

"I didn't want people to poke their fingers at my backbone and gossip about me. Some of them might even insult me right to my face. I can't stand that. But what I feared more was that the second husband might be cruel to my children. Beat them. Curse them. Let them eat leftovers. Give them cotton padded jackets with only reed catkins inside, like the Peking opera I told you about. I heard too many stories about mean stepparents. I didn't want to risk it."

So that was why for half a century Aunty remained true to her dead husband, whom she did not love. "He was so useless! When there was trouble, he couldn't deal with it. He died! Leaving us behind to fend for ourselves. Look at how much he made me suffer. Look at your other aunts (meaning her sisters). See what comfortable lives they've had. Love him? Humph! Who'd love a man like that?" When Aunty said this, she was bitter as if the death of her husband was his fault and his failure.

Since men were not as dependable as they seemed, Aunty decided to depend on herself. In the future, she would try to find work and bring in money. She would raise her children and protect them too. She would not let them down as her useless husband did.

From then on, Aunty began to make clothes for other people. Although she was a skilled dressmaker, first she had to conquer her shyness and fear to find customers. By and by, she learned to talk with people and deal with strangers. While she did this, she knew that she had to be extremely cautious, for she was a widow. Men might want to take advantage of her and women would "chase the wind and catch a shadow" to gossip about a poor widow. Yet she could not afford to stay home and sit idle. She needed customers, male and female. Life was always a dilemma. But this time Aunty handled everything well. Over the years, in front of her gate there was no wind, no shadow. Eventually she convinced her neighbors that she was a chaste woman with a lot of *zhiqi*.

As for her business, the price she charged was more than reasonable. The work was always done on time. Even the pickiest customers had a hard time finding fault with the clothes she made. So as time went by, her reputation grew in the neighborhood. Her customers kept coming back.

This was no small success for Aunty. Fate had dealt her a heavy blow, but it did not crush her. It made her stronger. After she climbed up, she stood on her own feet. She no longer needed to depend on a husband or to beg for help from his or her relatives, which was so humiliating. She could support herself and her children with her ten fingers.

The first time Aunty came to Nainai's house was to make clothes. After my great-grandfather died, she came to help the family's own tailor rush the so-called filial apparel. In old China a proper funeral should last forty-nine days, and during this period everything in the family must be white. The clothes, caps, and shoes worn by the family members and servants, drapes, curtains, tablecloths, chair-covers, bedding . . . A great deal of needlework had to be done in just a few days. Aunty worked conscientiously day and night. Her honesty, modesty, and competence left a deep impression on Nainai. Meanwhile Nainai gained Aunty's heart by her kindness and generosity. So years later, when Mother was pregnant and Aunty's old aunt suggested that her niece might be hired to take care of me, Nainai nodded her head and Aunty accepted the job.

Aunty earned handsome money during the funeral, but such good luck was hard to come by. In old Beijing, poor people who could not afford to make new clothes greatly outnumbered the rich ones who wasted their money on filial apparel. The rich families, moreover, had their own tailors. Unless it was an emergency, they did not have work for Aunty. So most of the time instead of making new clothes Aunty was altering old clothes for people who had less money and she had to charge a lower price for it. Then once in a while there weren't even old clothes to be altered; in that case Aunty would wash clothes for others to make ends meet.

Washing clothes the old-fashioned way was toilsome. Yet described by Aunty years later, it seemed quite beautiful to me. With a large bamboo basket, Aunty carried the clothes to a stream, where she soaked them and beat them gently piece after piece with a wooden stick against a flat rock. While she did this, the water flowed through the garments, carrying the dirt away. For the top of the rock was just an inch or so beneath the surface of the water. No "foreign soap" was applied. No funny smell. Dry the clothing in the sun. It smelled of the sun. To Aunty, this was always the best way in the world to wash clothes.

Aunty's nostalgia, however, did not make her forget the harsh reality. In fact, it was from her stories that I first came to know how difficult the lives of the working people had been in the old society, long before such narrative became fashionable in China. (In the sixties I sat through many "Recalling Bitterness Big Meetings" at my middle school. They got me into trouble. But when Aunty told her story, she was perfectly calm—unlike the speakers we had at school—and I felt no pressure to act out my hatred for the class enemies. We were both comfortable.)

Aunty said that for her the winter nights in Beijing were long and bitterly cold. The northwest wind from Mongolia howled over people's roofs. It shook and penetrated the thin window paper. It sneaked in from the cracks in the wooden doors. Rushing with clothes orders, Aunty sometimes had to sew far into the night. The light from her oil lamp shuddered and dimmed. The small fire in the stove was about to die out. Her fingers were so cold that they became stiff. Her feet felt like two pieces of ice. She kept her head lowered for so long, she felt a pain burning in her neck and shoulders. But she had no time to stretch or move.

The hot summer was equally hard for a seamstress. The sweat on her hands dulled the needle. The work went more slowly than usual. Aunty got behind in her orders. Many evenings while her neighbors were in the courtyard "riding the cool," she was by the oil lamp sewing. When the moon rose above the old date trees, the outside cooled down. But in the house it was still as hot and stuffy as in the afternoon. She had a palm-leaf fan lying next to her; but as she had only two hands, how was she to use it?

Hundreds of stitches, thousands of stitches, millions of stitches. Aunty's money did not come easily. Every cent had to be used at exactly the right place. Aunty told me that in old Beijing roasted peanuts were very cheap. For one big copper coin, you could buy a small packet, wrapped in old newspaper into the shape of an ice-cream cone. They were delicious! Many times Aunty's son and daughter begged her for it. Many times she had to harden her heart and say no to them.

All the year round, her family lived on a diet of corn flour bread. White flour was a luxury for birthdays and festivals. In summer, when vegetables were cheap and plentiful, Aunty would buy them from a peddler at the end of the day when they were on sale. The rest of the year, all they had were salted vegetables. Meat almost never appeared on their dinner table except on Chinese New Year, the biggest festival.

With such self-denial, Aunty not only survived, she put her son through elementary school. Later with her son's help, Aunty sent her daughter into high school. Like other old-fashioned Chinese mothers, Aunty placed all her hopes on her children, and they did not disappoint her. Though they grew up in poverty, they made no bad friend and acquired no bad habit. This, I guess, was to some extent attributable to

Aunty's talk about *zhiqi*. But more important was her own example. It turned out that her children were not only honest and modest, they were also filled with filial piety. Both hoped fervently that someday they would find good jobs, make enough money, so that Aunty would cease to toil. In her old age, she would be surrounded, loved, and waited on by her children and grandchildren.

Finally, Aunty's daughter graduated from high school. To Aunty's great satisfaction, she got a job in the Chinese Customs and later she married a young officer in the same department. In 1949 the daughter was pregnant. Aunty waited impatiently for her first grandchild to come. But before the baby arrived, the army led by the Communists came down from the northeast. All the Nationalist organizations including the customs were going to Taiwan. If Aunty's daughter and her husband stayed behind, both would lose their jobs. No one knew how many months or years they'd have to wait before they could find other jobs. The unemployment rate by then had reached an all-time high. It was even worse than in the late twenties. Meanwhile, the baby was coming . . .

History in China has a nasty habit of repeating itself. The same dilemma that Aunty and her husband had faced twenty-one years earlier returned to haunt the family, bringing back all the nightmares Aunty had tried to forget. Only this time it was up to Aunty to decide if she wanted her daughter to stay or to leave, and there was no time to hesitate. She had to make a decision in just a few days. Such a decision, Aunty knew from her past experience, could be a matter of life and death.

In the past, her husband died in poverty and despair. Now history mustn't be allowed to repeat itself in her family! So after a few sleepless nights, a red-eyed Aunty told her daughter that she ought to go to Taiwan, together with her husband. They did what she said. After they set off for the southern island, communication between mainland and Taiwan was cut off. When Aunty died in 1978, she had never received a single letter from her daughter. She had no idea whether she was alive or dead, nor did she know anything about what happened to the grandchild she dreamed of holding in her arms.

After her daughter was gone, Aunty began to think about her son more and more. In the fourteen years after he graduated from elementary school, he spared no effort to help her support the family. At first he was a newspaper boy and an errand boy. Next he apprenticed and worked in a bicycle store. A few years later he became an assistant in a camera shop, because the pay there was a little better, even though it was much farther from home for him to walk. Finally he became a worker in Beijing zoo.

From 1935 to 1949, these were fourteen disastrous years for the ordinary Chinese. The Japanese occupation was followed by the large-scale civil war. The prices of food and other necessities rose from month to month until in the end it shot up from morning to the afternoon. In 1949 a sack of banknotes could not buy a sack of flour. Numerous people were jobless. Many lost their homes. People starved to death in the street. Amid all this, Aunty's family not only survived but her daughter graduated from high school. All this would not have been possible, Aunty knew, had it not been for the tremendous effort and self-sacrifice made by her son.

After 1949, there was no more civil war and the inflation was brought under control. Slowly people's lives returned to normal. But time was running out for Aunty's son to get married. At the age of twenty-eight, he never had a girl friend. Although he was not so ugly, he would not attract a young woman unless he had something else, such as money. Aunty knew that her son had not saved any money for himself. She worried about his future happiness, knowing romantic love between beauty and talent existed only in operas on the stage. In real life, marriage was a practical matter. She decided that she should help him.

That was why Aunty went to Switzerland. The agreement she had with my parents said once they got her there she had to work for us for five years. By so doing, of course, she would make money, a lot of it, according to the Chinese standard of the time. But if it had not been for her son, she would not have accepted the job.

In the past she had never been away from Beijing. The sound of an airplane scared her to death and all the trains, buses, and ships made her dizzy and sick. Now she was going to take all these to a foreign country she knew not where it was. She would have to live among foreign devils who were frightful and smelly, eat their food, and live in their houses. Listen to their language but not understand even a single word. And they would not understand her Mandarin Chinese. Aside from these obstacles, what Aunty feared most was that in Switzerland people might treat her like a servant, ordering her around, looking down on her. Once she'd left China, she would have to put up with everything. There was no way she could quit the job and go home. But all these fears put together did not carry as much weight as the future happiness of her son. So Aunty bade her son farewell and took off for Europe.

In Switzerland, she worked hard and saved all the money. Four years passed, her savings in the bank grew to the equivalent of nearly two thousand yuan. Holding the money in her hand, she dreamed of the blissful day on which she would return home. She would give all the money to her son, and he would be happily married. The wife would be a gentle, loving young woman. At first, she'd be a little shy. Soon she would merge into the family as honey blends into milk. Thus thinking, Aunty fell in love with her future daughter-in-law. The next day she purchased an expensive Swiss watch for her future daughter-in-law, a Longines it was, and put it side by side with the one she had already purchased for her son.

Just as Aunty was having such happy dreams and looked forward to the day on which my father's term of office would expire, fate played another dirty trick on her. In Beijing, her son suddenly came down with a mysterious illness. Later I heard people say that he probably got it from the animals in the zoo. As the doctors were unable to diagnose it, they could not help him. He died in just a few days.

When the leaders of the ministry learned about this, they decided to keep it a secret from Aunty for the time being. They were afraid that if Aunty heard the bad news, she might not be able to work anymore. Then they would have to send someone else halfway across the world to replace her.

A few months later Aunty was back in Beijing. She found her house empty. The neighbors and relatives were embarrassed when she asked them about her son. They did not know how to break the sad news to her. So instead of telling her the truth, they invented stories: her son was out of town. He went to the northeast. It was some urgent business. He would be back soon.

But of course he never returned. Nor was there any letter from him. Staying home alone, Aunty grew more and more uneasy. A premonition oppressed her heart like a big snake. She was scared by the dead silence of the house. It was so empty, so cold. After a while, she decided that she'd stay at Nainai's home and go on working for us until her son came back. To comfort herself, she invented all kinds of excuses for her son.

Then one night Aunty finally heard about her son's death. It was from a woman she hardly knew, a cook's help newly hired by Nainai. The woman never suspected that Aunty did not know about the death of her own son. Everybody else knew it. It was no secret. She was merely trying to offer her some condolence. But her words struck Aunty down like a thunderbolt.

In the sudden blinding light, all became clear. There was no more doubt, and at the same time there was no more hope. Of course he was dead! What else could keep him from rushing back to see his old mother? The mother who had brought him up in widowhood with millions of stitches. The one who had just worked in a foreign country for five years to help him get married. Only death had the power to keep him away! She should have thought of it a long time ago!

Maybe her son had tried to resist death in his last days? He could not die without seeing his mother one more time. He wanted at least to say good-bye to her and tell her to take good care of herself in the days to come. He wanted to apologize to her, for he had promised to support her in her old age and bury her after she died. Now all this had become impossible. Who would be looking after her when she was too old to work? He could not close his eyes! But death was too strong. His strength was exhausted. His mother was too far away. He could not hold out any longer. Despair seized him. His willpower collapsed. His soul drifted away from his body with a gust of wind. It flew across the ocean and over the mountains to look for her dreams, in which they would be reunited. But the world was so vast, and people's dreams were like millions of fireflies. He could not catch them. He had to go. So Aunty never got a dream from her son.

I still remember the night I saw Aunty wailing and rolling on her bed. Her face was as white as a sheet of paper. Large tears rolled down from her eyes. Her voice was hoarse. Her hair fell out of the bun. Everybody in Nainai's household was in her room, trying to calm her down. At that time, I did not quite understand what had happened and why Aunty was crying. Before this I had never seen an adult cry like that. I was frightened. Perhaps that was why I remembered the scene so vividly.

When I grew up and learned from Aunty and others about what had happened, my heart grew very heavy. In China, people liked to say "bringing up a son to provide for one's old age." In her life, Aunty had brought up both a son and a daughter. For this she had "eaten a lot of bitterness." Now her old age was near, there was no one to provide for her. Although my parents had promised to support her when she was too old to work, I knew that Aunty would not count on it.

From 1958 to 1966 I slept in the same room with Aunty. Sometimes I woke up in the middle of the night and heard her deep sighs. I knew she was unable to sleep. Her sadness touched my heart. But I did not know how to comfort her. Finally one night I went over to her in the dark, put my arms around her, and said gently: "Aunty. Don't you worry! When I grow up, I will earn a lot of money. I will support you and take care of you when you are old. I am your own daughter!"

When Aunty heard this, she started to sob. Putting her arms around me, she said: "My good daughter! My dear daughter!" She had never called me daughter before. Nor did she dare call me that afterwards in front of other people. But I knew that in her heart of hearts she had taken me to be her own daughter from that moment on. This bond between us would last forever.

11

Beijing 101 Middle School

Fifth grade was a turning point for me. I was eleven years old. One morning when I opened my eyes, I found that my mind, which had been thick and heavy like mud, suddenly became light and clear. It started to run like a mountain stream. The golden sun danced on it, accompanied by the silver moon, five-colored stars, and the rainbow—a miraculous moment. I woke up as Sleeping Beauty did. Even today I still can't tell what triggered the change. "The apertures of your heart opened" was Aunty's explanation. For the Chinese have always believed that intelligence comes out of a person's heart, as the twin sister of emotion.

From then on mathematics became my favorite subject. The grades I got rarely went below 100. The questions became so easy that I really couldn't understand why in the past they had frustrated me so much. As for my Chinese, some characters I wrote still had problems. That could not be fixed overnight. But by this time such mistakes had become less important. What really counted were the essays and stories we wrote, which depended on ideas and style.

After I figured this out, my papers began to catch the fancy of our Chinese teacher, Mr. Wang. Once in a while he would read my paper in front of the fifty students in our class. He spoke with emotion and intonation, adding favorable comments every now and then. At such time, my heartbeat quickened and my cheeks were burning. I would lower my head to hide my smile, while my ears were wide open, like a pair of antennas, catching the sweet music, note by note.

Amid such delightful reassurance that I was after all not so stupid, I reached the age of twelve. Suddenly I grew much taller. My breasts started bulging. Blood began to come out of me as it did Mother. In old China, this would mean that I had reached marriageable age. Perhaps a few matchmakers had already visited my parents and they had discussed my "lifelong big affair" behind my back.

Or else perhaps Father had made a "belly engagement" for me before I was born. This was a time-honored Chinese custom: in the olden days fathers-to-be who were friends would point at their wives' protruding bellies and say: "If this is a girl and that is a boy, they will be husband and wife. She will be your daughter-in-law. He will be my son-in-law." Such pledges made by the fathers were almost as good as the engagement itself. A man who went back on his words in such important matters shamed his ancestors. Henceforth he would be despised by everybody.

But I lived in new China. So in 1963, instead of doing needlework to get my dowry ready and praying to heaven for a decent husband, I had something else on my mind: the upcoming unified entrance examination for junior middle school. The examination was extremely competitive. Among some two hundred middle schools in Beijing, only four were considered at the very top. Two were in the city: Male Fourth Middle School and Female Middle School attached to Teacher's University. The other two were in the west suburb: Beijing 101 Middle School and Middle School attached to Qinghua University. Although both were quite close to the big yard where we lived, somehow my classmates and their parents all set their minds on 101.

This 101, I was told, was not only the best middle school in Beijing, it was without equal in China. In this school, the teachers were chosen from among thousands of middle school teachers. They were the most experienced and worked most conscientiously. The facilities were the best. As for the students, they were the most ambitious and brilliant youths from all over Beijing, not just the west suburb. At the time more than 80 percent of the students were boarders.

So if I could gain admission to this middle school, a bright future was almost guaranteed for me. Three years' study in the junior section would give me a great advantage over those who got themselves into second-rate or third-rate middle schools. So at the next unified entrance examination, this time for senior middle school, I would have no problem regaining admission to 101. Another three years, the gate of any university in China would open for me. The statistics were no secret: each year over 90 percent of the students who graduated from 101 went on to key universities and elite colleges such as Qinghua University, Beijing University, and Harbin Military Engineering College. Whereas in a second-rate middle school, sometimes only 20 percent of the graduates could go to college. As for the third-rate schools, the percentage was so low that most students simply gave up.

This kind of talk I heard day in and day out when I was in the sixth grade. Everyone was singing the same tune. My parents, other parents, the school principal, the teachers, and all the neighbors. It really brainwashed me into believing that the forthcoming entrance examination was a matter of life and death for me. If I failed to get into 101, I would be doomed once and for all. No college education. No future. The glorious jobs such as scientist, doctor, engineer, professor, diplomat would all be beyond my reach. I would end up selling groceries, sweeping streets, repairing smelly shoes or dirty bikes. And it was all my fault! I knew it. Others knew it. The word SHAME would be branded onto my face. Never to be washed off.

Such a prospect put a great deal of pressure on me. As summer drew near, lazy and arrogant as I was, even I began to study hard. Each morning without anybody urging me, I jumped out of bed at the crack of dawn. After a simple breakfast of Aunty's pancakes, I went to the schoolyard to learn the Chinese lessons by heart. Usually I'd arrive at around six thirty, and most of my classmates were already there. Each person had a favorite spot; mine was on the swing. From there I competed with others with closed eyes and a loud voice. Our chanting of the texts converged into a river that flowed far and wide in the cool morning breeze. In an hour and a half, the sun would grow hot and the school bell would ring. Classes started at eight o'clock.

In mid-July, the decisive moment came. I charged headlong into the battlefield with a determination either to carry off the palm or to lay down my dead body. After that, a whole month of restless waiting. Sometimes I was very confident and painted rosy pictures in my head about a great future. Then suddenly doubts gripped my heart and I fell from the top of the rainbow into a bottomless abyss. I missed sleep at night and a lot of good humor by day. This state of mind, the Chinese called "fifteen buckets drawing water from a well, seven moving up and eight going down."

As for my parents, although they pretended to be calm, I knew that they were as uneasy as I was. Then one day a letter arrived. It was the admission notice! Strange! Such an important letter was so small and looked so ordinary. Yet my life depended on it! I could hardly breathe when Mother eagerly tore it open. "Beijing 101 Middle School!" Tears of joy welled up in Mother's eyes. At that instant, a rock of a hundred tons that had been sitting on my heart turned into a thousand butterflies. They whirled around the room. They flew out into the sunny sky. The next thing I knew I was on my way to see my classmates.

On that day I witnessed some of the happiest smiles as well as very bitter tears. It turned out that about 10 percent of the graduates from West Garden Elementary School were going to 101. Not a bad record. The principal was smiling and very proud. The teachers, whom we went to thank, thanked us also because we had won honor for our mother school.

Later when the good news spread, many neighbors came to congratulate us. Some of them used this as a good opportunity to brainwash their own children who were to take the entrance examination the next year. Aunty served them tea and candies. A big smile was on her face all the time. Later that evening she surprised me with a fancy pencil box that she had bought a while back and kept in a secret place. The next day, Father and Mother took me out to dinner and Father rewarded me with a novel, the original three volumes of *Water Margin,* which I had wanted. For the rest of the summer I was the star in our family once again. My parents and Aunty were all proud of me. Lian was eclipsed. Too bad. But there was nothing he could do except to wait for five years to have such a chance. Let us wait and see if he could get himself into 101.

On September 1, I reported to the new school. On that day we each got a school badge, which had bold red characters against a shiny white background. From then on everywhere I went, I wore the badge. It always drew people's attention to me. Some looked at me with approval, others with envy, depending on who they were. That gave me quite a lot of satisfaction.

Before long I discovered that 101 was just like the elementary school I went to. Here most students were from revolutionary cadres' families. The rest had parents who were scientists, professors, writers, and artists, since the Chinese Academy of Sciences and a number of key universities were all in this area. Some students even had parents who were famous nationwide. But they, I must add, were admitted to 101 because they did well in the examination. As far as I know, in the early sixties, no one came to 101 through back doors.

Even though the competition seemed fair, out of the fifty students in my class, only two girls were from workers' families and one boy was from a nearby village. The latter's name was Jin. For a year and a half, we shared a desk. As time went by I got to know him. Not really well, but probably better than others. For Jin was very quiet and seemed to have no good friend in our class.

Perhaps it was because he was slightly older? Or was it something else that made him "a camel among a flock of sheep" in this group? His clothes, for example, were made at home, while ours were bought from stores. The patches on them did not give him the same air as they did the high-ranking officials' children, who in those days deliberately wore patched clothes to show off their families' plain living style. I had also heard that his family was unable to pay the five yuan tuition. Each year they had to ask for an exemption.

Despite all this, Jin was very bright and good-natured. Sometimes when we felt the class was boring, we would read other books together under our desk. We read fast, competing for speed, leaving the comments and questions to the recess. Meanwhile we had to watch out for the teacher's sudden questions. We needed to make sure that we always had the right answers. The secret reading gave us a lot of fun. The teachers never found us out, as our desk was at the back of the classroom. But in the middle of the second year, Jin told me that he had to quit school.

He said that his father's health was not good. The family needed him to work in the fields to earn labor points. He was probably the oldest child. I didn't ask him. I didn't know what to say to him. I was puzzled. I was sad. At the time Jin was only fifteen, and being admitted to 101 was something! What could he do in the fields? If his family needed help, why wouldn't the people's commune help them? Why did he have to quit school? But as Jin said the decision was final and he was not coming to school tomorrow, I said good-bye to him. He did not tell me or anybody where he lived. So we couldn't visit him afterwards.

The rest of the class went on with our studies. The curriculum at 101 was actually not that different from other schools. Yet as time went by I realized that there was something extra which we learned from 101. This something extra one could not see or touch. It was not written in textbooks. Yet it was everywhere in the atmosphere. Each day we breathed it in. It blended into our blood. It seeped into our subconscious. To explain this, perhaps I should start from the name of this middle school.

The name, 101, was deliberately chosen by Wang Yizhi, our seventy-year-old principal, whom the students revered. (Other schools, by the way, did not have the privilege of choosing the numbers that were to become the names of their schools, which the municipal bureau of education gave out in sequence.) I was told that she chose the name because she wanted us never to be content with what we had accomplished. Even after we got the perfect grade of one hundred, we should still strive for something better, which was symbolized by 101.

Our school, the teachers often told us, was not for ordinary students. It was for the most reliable, most courageous, and most brilliant youths who were to become the nation's political leaders, top scientists, and finest artists. "You are the best. You are the chosen ones. But we will still challenge you and make you even better." This kind of talk convinced me that I belonged to an elite group. I remember in those days there were three kinds of people whom we especially looked down on.

The first group was the provincial folk, whom we liked to ridicule behind their backs. It included all those who did not grow up in Beijing. The Mandarin they spoke was absurd and sometimes hard to understand. Their clothes, taste, and demeanor were laughable, giving off an earthy smell. As for their way of thinking, it was hopelessly simple and naive. They hardly knew anything about what was going on behind the scenes on China's political stage, while we always heard a great deal on the grapevine from our privileged schoolmates.

Another group of people we held in contempt was the "petty-city dwellers." It included all those who grew up in Beijing but were neither officials nor scholars. These people were despicable because of their pettiness. Poorly educated, they were cowardly, selfish, gossipy, oily, and often downright mean. Day in and day out, they played little tricks on one another for little gains or no gain at all. Their heads, from morning till night, were filled with "chicken feathers and garlic skins." Thoughts of China's future and the fate of humankind probably never crossed their minds.

As for the third group we looked down on, they were our peers. The students who failed to get into the four top schools were definitely inferior. Even those who were in the other three top schools were less fortunate. Academically, their schools might be as superb as ours, yet none of them could boast of a glorious revolutionary history dating back to the liberated area of Jinchaji before the civil war. Nor were their schools linked to so many important names in modern Chinese history.

Our principal, Wang Yizhi, for instance, was the widow of a famous Chinese revolutionary martyr, Zhang Tailei, who organized the well-known Guangzhou uprising in 1927. Wang herself joined the Chinese Communist Party as early as 1922, when the party was only one year old. The person who recommended her for party membership was none other than Liu Shaoqi, by then the president of the People's Republic of China. In 1957 Premier Zhou Enlai visited 101 in person. Chairman Mao, though his own son Mao Anying studied in Russia before our school was set up, sent his nephew Mao Yuanxin here for six years. Later during the Cultural Revolution, this nephew of Mao's became a rather notorious political figure who eventually fell with the "Gang of Four." Nowadays people in China don't talk about him anymore. But back in the early sixties we were quite proud to have him as our alumnus. The lyric of our school anthem was written by a famous poet, Guo Moruo, who was by then the president of Chinese Academy of Sciences. This list of VIPs could go on and on, and it served to feed our pride.

So I felt lucky that I was in 101 when I was awake. When I was asleep, however, I was unable to control my dreams. One dream haunted me like a ghost. At the start I was always happy, running on a broad road or a flower-strewn meadow. I took a step forward. When my foot touched the ground, suddenly I seemed to lose all my weight and up I went. I was above the ground, at about twice the height of a person. My whole body tightened in fear. Then, fortunately the upward movement slowly stopped. For a second or two I hung suspended in the air. Then I started to fall.

As soon as my feet touched the ground, however, the impact sent me up again. This time I reached the height of a big tree, hanging there like a kite with a broken string. My heart leaped into my mouth. I wanted to cry out for help, but I couldn't. No one was in sight anyway. My eyes were fixed on the ground as if by a spell. The height was frightful and I could not turn my eyes away from the earth.

Then once again the upward movement reversed itself. As I dropped down, I tried desperately to find something on the ground to get hold of: a rock, a plant, a rat hole, anything. But nothing was there. Up I went, once again. Pulled by an irresistible force, I flew higher and higher. The trees vanished from my sight. The blue horizon was half hidden in a thin mist. Anticipating the fall, I knew this would be the end of me. When I woke up, it took me a long time to calm my heart.

I did not understand why I had such dreams, not just once or twice, but many times in those years. I thought of the old saying, "Whatever one thinks during the day, one dreams it at night." But as far as I remembered, I never had any experience similar to this. Maybe the dream showed I was uneasy at 101, among the confident group of youths whose hopes in new China were sky-high. Academically, I dare say, I was still doing better than most of my classmates. But politically, I had some serious doubts about myself. Looking back on it, I believe my doubts were triggered by three things: Lei Feng, physical labor, and the Recalling Bitterness Big Meetings.

Lei Feng was a shining example Chairman Mao set for all the Chinese in the early sixties. He was perfect. He loved the Party and Chairman Mao more than he did his own parents (who died in the old society). In his whole life he never did anything to benefit himself. He always did things that benefited others. For example, he lived very frugally and saved every cent of his soldier's allowance (which wasn't much). When he heard that somewhere there was a flood, he donated his money to the people there, hundreds of yuan at a time, anonymously. He did numerous good things like this and wrote a wonderful revolutionary diary. If he was 100, how could I possibly be 101? Compared with him, I was not even 90 or 80. When something happened, instinctively I would think of myself first. Then on second thought, hopefully I could take others into consideration. Besides, if I was honest with myself, I was not sure if I could love the Party and Chairman Mao more than Aunty and my parents. So I bore Lei Feng a secret grudge, because he was too perfect. He made it impossible for me to live up to the expectation of our old principal and be 101.

Besides Lei Feng there was physical labor, a required course at 101. All students had to take it once a week for an entire afternoon. The aim of the course, I was told, was to help us cultivate proletarian thoughts and feeling. "All workers and peasants love physical labor, while landlords and capitalists hate it" was the theory. I accepted the theory. Nonetheless, I found the course terribly boring. For an entire afternoon, all we did was carry coal cinder from one corner of the schoolyard to another. A few weeks later we might be carrying it all the way back. What a waste of time! The work made me dirty and uncomfortable all over. By the end of an incredibly long afternoon I was totally exhausted. As a result, I could not read or do anything in the evening. Looking back on it, the class only taught me to dislike physical labor. Moreover it made me doubt myself, for I kept wondering if my classmates were really as happy as they seemed while they were taking this class. I could not ask them. They could not ask me.

In addition to the labor class on campus, each semester we were required to work in a factory or a people's commune for two weeks. At first the idea seemed exciting. *In the past I never had a chance to get in touch with workers and peasants. This time I will be living among them.*

See their lives with my own eyes. Talk to them face to face. Hopefully I can make a few friends among them. Won't that be wonderful? But what happened afterwards proved that my expectation was unrealistic.

Each time my classmates and I went to a factory or a people's commune, we were put up in some empty conference rooms or classrooms. By day we were an isolated group, doing some quite indispensable odd jobs that the grass-roots units managed to find for us. In the evening no one was allowed to wander away from our temporary quarters. Revolutionary discipline had to be observed. In fact, the teachers didn't need to worry. Where on earth could we go? As we made no friends among local people, nobody invited us to visit them. The evenings were really tedious.

Soon I got fed up with going to factories and people's communes. In my opinion, such trips were worse than futile. On our side, we had to put up with a great deal: the interruption of our studies, the fatigue, the damp floors we had to sleep on, the mosquitoes and fleas that feasted on us, the bad food produced in our makeshift kitchens, the lack of showers and modern toilets . . . As for the grass-roots units that received us, we were never much help to them. Yet it was such a lot of trouble to accommodate us and make sure that we were safe. Sometimes they had to dismiss the children from school so that we could live in their classrooms. For the local people, we must have been a real pain in the neck! But in those days, of course, no one dared complain. Receiving us was a political task they had to fulfill.

Then in 1964 suddenly class struggle was of great importance. Chairman Mao spoke about it first. Other leaders quickly followed suit. The media spread the message all over the country. Millions of people were mobilized. Our school, which had never fallen behind in any political campaign, tried to heighten the students' class consciousness by inviting old workers and peasants to talk about their hard lives in the old society. Each guest speaker had a tragic story to tell. Some scenes they described left a deep impression on me.

I remember one old peasant talked about how his family sold his younger sister during a famine. The girl, at the age of six, was unusually bright and sensitive. She knew that dealers of children had arrived at the village and her parents were about to give her up. She pleaded with tears streaming down her face: "Please don't sell me! I will never say I'm hungry again! I will let my brother eat all the food. And I will work so hard. I promise. Please, oh, please! Take pity on me! . . . " This broke the hearts of the parents, yet they had no choice. The family was starving. There was nothing else they could sell. So the little girl was sold for a few silver dollars to a dealer who later sold her to another for more money. Nobody knew where she went and what became of her. Maybe she became a prostitute, or a rich man's concubine, or a slave girl? Maybe she didn't survive after all? But the tearful pleading she made before she was dragged away by the dealer never ceased to ring in the ears of her brother.

Another story I remember was told by a poor peasant who was brought up by his widowed mother. The two were devoted to each other. When the mother fell ill one winter, the son had no money to send for a doctor or buy medicine for her. So as her illness went from bad to worse, he could only watch helplessly and blame himself. One day, she woke up from a coma and murmured: "If only I could have some hot, thick corn-flour porridge before I die . . . " Hearing this, the son rushed out to a landlord's home and begged him for a bowl of corn flour. But the landlord's heart was made of iron and stone. In his desperation, the son begged from door to door. It took him a long time to get the food, for the villagers were very poor. When he ran home with it, he found that his mother had already passed away. She died with an empty stomach in an icy cold room all by herself. The son could never forgive himself for this.

The tragic stories went on and on. The one that got me into trouble was told by an old worker who used to be a rickshaw puller. Once he was laid up by a serious illness. The family had no savings. So while he was unable to work, his wife and children starved. Seeing this, the man forced himself out of bed and went out with his rickshaw. On that day he got a customer who was a rich young lady. She was going to an opera. The theater was quite far away. The man tried to run, but soon he was out of breath and his feet seemed to be treading on cotton. Sweat soaked his clothes, but he was not warm. He was shivering all over. By the time he dragged the rickshaw to the theater, the opera had already begun. The young lady was angry. The man tried to explain, but she wouldn't listen. She went into the theater without giving him a cent. The man was too feeble to argue with her. He dropped to the sidewalk coughing blood. That night he got home very late. He had brought back no food, no coal, nothing. The children were so disappointed. The whole family huddled together and cried . . .

Hearing this sad story, I was deeply moved. "How cruel that young lady was! How heartless!" I thought to myself, If I were that young lady, I would never do such a thing. I would be as kind and generous as Nainai had been in the olden days. I would give all the money in my purse to this man and send him home in a warm taxi. Imagine how happy his children would be to see all the good food and new clothes their father had brought back! And his wife would be so relieved that she'd suddenly look ten years younger. The next morning, an unexpected visitor would knock on their door: the best doctor in town. He'd say that someone had paid him to make a house call here. He would cure the man's illness. That someone, of course, would be no one else but me . . .

When the Recalling Bitterness Big Meetings went on, I was half listening and half daydreaming. My imagination took over the narratives, worked on them, and turned them into stories of my own liking. I rather enjoyed doing this, until one day it suddenly dawned on me that I had always imagined myself to be a kindhearted young lady who was rich! In all the stories I made up, I had never identified myself with the poor workers and peasants!

Thinking of this, I broke into a cold sweat, for now I realized that I had a serious problem with my class stance. In class struggle, the most important thing was on whose side one stood. Without noticing it, I had sided with the wrong group of people! It was most dangerous! Luckily I realized the problem before it was too late. From then on I drove such nonsense out of my head and brought my imagination under control.

By and by I was able to put this accident behind me. Just as I was beginning to feel better about myself, a new campaign started at 101. It was called "Exposing the Third Layer of Thoughts." What was the third layer of thoughts? Our political teacher Qian explained.

"The first layer of thoughts you would not hesitate to tell your teachers and classmates. The second layer of thoughts, however, you only reveal to your bosom friends behind closed doors. As for the third layer of thoughts, it flies across your minds in the wink of an eye. Most of the time, you will simply forget it. But if you grasp it, look at it carefully, it will shock you. You will never tell anyone about it! You don't even want to admit to yourself that such terrible thoughts were yours!

"This third layer of thoughts," the political teacher continued, "is the most dangerous. It is like cancer hidden inside you. If you cover it up and keep it a secret, it will find the environment agreeable. It will grow and spread and proliferate! It will take you over and kill you!"

Hearing this, I gave a shudder and saw gooseflesh coming up on my arms. But at that instant, his voice changed as he spoke coaxingly.

"So if you find that you have this third layer of thoughts, what do you do? When you find a tumor in your body, you tell the doctor so that he can treat it, by operation or medication—only he can give you professional help. Only he can cure you. As for your third layer of thoughts, I want you to think very carefully about it, write it down in a thought report, and hand it in to me next week."

Thus his talk ended; but the turmoil in my mind had just begun. I recalled the thoughts I had about physical labor and the stories I made up during the Recalling Bitterness Big Meetings. I knew I had this third layer of thoughts and they were dangerous. *What should I do? Should I write them down and hand the report to the political teacher or should I hide them from him? If I hide them, am I hiding something from the Party? But if I am honest, I will incriminate myself. It is a foolish thing to do!*

This was the first time I was tortured by the "thought struggle." It was a terrible experience. I was fourteen. Too young to look at things in perspective. Moreover, up to that point, all my education told me that the teachers were always right. My parents could be unfair, they could be mistaken. But not the teachers. Especially not our political teacher Qian. For us, he was almost the Communist Party incarnate. I had heard quite a few students say that he had the magic power to read people's minds. It was hard to believe. Yet my schoolmates were not stupid kids.

So what if he already knew of all my terrible thoughts? Maybe he is merely testing me to see if I am honest or not? I will fail the test. And henceforth everybody will know that I am a coward, a liar, and a person with very dangerous thoughts!

The prospect scared me. Yet I was unwilling to betray myself. Toward the end of the week, one night, I was awake for a long time. When I finally fell asleep, I had a dream.

It seemed that I was back in my childhood. Instead of being fourteen, I was only nine or ten. It was a sunny day. I was in a beautiful park. I had never been to this place before. Everything was unfamiliar. *Why am I here? Is this a spring outing? Where are the teachers and other students?* Suddenly it occurred to me that we were playing hide-and-seek. My classmates had all disappeared. *Where should I hide myself?* I became very anxious.

With frenzied eyes, I looked around me: the flower bushes were very low. The young trees were too slender. In some distance I spotted a pavilion. But when I rushed into it, I found it was made of bamboo. The delicate banisters could not hide anyone. Besides, it was on top of a naked hill. Anyone in the park could see me, from any direction. Their eyes. Sharp long nails! They'll pierce me, punch holes through my body. But I mustn't give up. There's still time. I have to find another hiding place. Hurry up! Time's running out! The seeker might be here at any moment!

In despair, I looked around me once again. This time to my great joy I discovered a small shack at the foot of the hill—somehow, it had escaped my attention. I ran toward it. In no time I was inside. In the shack, it was dark. Just as I heaved a sigh of relief and thought that I was safe at last, I lowered my eyes and saw that my feet were stuck in a big pile of dung!

I woke up with a start, utterly disgusted. Unable to go back to sleep, I thought about this dream. It was a bad omen. No doubt about it. In the past I had heard people say that dreams would foretell a person's luck. If one dreamed of water, for instance, it meant that one was going to have money. If one dreamed of fire, it meant success. There were bad dreams too. Shoes, for instance, were bad luck. Teeth falling out of one's mouth meant that someone in the family was going to die. But excrement was worst of all. It was a sure sign that the person would run into some very big troubles. The cursed dream made me even more nervous than before.

Yet in the midst of all my troubles, somehow I never thought of discussing it with my parents. I knew they would laugh at me if I started talking about dreams. And if I told them that I was serious, they would be ashamed of me. Besides, at the age of fourteen, although the crisis between my parents and me had been over for some years, I was still afraid that if I told them about my dangerous thoughts, I would give them new evidences of my wickedness. So I kept my problem to myself. The third layer of thoughts, Qian was right, one would not tell anybody.

On the last evening I sat down with a pen and a piece of paper. For a long time I wrote nothing. When the clock struck twelve, my hand jotted down a few insignificant things. The next day, without reading it a second time, I handed the thought report in. After that I waited for the political teacher to send for me. A talk in his office. A guilty verdict . . . For several days my right eyelid kept jumping. Another sign of some forthcoming disasters, for didn't the Chinese say, "The left eye jumps for wealth; the right eye jumps for disaster"?

But as time went by the political teacher did not send for me and after a while my eyelid calmed down. My heart, which had been hanging at the top of my throat, gradually returned to its normal place. I was relieved. I even grew a little complacent. After all, the political teacher was not a god! So I had deceived him and got away with no loss of face! At that instant, however, I remembered what he said about cancer and my heart sank again. Perhaps by concealing my third layer of thoughts, I had already created a favorable environment for the cancer to grow inside me. Someday I would be eaten up, the result of my cowardice and dishonesty. I could not blame others for not trying to save me. It was me who let them down.

Even today I am not sure where this Exposing Third Layer of Thoughts campaign came from. I checked with others who were in middle schools in Beijing and elsewhere at the time; they had not heard of such a thing. So I suspect that our political teacher took the initiative to create such a campaign. Thanks to him, at the age of fourteen I had a nightmare that I would never forget. The teachers at 101 worked conscientiously indeed. What wonderful teachers we had! When the Cultural Revolution broke out, I would have my revenge.

12

The Hero in My Dreams

The political campaigns made me increasingly uncomfortable, and I began to regret that I went to a school with such a glorious revolutionary history. As an option, I thought of the nearby middle school attached to Qinghua. Perhaps they would not emphasize physical labor and thought reform as much? I secretly decided that when the next entrance examination came round I would apply to that school. From there I would go on to Qinghua University and eventually become a woman scientist.

For 101 did not make me feel good about myself. Nor did it make me feel good about my parents. In the past I had been very proud of Father because he was an old revolutionary. Now I did not know what to think of him. In the early sixties, he decided that he did not want to be an official anymore. He wanted to be a college teacher instead. It was a strange request, from an old comrade like him. The leaders of the ministry were not pleased. It was not hard to imagine what they thought of him. "This old comrade's revolutionary will has waned." "Well, he was from a capitalist family, and when he was in college, he was influenced by Western ideas." So after a while, they let him go.

He was transferred to International Relations College, which was attached to the ministry anyway. At the college, Father was asked to be the dean. He refused, saying that he just wanted to be an ordinary teacher. So in the end he got what he wanted. He became an ordinary teacher.

As for Mother, in old China there was a saying: "Married to a rooster, follow a rooster; married to a dog, follow a dog." In new China somehow this was still true. Soon she followed my father into the same college where she too became an English teacher. Meanwhile, we moved out of the big yard. That made me rather sad. I missed our comfortable apartment there and my friends. Without the special pass, I could no longer go to the auditoriums to see operas and movies on Saturday nights. But I said nothing. Between my parents and me, there were things we did not talk about. This was one of them.

Officially, of course, I was still a revolutionary cadre's child. Father's source of income before 1949 decided that once and for all. Yet after my parents became teachers, each time I said I was from a revolutionary cadre's family, my voice was a little thin. Nobody noticed this, of course. I did not bother to tell my classmates that my parents had changed jobs. Yet somehow I began to feel lonely at school. Among those blue-blooded, high-ranking revolutionary cadre's children, I felt that I was "a fish eye mixed in a pile of genuine pearls." Secretly I was ashamed of my parents; I was ashamed of myself. Thus I tried to stay away from 101 as much as possible.

Some of my classmates soon noticed this. Jokingly they said that I had become the teacher's forerunner. In the morning I always entered the classroom just one minute or two before the second bell rang. In the afternoon as soon as the class was over, I jumped onto my bike heading home. Neither the violent spring wind nor the thunderstorms in summer could stop me. In winter I slipped and fell on ice and snow, but I had no complaints. In fact, I thought I was really lucky that I could go home every day. How miserable I'd be if I were a boarder—sharing a room with five other students, I'd have to live under the teachers' noses twenty-four hours a day, six days a week. At home, at least I could relax behind closed doors and indulge in the two things I loved most: the books I read and the dreams about my hero.

I began to read novels when I was about ten, skipping difficult words and lengthy descriptions of the landscape: I read for the stories. At home my parents had a sizable collection of Chinese and foreign books. I started with Chinese novels: *Song of Youth, Genealogy of a Red Flag, Red Sun, Seeds of Fire, Railroad Guerrillas, Wind and Rain of Tong River, Spring and Autumn of a Small Town, Reports of Guns on the Plain, Red Rock, Wild Fire and Spring Wind, Fight Over an Ancient City* . . . These were all revolutionary novels popular in China in the sixties, as their names show. Such books were the spiritual diet on which people of my generation fed. They shaped our imagination.

While reading novels, I also dug into my parents' nonfiction books: memoirs of old revolutionaries who had been Red Army men or underground workers, biographies of famous revolutionary leaders and martyrs, foreign as well as Chinese. After I finished these, I turned to translations of foreign masterpieces. Some of the books I borrowed from the library of 101. Others Mother borrowed for me from her college. (My parents' foreign books were no good, because at the time I could not read English or French. In fact I never read them; in 1966 after the

Cultural Revolution broke out Mother sold the books by the pound, several hundred copies, to a waste recovery station.)

Of the foreign books I read in translation, my favorite ones were *La Dame aux camélias, Les Misérables, Wuthering Heights, Jane Eyre, A Tale of Two Cities, War and Peace, The Captain's Daughter, The Gadfly, How Steel Was Made, The Scarlet Letter, Life on the Mississippi, Twenty Thousand Leagues Under the Sea* and all the rest of Jules Verne's science fiction, plus the detective stories by Arthur Conan Doyle, *The Thousand and One Nights,* the Greek myths, and Shakespeare's tragedies. This list not only reflected my taste, it also showed what was available to me at the time.

When I was in middle school, no libraries in Beijing would allow students to enter the stacks to look for books. Instead, I had to write down the call number of books I wanted to borrow, but only one at a time, hand the slip in to a librarian through a hole in a thick wooden door, and wait for my name to be called. If the book was not there (which happened often when the book was popular), I might try again a week or two later. The library would not recall books for students. Thus some books I would have loved to read I never got hold of.

Buying books was not easy either. First of all, I did not have the money. Second, many good books were either sold out or out of print. Because of such difficulties, each time I got hold of a good book, I spent hours copying parts of it down into a notebook. The book itself I had to return to the library within a fortnight or else pay a fine.

As time went by, my notebook filled with excerpts from my favorite books. I became very attached to it. By day I kept it at home in a drawer, knowing that Aunty would guard it for me like a dragon. At night, I let it stay next to my pillow so that I could read parts of it before I went to sleep. I rehearsed the tragic love and noble deaths of the heroes in my head. After I crossed the threshold to the "dark, sweet homeland," the boundaries of the stories melted away. A hero, like a bright star, came into being in my dreams.

Looking back on it, I think it is strange that the hero I dreamed about was so different from myself. Actually he was the opposite of me in almost every aspect. For example, while I was plain, he was very handsome. I can still see him now.

*   *   *

Tall, slender and vigorous, he is like a Greek warrior. His every movement is nimble and graceful. His voice is sweet and mellow, like music from heaven. His hair is pitch-black. His eyes are the brightest stars in the sky of a clear autumn night. His lips are warm and rosy, as intoxicating as the finest red wine.

Unlike me, he has a great deal of charisma. I always shun crowds, but in the largest gatherings he is in his element. Everywhere he goes, he is a magnet, he is the sunshine. He gains people's hearts by his kindness and generosity, risking his life many times to rescue others. Where I am cowardly, he is brave and resolute. If the situation demands that he cut off his left arm, he will clench his teeth, pick up a knife, and do it himself. He will not faint or even utter a groan.

He is, of course, a revolutionary hero. He joins the Chinese Communist Party when the fire of revolution is yet as tiny as sparkling stars, and the counterrevolutionary forces are raising storms of blood in their attempt to put it out. Their slogan is "Better to kill a thousand by mistake than let one Communist escape." White terror shrouds the whole country. Thousands of intellectuals and workers are put in prison and executed. Others bury their heads in books or go abroad. At this juncture my hero, saddened by the backwardness of his country and enraged by the slaughter of innocent people, commits himself to the revolutionary cause.

Henceforth he fights for the people's liberation. He climbs down the deepest shafts, lighting torches within the hearts of coal miners who are buried alive in poverty and oppression. He organizes strikes among railroad and factory workers. Red band around his left arm, he stands in front of them in the picket line. Tear gas, fire hoses, mounted troops, sabers, nothing will force him back. His blood is mixed with that of the workers, who respect him as a teacher and love him as a brother.

He also goes up into the green mountains to fight guerrilla wars. He is a brilliant military strategist. Amid the enemy's ruthless attacks, his army not only survives but grows. When spring comes, he rides a black steed on the mountain slope and shoots at copper coins thrown up by his bodyguards by the handfuls from a hundred paces away. The coins glitter in the sun, falling like sparking rain through willow twigs that sway in the wind. With a pistol in each hand, he fires twenty shots in one breath. Not a single shot misses the mark.

As time goes by, his fame spreads. The Robin Hoods of the mountains and marshes, proud and tough men they are, hear of it. They come to challenge him. First he wins the contest on their terms and gains their respect. Later he talks to them heart to heart and opens their eyes to the revolutionary truth. In the end they all join him. Men, horses, and guns.

His strength, however, comes mainly from the ordinary peasants who have been driven by famines and the bullying of local tyrants to desperation. For them, he is the only hope. If he wins, every family will have a piece of land to farm and all will have enough to eat. The old men will not lose their dignity begging in the streets. The young girls will not be kept home by shame because they have no decent clothes to cover their bodies. The children will laugh instead of cry. There will be peace and justice in China for ten thousand years to come. For such a dream, the peasants give him all they have: their sons, grain, protection, and information.

My hero, though he is devoted to the liberation of workers and peasants, is not from a poor family. His family is rich and powerful. He is well educated. He has studied in London and Paris, where beautiful and wealthy young ladies fell in love with him. Old men in the reactionary government recognized his genius. They promised him a "great future"—in politics or in the military—if only he would join them. But my hero does not want to live for himself. He was born for the salvation of millions who are living in deep water, hot fire.

Under the hero's leadership, people are winning the war. Each day young peasants join his army by tens of thousands, while workers and students hold demonstrations in big cities. Even those who work in the enemy camp come over to his side secretly and help him with intelligence. The old world is crumbling. The reactionaries are desperate.

Among those who hate my hero, none is more shrewd or cruel than his own father. In that old man's heart, there is no love, only hatred and an insatiable desire for power. Seeing that his only son is tearing down what he and his ancestors have built up over centuries, he wants to destroy him: strangle him slowly with his own hands. Cut his flesh with a razor blade and see blood gush out from the wounds. Stamp on his chest and break his ribs. Slash open his abdomen and see him struggle in his death throes.

To satisfy these desires, the old man lays a snare for my hero. Knowing how much his wife, who is in poor health, misses her son and vice versa, he sets himself to convince her that he can arrange for them to meet at a secret place. No one will find out. Their son can come in disguise and return safely. The only thing she needs to do is to write him a letter, saying that she wishes to see him for the last time. The old woman is taken in. She does exactly what her husband tells her to do. As a result, the hero falls into an ambush. In crossfire, he is wounded in the chest. He loses consciousness and is seized by the enemy.

The hero's fiancée, who comes with him to see her future mother-in-law, is also captured by the enemy. Many people know their love story. She is the only daughter of an excellent scholar, a true intellectual who was the hero's beloved teacher. She and the young man studied together. In their quest for knowledge and pursuit of truth, they fell in love. Since then, neither time and distance nor human beings are able to separate their hearts.

But now they fall into the hands of their enemies, their love is doomed. The young man regains consciousness and sees the enemies begin to torture his fiancée in front of him. They hang her up and whip her until blood drips from all over her body and she passes out. They tie her to a bench and pour red pepper juice down her nose and throat. When she coughs it up, it is mixed with her blood . . . The torturers tell the young man that his fiancée's life is in his hands. He can make them stop at any moment, if he will denounce the Party and reveal the names of the underground workers. Of course he cannot do this. So he has to watch her suffer, raped by those beastly torturers, attacked by ferocious wolfhounds, drowned in a glass water tank . . . The only thing he can do is pretend that he does not care.

"In China's history what is a woman to a man? She is a garment. Nothing more. If you tear her to pieces today, tomorrow I'll have another one, who is younger and even more beautiful. A man can have as many women as he likes, while a woman can have only one man.

"Or if you think you can scare me with such a spectacle, you pick the wrong man! This is a pretty sight compared to the scenes I faced on the battleground. A commander in chief has nerves as strong as steel, who uses human lives as chips to buy victory. If necessary, I will send ten thousand men to death—my own brother among them—without batting an eye."

Such is the facade he puts up, knowing that things will be ten times worse for him and his fiancée if he lets the enemies guess his true feelings. His acting works. The enemies are disappointed. But they persist in the hope that something might come from the torture.

Meanwhile only the young woman knows what is going on inside her lover. They put his heart in boiling oil and fry it for hours on end, day after day; yet he cannot cry out with pain. He has to sit there and watch her suffer without changing his facial expression. He cannot allow his lips to tremble. He cannot turn his eyes away. Or sweat. His heartbeat has to remain normal. His willpower may be strong, but his strength is not limitless.

Though his face does not betray him, she can read his thoughts from the depth of his eyes: he hates the fact that he is still alive and has to watch all this. Living like this is worse than death. In the past, he has always been a leader, a winner, a national hero. No matter how difficult the situation, he was in control. He always managed to outmaneuver his opponents. Now he and she are at the mercy of their enemies. They are like meat on a chopping board as the butcher's knife hacks at them. The butcher's knife is ruthless, striking her in the body and him in the heart. He will not be able to stand this much longer. Within his skin the concealed agony turns him into ashes inch by inch.

She must take action immediately, she decides, or it will be too late. The next morning when they are brought together, she looks him deep in the eye and gives him a dazzling smile. The next moment she manages to break from the guards, runs to the window, and jumps out. No one is quick enough to seize her. She flies down like a bird, wild and free. The building is tall; her flight is short. Yet to him it is an eternity. Time is frozen in horror. Sound is lost. The world ceases to exist. He himself ceases to exist, except for his eyes, which are fastened on her. In the end, she lands on the concrete pavement where she bursts into a tiny red flower. The fragrance of it will remain for a thousand years.

At this instant, red blood spurts from the young man's throat. So much of it. Unstoppable. It chokes him. He falls to the ground. Someone has grabbed his heart, pulled it out of his chest, and dashed it against the granite floor. It bursts into a thousand pieces. Heaven and earth turn upside down. Daylight fades out. Darkness drowns the world. In the middle of immense darkness, a tiny red flower . . .

For several months the young man is on the brink of death. A high fever consumes him. His heart fails. The best doctors are flown in by special airplanes. They operate on him several times and bring him back to life.

When the young man wakes up again, he feels a void in his heart. His mother is dead too, he knows. Having found out what happened to her son and her would-be daughter-in-law, she could not forgive herself. Nor could she face the truth about her husband. With remorse, abhorrence, and bewilderment, her heart could not find a moment's peace until she was buried in the yellow earth. The young man takes his mother's death calmly. Yet deep down he feels that fate has played a cruel joke on him. After all the risks he and his fiancée have taken, neither of them was able to see the old woman while she was alive. Now the two women he loves most have vanished from the surface of the earth, leaving him behind, alone, with a bleeding heart in this hateful prison. The thought of joining them under the nine springs seems a sweet dream. But the doctors have no mercy. They will not let him die.

Pondering his situation, my hero sits in the yard of a special hospital. Over his head white clouds drift across a sky framed by electrified barbed wire and bayonets. Around him dead leaves dance in swirls like the ashes of paper money. He is all skin and bones in a white silk robe, the color of infirmity, the color of mourning . . .

But the young man is a revolutionary hero. He cannot be heartbroken forever. Something will stir him, pull him into action—yes, a secret plan imparted to him by an underground worker he protected. It says the enemy will secretly exterminate all the political prisoners in the concentration camp, hundreds of men and women. Tested in blood and fire over the years, they are the most courageous and steadfast. Precious property of the Party. In the future they will prop up the great mansion of a new China. The hero must save their lives.

He organizes the political prisoners and puts them in touch with the underground. A plan to rescue them is worked out. It is a perfect plan, but its success depends on its secrecy. In a dungeon under this prison camp there exists a secret tunnel, dug by an old revolutionary martyr for the sake of others years ago. Now all the prisoners are to escape through this tunnel with the help of the underground workers and guerrilla fighters.

The plan is known only to a few, who are most reliable. Thus when a prisoner betrays the group, he can only suggest vaguely that there might be such an attempt. The enemies are not convinced, yet they are alarmed. They figure if there were such a plan, the hero would be the first one to know it. So they torture him for a confession.

They take him to the "tiger bench." Tie his legs to it at a place just above his knees and put bricks under his feet, one after another. Sweat of pain rolls down his ashy face, the drops as large as soybeans. To endure the pain, he bites his lips until blood trickles from his mouth. He knows that his comrades are unable to sleep, they are listening in the dark. He does not want to agonize them. He keeps his silence until his legs are broken.

After that the torturers tie his hands to the arms of a special chair and knock sharp bamboo sticks into his fingertips. They split when they hit the bone. Then the torturers pull them out, one by one. The excruciating pain in his fingers makes the hero faint again and again. Each time when he wakes up in cold water, he denies that he knows any plan for the prisoners to escape.

But the enemies are still not convinced. So they take him to an electric chair and run the current through him. A minute is as long as a century. An hour is eternity. The torturers have experience. They know how to increase and decrease the current to keep him from losing consciousness. That way the pain accumulates. It shoots through his veins, throbs in every cell of his body, and pours into his heart. The young man gasps for breath. His face is as white as a sheet of paper. Cold sweat drips from it. But he does not confess to make them stop.

Finally the hero is dragged into a dark dungeon. There at first he sees only a roaring furnace. At the sight a shudder runs through his body, but his heart is firm. The torturers bind him to a pillar beside the furnace. Next they take out a white-hot iron from the fire and press it against his chest.

When the iron touches his skin, the skin turns black instantly. A sickening smell spreads out and fills the room. The torturers laugh in excitement and press harder. The burning iron sizzles through his flesh. The pain is too much for a human being to bear. The young man can no longer hold back his screams. In despair, he prays to heaven for death. Any death, no matter how painful, is a mercy. Anything is better than this! But it is of no avail.

The torture continues. After one iron cools off, another is taken out. They put it to his thighs, his armpits . . . Then they bring it up to his eyes and tell him this is his last chance. If he does not make a clean breast of the whole thing immediately, he will regret it for the rest of his life. The hero insists, with whatever strength he still has, that he has nothing to confess. His words are cut short by a savage scream forced from him by a horrible pain in his eyes . . .

A gust of wind rises from the grass. Sudden, violent wind. It makes the sand fly, the stones walk. Two bright stars from the night sky are blown out. From then on, perpetual darkness . . . The enemies' doubts at last come to an end. They believe that no human being of flesh and blood can go through such torture without confessing the truth. Their vigilance lapses. Then one night the rescue is carried out. The political prisoners escape into the mountains. All are safe except my hero, who was taken to a secret place the day before.

The next morning, from the stir in the air the hero knows that the plan has worked. He has not suffered in vain. His last wish on earth is fulfilled. His heart is serene and content. He knows that the enemies will not let him off. They will vent their anger on him, but he doesn't care. Let them do whatever they want with him. He'll gladly take it all. He has only one life to lose, no matter how many times they make him die.

His death sentence comes before dawn, signed by his own father. Before he goes to the execution ground, he gets no wine, no final meal, as Chinese custom requires. But he does not need these to help him face his final moment. He dies with a smile on his face, for though he cannot see the first ray of light breaking the darkness in the east, he hears the booming sound that grows louder and louder: the Liberation Army is coming! Its advance is irresistible. A new China, like a precious infant, will soon be born.

*　　*　　*

At this point it must seem that my hero's story had come to an end. But it didn't, because the story I dreamed about was not linear. It became so only when I wrote it down. Originally the story had no beginning, no end. The various scenes floated and revolved around me like stars in a galaxy, waiting for me to pick them up and animate them, one at a time. Later when I put them back into their orbits, they were always a little changed. And each time I read a book, saw a movie, or heard a story from someone, a few new episodes would appear in my story. Old episodes, on the other hand, if I neglected them too long, would grow pale, lose weight, and vanish. Thus the story was fluid and the hero was not always as I describe him. One night he was a passionate lover, the next a loving father to a little girl. Or a loyal friend, a devoted student, a gallant sworn brother, a filial son to a working-class foster mother, and much, much more. No matter what role he played, the hero always suffered and died young. I could not imagine him any older than thirty.

Thanks to this hero, for several years I lived two lives at once. On the one hand, I attended classes, ate lunch at the school cafeteria, did physical labor, and went to meetings just as others did. I dare say I functioned quite well. At least no one had noticed anything strange about me. Yet whatever I did in the outside world, my heart and soul were not in it. Day and night, the hero's dream wrapped me in an atmosphere no one else could see. Within it, the hero and I were one. His excruciating pain vibrated through my body; his anguish pierced my heart. How sweet the heartbreaks! How pleasurable the torture! Playing the hero in my mind, I forgot my loneliness and inferiority. I forgot that I was a girl. I could be a man as well as a woman. Whatever the hero accomplished, I did. There was no limit to my power, as long as I had the power to imagine it.

After the campaign of Exposing the Third Layer of Thoughts, of course, I knew the danger of indulging in one's imagination. Things could go wrong in the wink of an eye and the damage done to me might be irretrievable. Yet I would rather take the risk. Without the hero, life was so dull, so cold. It was not worth living. Thus I went on dreaming about him until the Cultural Revolution.

In the summer of 1966, for a few months I was so busy making revolution that I forgot the hero. In fact, in those days my mind was taken over by another hero, who was not a product of my imagination but real. This hero was Chairman Mao, whose story became known to us shortly before the Cultural Revolution broke out.

Mao was from a peasant's family in Hunan Province. In his youth he cherished a great ambition to reform China. To prepare himself for the struggles ahead he studied hard, both at school and on his own, especially on his own in public libraries. Sometimes he and his friends read books at noisy marketplaces so as to practice concentration. Sometimes they ate only one meal a day and slept in the open air to temper their bodies. When it rained hard or the wind was strong or the sun was blazing hot, they'd take off their shirts to have "rain baths," "wind baths," and "sun baths." One summer he and a friend traveled on foot through Hunan to make social surveys. On this trip they talked to all kinds of people: peasants, merchants, Buddhist monks, Confucian scholars, a county magistrate, a fortune-teller . . . Between the two of them, they did not have a single cent. They did this deliberately to see if they could survive in difficult situations. Yet their minds were so rich and broad that they embraced the entire world.

These stories fascinated me. This was what youth should be: creative, exciting, with heart-warming friendship! It was utterly different from the boring reality we had to face daily at 101, where independent thinking and taking initiative met with disapproval; freedom was suppressed in the name of revolutionary discipline; friendship was killed in competition when no one looked beyond grades. But the contrast does not explain why I loved Mao at the beginning of the Cultural Revolution.

I loved him because of the tremendous sacrifice he made for the Chinese people: in the past four decades, he had lost six family members. His first wife, Yang Kaihui, was the daughter of his beloved teacher, Yang Huaizhong. She was arrested by the Nationalists in 1930, while Mao was fighting guerrilla wars at the famous Jinggang Mountain. The enemy told her if she would break off with Mao, they would set her free. She refused to do so. As a result, she was executed. By then she was only twenty-nine years old.

In 1956, twenty-six years after she died, Mao wrote a beautiful poem to commemorate her. In that poem he describes her imagined ascent to the moon palace. There a god named Wu Gang welcomes her with cassia wine and Chang E, the lonely celestial beauty, waves her long sleeves to dance for her. Later when she hears the news that in the human world the revolutionary people have won the war, Yang Kaihui is so happy that she weeps. Her tears fall from heaven to shower the earth.

Beyond this poem I really did not know much about Mao's private life and his relation with Yang Kaihui. But that was not a problem. I filled the void with my imagination. I saw in my mind's eye his sleepless nights: a lone lamp is burning; bells ring in the rain. Fireflies take his thoughts to the woman he loves. The tears he would not let others see . . .

In addition to his wife, Mao had lost his younger brother, Mao Zemin, and his oldest son, Mao Anying. The former was arrested and killed in 1943 by a warlord named Sheng Shicai in Xinjiang. The latter was sent by Mao himself to the front during the Korean War, where he died in an air raid. Mao and Yang Kaihui had had two more sons; one was lost after Yang's execution and the other became mentally ill, probably traumatized by his childhood experiences.

When I heard these stories, I was deeply moved. Henceforth I loved Mao in two different ways. He was, on the one hand, the radiant sun in the sky, giving life to everything on earth. This Mao I loved as millions of Chinese did at the time, as our great leader, great commander, great teacher, and great helmsman. In 1966 he was seventy-two years old, tall and stout, with a receding hairline and rosy cheeks, which were evidence of his great wisdom and excellent health.

But behind this Mao there was another: a secret, sweetheart hero of a fifteen-year-old girl. This Mao was perpetually young and handsome. He was tall and slender, with thick black hair and slightly knit eyebrows. Perhaps he was thinking about the future of China and the fate of humankind? Or was he sad because he had lost his beloved wife and children? His eyes were gentle and somewhat melancholy, with double-fold eyelids. This Mao, to me, was not the radiant sun but a vulnerable man, a tragic hero. Like Prometheus, he had given fire to humankind and, as a result, had to withstand the wrath of Zeus. Chained to the top of a mountain and tortured by an eagle night after night, he was glad nonetheless. He never regretted what he had done.

For such a hero I was willing to do anything he might want me to do. Sleep in a graveyard. Drink a bottle of poison. Stab myself in the chest. Like Juliet? No! I mean I would continue to make revolution under proletarian dictatorship and defend his revolutionary line. Climb a mountain of knives. Jump into an ocean of raging fire. Face a forest of rifles and charge forward into a shower of bullets. I would do it for his sake. Proudly and gladly. Let my body be pierced a hundred times and my bones be shattered. My heart would remain true to him. With my last breath I would cry, "Long Live Chairman Mao!"

Looking back on the two kinds of love, I don't know which was stronger. But I know that when they joined forces in my heart, they turned me into a burning coal, radiating heat from the red sun. When the red sun rose in the east, it eclipsed the bright star of the hero I had dreamed about. I did not even realize the change until a few months later he came back in a different dream.

This time I was at a struggling rally. I had attended such a rally at Beijing Workers Stadium earlier. Was it in July or August? Who did we struggle against? I could not recall. Too many rallies occurred in 1966. Too many people we struggled against. After a while I got them mixcd up. All I remember about this rally was the fact that it was held at night in pouring rain that did not taper off in three or four hours. The rain poured down on the heads of eighty thousand people who came from all over Beijing. It was like pouring oil on flames. The revolutionary masses were in a great rage. Their voices, "Down with so and so!" overwhelmed the sound of thunder. From time to time people got so angry that they rushed down from the stand to the middle of the football field to grab the "enemies" who stood in a thin line. They kicked their legs to make them kneel on the ground. They punched their heads to make them bend even lower. The speech was interrupted. No one was listening to it anyway.

The rally goes on. I stand in the rain, shivering from head to feet. Why am I so cold? I am scared! Why do all these people hate me so much? What have I done? Oh yes, old revolutionaries are now capitalist-roaders. The struggle and sacrifice we made in the past have become our crimes. Around me, people are furious. Yelling at the top of their voices: "Smash your dog head!" "Bombard you with cannonballs!" "Fry you in boiling oil!" "Condemn you forever!" Hatred is what I inspire. Revenge is what they want. Blood for blood. Life for life.

The revolutionary masses close in on me. They grab my arms, twist them back to force me to bend lower. Famous jet-plane style. They unbuckle their army belts. They begin to thrash me. Blood splashes out. Heavy army boots fall on my back. The old wounds in my body burst open. The wounds left there by the enemies. I want to talk. I can't. Blood wells up into my mouth. No one is willing to listen. From my neck they hang a heavy board on which my crimes are written. The thin wire bites into my flesh. I feel no pain. Yet I am crying. In the past when I was tortured by the enemies, I shed blood but no tears. Now the people I love are the ones who hate me so much, the agony in my heart is insufferable. "People, I love you! But you do not understand me! You are deceived and used by a small group of opportunists inside the Communist Party. You are in great danger! Our country is in great danger! Open your eyes and guard against hidden enemies!" I do not care what happens to me. But I must endure the torture and humiliation. I must survive so that someday I will regain the trust of the people and reveal the truth to them. The revolution must be saved . . .

This was how the hero came back and reclaimed my dreams. From then on I loved Mao by day and played the role of the hero at night. The two heroes of mine did not seem to get along. I began to have insomnia.

My mother on her graduation from Yanjing University: 1948.

My father wearing an army uniform: June 1950.

My parents six months before I was born: May 1950.

Nainai, my paternal grandmother, holding me in her arms
after Mother left for Switzerland
to join my father: March 1951.

Aunty (my nanny) and I out for a
walk in a courtyard inside Nainai's
house: June 1951.

My mother and father in Switzerland, one month after I was born:
January 1951.

A happy reunion—my father and I.

My home in Switzerland: many toys, no playmates.

Mother and I in Geneva: March 1954.

With my brother
Lian, back in
Nainai's house in
Beijing: 1956. I was
really happy there.

With my cousins
Little Ox (*left*) and
Little Dragon (*right*):
1956. We all seemed
very happy.

In the big yard, the top-secret Ministry of Investigation, where we lived after we moved out of Nainai's home: 1957.

During the Cultural Revolution: Mao was the red sun and the great
helmsman.

Standing in front of the Monument to the People's Heroes at
Tian'anmen Square during the Cultural Revolution.

On Farm 850 in Heilongjian
province in the northeast:
winter 1968.

Fang with Capitalist, a
pig we loved: 1969.

My little brother,
Yue, visiting my
parents in the
countryside:
Hebei province,
1970.

Aunty and my brothers, Lian and Yue, who lived with her after our parents went to the countryside: Beijing, 1970.

With Aunty during my only visit home in five years: 1971.

13

At the Center of the Storm

From May to December 1966, the first seven months of the Cultural Revolution left me with experiences I will never forget. Yet I forgot things almost overnight in that period. So many things were happening around me. The situation was changing so fast. I was too excited, too jubilant, too busy, too exhausted, too confused, too uncomfortable . . . The forgotten things, however, did not all go away. Later some of them sneaked back into my memory, causing me unspeakable pain and shame. So I would say that those seven months were the most terrible in my life. Yet they were also the most wonderful! I had never felt so good about myself before, nor have I ever since.

In the beginning, the Cultural Revolution exhilarated me because suddenly I felt that I was allowed to think with my own head and say what was on my mind. In the past, the teachers at 101 had worked hard to make us intelligent, using the most difficult questions in mathematics, geometry, chemistry, and physics to challenge us. But the mental abilities we gained, we were not supposed to apply elsewhere. For instance, we were not allowed to question the teachers' conclusions. Students who did so would be criticized as "disrespectful and conceited," even if their opinions made perfect sense. Worse still was to disagree with the leaders. Leaders at various levels represented the Communist Party. Disagreeing with them could be interpreted as being against the Party, a crime punishable by labor reform, imprisonment, even death.

Thus the teachers created a contradiction. On the one hand, they wanted us to be smart, rational, and analytical. On the other hand, they forced us to be stupid, to be "the teachers' little lambs" and "the Party's obedient tools." By so doing, I think, they planted a sick tree; the bitter fruit would soon fall into their own mouths.

When the Cultural Revolution broke out in late May 1966, I felt like the legendary monkey Sun Wukong, freed from the dungeon that had held him under a huge mountain for five hundred years. It was Chairman Mao who set us free by allowing us to rebel against authorities.

As a student, the first authority I wanted to rebel against was Teacher Lin, our homeroom teacher—in Chinese, *banzhuren*. As *banzhuren*, she was in charge of our class. A big part of her duty was to make sure that we behaved and thought correctly.

Other students in my class might have thought that I was Teacher Lin's favorite. As our Chinese teacher, she read my papers in front of the class once in a while. That was true. (Only she and I knew that the grades I got for those papers rarely went above 85. I could only imagine what miserable grades she gave to others in our class.) She also chose me to be the class representative for Chinese, which meant if others had difficulties with the subject, I was to help them. In spite of all these, I did not like Teacher Lin! She had done me a great wrong in the past. I would never forget it.

In my opinion, Lin was exactly the kind of teacher who, in Chairman Mao's words, "treated the students as their enemies." In 1965, we went to Capital Steel and Iron Company in the far suburb of Beijing to do physical labor. One night there was an earthquake warning. We were made to stay outdoors to wait for it. By midnight, no earthquake had come. Two o'clock, still all quiet. Three o'clock, four o'clock, five . . . The night was endless. Sitting on the cold concrete pavement for so many hours, I was sleepy. I was exhausted. My only wish at the moment was to be allowed to go into the shack and literally "hit the hay." Without thinking I grumbled: "Ai! How come there is still no earthquake?"

Who should have thought that this remark was overheard by Teacher Lin? All of a sudden she started criticizing me in a loud voice.

"The workers and the poor and lower-middle peasants would never say such a thing! Think of all the property that will be damaged by an earthquake. Think of all the lives that may be lost! Now you are looking forward to an earthquake! Only class enemies look forward to earthquakes! Where did your class feelings go? Do you have any proletarian feelings at all? . . . "

She went on and on. Her shrill voice woke up everybody, my classmates as well as students in the other five parallel classes. All were sitting outside at the moment. Everybody turned to watch us. Three hundred pairs of eyes! It was such a shame! I felt my cheeks burning. I wanted to defend myself. I wanted to tell Teacher Lin that although there might be some truth in what she said, I had never been in an earthquake. I was merely tired and wished the whole thing over. Besides, I was only half awake when I said that. I was not looking forward to an earthquake!

In fact, what I really wanted to tell her was that I knew why she was making such a fuss about my remark, which if she had not seized would have drifted away and scattered in the morning breeze like a puff of vapor: she was using this as an opportunity to show off her political correctness in front of all these teachers and students. At my cost! Later she might be able to cash in on it, using it as her political capital . . .

But of course I knew it would be crazy for me to talk back like that. Contradicting the teacher would only lead me into more trouble. So I swallowed the words that were rolling on the tip of my tongue and lowered my head. Hot tears assaulted my eyes. Tears of anger. Tears of shame. I bit my lips to force them back. *Let's wait and see, Teacher Lin. Someday I will have my revenge. On you!*

Now the time had come for the underdogs to speak up, to seek justice! Immediately I took up a brush pen, dipped it in black ink and wrote a long *dazibao* (criticism in big characters). Using some of the rhetorical devices Teacher Lin had taught us, I accused her of lacking proletarian feelings toward her students, of treating them as her enemies, of being high-handed, and suppressing different opinions. When I finished and showed it to my classmates, they supported me by signing their names to it. Next, we took the *dazibao* to Teacher Lin's home nearby and pasted it on the wall of her bedroom for her to read carefully day and night. This, of course, was not personal revenge. It was answering Chairman Mao's call to combat the revisionist educational line. If in the meantime it caused Teacher Lin a few sleepless nights, so be it! This revolution was meant to "touch the soul" of people, an unpopular teacher in particular.

Teacher Lin, although she was not a good teacher in my opinion, was not yet the worst. Teacher Qian was even worse. He was the political teacher who had implemented the Exposing Third Layer of Thoughts campaign. In the past many students believed that he could read people's minds. Now a *dazibao* by a student gave us a clue as to how he acquired this eerie ability. Something I would not have guessed in a thousand years! He had been reading students' diaries in class breaks, while we were doing physical exercise on the sports ground. The student who wrote the *dazibao* felt sick one day and returned to his classroom earlier than expected. There he had actually seen Qian sneak a diary from a student's desk and read it. The student kept his silence until the Cultural Revolution, for Qian was his *banzhuren*.

So this was Qian's so-called "political and thought work"! What could it teach us but dishonesty and hypocrisy? Such a "glorious" example the school had set for us, and in the past we had revered him so much! Thinking of the nightmare he gave me, I was outraged. "Take up a pen, use it as a gun." I wrote another *dazibao* to denounce Teacher Qian.

Within a few days *dazibao* were popping up everywhere like bamboo shoots after a spring rain, written by students, teachers, administrators, workers, and librarians. Secrets dark and dirty were exposed. Everyday we made shocking discoveries. The sacred halo around the teachers' heads that dated back two thousand five hundred years to the time of Confucius disappeared. Now teachers must drop their pretentious airs and learn a few things from their students. Parents would be taught by their kids instead of vice versa, as Chairman Mao pointed out. Government officials would have to wash their ears to listen to the ordinary people. Heaven and earth were turned upside down. The rebellious monkey with enormous power had gotten out. A revolution was underway.

Looking back on it, I should say that I felt good about the Cultural Revolution when it started. It gave me a feeling of superiority and confidence that I had never experienced before. Yet amidst the new freedom and excitement, I ran into things that made me very uncomfortable.

I remember one day in July, I went to have lunch at the student dining hall. On the way I saw a crowd gathering around the fountain. I went over to take a look. The fountain had been a pleasant sight in the past. Sparkling water swaying in the wind among green willow twigs, making the air fresh and clean. In Beijing it was a luxury ordinary middle schools did not enjoy. When the Cultural Revolution broke out, the water was turned off. Now the bottom of the fountain was muddy, littered with wastepaper and broken glass.

On this day I saw a teacher in the fountain, a middle-aged man. His clothes were muddy. Blood was streaming down his head, as a number of students were throwing bricks at him. He tried to dodge the bricks. While he did so, without noticing it, he crawled in the fountain, round and round, like an animal in the zoo. Witnessing such a scene, I suddenly felt sick to my stomach. I would have vomited, if I had not quickly turned round and walked away. Forget about lunch. My appetite was gone.

Sitting in an empty classroom, I wondered why this incident upset me so much: *This is the first time I've seen someone beaten. Moreover this person isn't a stranger. He's a teacher at 101. Do I pity him? Maybe a little? Maybe not. After all I don't know anything about him. He might be a counterrevolutionary or a bad element. He might have done something very bad; thus he deserved the punishment. Something else bothers me, then—not the teacher. What is it?*

Then it dawned on me that I was shocked by the ugliness of the scene. *Yes. That's it! In the past when I read about torture in revolutionary novels, saw it in movies, and daydreamed about it, it was always so heroic, so noble; therefore it was romantic and beautiful. But now, in real life, it happened in front of me. It's so sordid! I wish I'd seen none of it! I don't want the memory to destroy my hero's dream.*

This teacher survived; another was not so fortunate. Teacher Chen, our art teacher, was said to resemble a spy in the movies. He was a tall, thin man with sallow skin and long hair, which was a sign of decadence. Moreover, he seemed gloomy and he smoked a lot. "If a person weren't scheming or if he didn't feel very unhappy in the new society, why would he smoke like that?" a classmate asked me, expecting nothing but heartfelt consent from me. "Not to say that in the past he had asked students to draw naked female bodies in front of plaster statues to corrupt them!" For these "crimes," he was beaten to death by a group of senior students.

When I heard this, I felt very uncomfortable again. The whole thing seemed a bad joke to me. Yet it was real! Teacher Chen had taught us the year before and unlike Teacher Lin and Teacher Qian, he had never treated students as his enemies. He was polite and tolerant. If a student showed talent in painting, he would be delighted. On the other hand, he would not embarrass a student who "had no art cells." I had never heard complaints about him before. Yet somehow he became the first person I knew who was killed in the Cultural Revolution.

Living next door to Teacher Chen was Teacher Jiang, our geography teacher. While Teacher Chen was tall and lean, Teacher Jiang was short and stout. Both were old bachelors, who taught auxiliary courses. Before the Cultural Revolution Teacher Jiang was known for two things. One was his unkempt clothes. The other was the fact that he never brought anything but a piece of chalk to class. Yet many students said that he was the most learned teacher at 101. He had many maps and books stored in his funny big head.

If Teacher Jiang had been admired by students before, he became even more popular after the revolution started and Teacher Chen was killed. Since August 1966 Red Guards were allowed to travel free of charge to places all over China. Before we set off, everybody wanted to get a few tips from him, and afterwards we'd love to tell him a few stories in return. It was our chance to show off what we had learned from the trips. Thus from August to December, Teacher Jiang had many visitors. Happy voices and laughter were heard from across the lotus pond in front of his dorm house. At night lights shone through his windows often into the small hours. Geography turned out a true blessing for Teacher Jiang, while art doomed Teacher Chen.

In contrast to the teachers who lost control over their lives in 1966, we students suddenly found power in our hands. Entrance examinations for senior middle school and college were canceled. Now it was entirely up to us to decide what we would do with our time. This was a big change. In the past, decisions had always been made for us by our parents, teachers, and leaders. At school, all courses were required and we took them according to a fixed schedule, six classes a day, six days a week. College was the same as middle schools. After college, the state would assign everybody a job, an iron rice bowl. Like it or not, it would be yours for life.

Now those who had made decisions for us—teachers, parents, administrators—were swept aside by the storm. We were in charge. We could do things on our own initiative. We made plans. We carried them out. So what did we do? Instead of routine classes, we organized meetings at which we shared our family history. (People who spoke up at such meetings were of course revolutionary cadres' children. Others could only listen.) I remember Wu, a girl from a high-ranking cadre's family, told a story that left a deep impression on me.

In 1942 Japanese troops raided the Communist base in the north. At this time Wu's older brother was only several months old. He was a beautiful baby boy, with a chubby face and the mother's large brown eyes. The mother gave him the name Precious. Day and night she longed for the father to come back from the front to meet his firstborn.

But before the father returned, the Japanese invaders came. Wu's mother took the baby and fled to the mountains. She and many others hid in a cavern. The enemy soldiers came near, searching for them. At this moment the baby woke up and was about to cry. Her mother had no choice but to cover his mouth with her own hand. Or else all would have been found and killed by the Japanese.

The baby was in agony. He struggled with all his might for his life. His lovely little face turned red and then blue. His tiny hands grabbed at his mother's, desperately trying to push it away so that he could breathe. His plump little feet kicked helplessly. The mother's heart was pierced by ten thousand arrows, but she did not dare loosen her grip. Finally the Japanese went away. By then the baby had turned cold in her arms.

Wu burst into tears and we all cried with her.

Why does she cry like that? Yes. I understand. The brother! Because he died so tragically, he will always be loved most by the parents. The perfect child. The most "precious" one, the one they sacrificed for the revolution. Wu and her other siblings cannot rival him, no matter how good they are . . .

But of course that was not why she cried or why we cried with her on that day. We cried because we were deeply moved by the heroic struggle and tremendous sacrifice made by our parents and older brothers and sisters. The stories we told at such meetings convinced us that our lives were on the line: if we should allow the revolution to deteriorate, the evil imperialists and beastly Nationalists would come back. As a slogan of the thirties went, "Cut the grass and eliminate the roots"—if we did not act, they would kill our parents who were revolutionary cadres and make sure that none of us would survive to seek revenge on them.

Suddenly I felt that these classmates of mine were dearer to me than my own brothers and sisters. I loved them! They loved me! Today we shed tears in the same room. Tomorrow we would shed blood in the same ditch. I was willing to sacrifice my life for any of them, while before the Cultural Revolution I mistrusted them, seeing them as nothing but my rivals.

In fact, it was not fear for our lives but pride and a sense of responsibility that fired us up. Chairman Mao had said that we were the morning sun. We were the hope. The future of China and the fate of humankind depended on us. The Soviet Union and East European countries had changed colors. Only China and Albania remained true to Marxism and Leninism. By saving the revolution in China, we were making history. We must uproot bureaucracy and corruption in China, abolish privileges enjoyed by government officials and the intelligentsia, reform education, reform art and literature, reform government organizations . . . In short, we must purify China and make it a shining example. Someday the whole world would follow us onto this new path.

Aside from sharing family history, we biked to universities and middle schools all over Beijing to read *dazibao* and attend mass rallies where

Lin Biao, Zhou Enlai, and Mao's wife, Jiang Qing, showed up to give speeches. I first heard the term "Red Guard" in late June at Middle School attached to Qinghua University, two months before most Chinese would hear of it. It was an exciting idea. On our way back, my schoolmates and I were so preoccupied with the notion that our bikes stopped on a riverbank. Next thing I remember, we were tearing up our red scarves, which only a month before had been the sacred symbol of the Young Pioneers. Now they represented the revisionist educational line and to tear them up was a gesture of rebellion. We tied the strips of red cloth around our left arms in the style of workers' pickets of the 1920s. When we rode away from the spot, we had turned ourselves into Red Guards.

People in the street noticed our new costume: faded army uniforms that had been worn by our parents, red armbands, wide canvas army belts, army caps, the peaks pulled down low by girls in the style of the boys . . . Some people smiled at us. Some waved their hands. Their eyes showed surprise, curiosity, excitement, admiration. I don't think I saw fear. Not yet.

When people smiled at us, we smiled back, proud of ourselves. Our eyes were clear and bright. Our cheeks rosy and radiant. Red armbands fluttered in the wind. We pedaled hard. We pedaled fast. All of us had shiny new bikes, a luxury most Chinese could not afford at the time. (In my case, Father had bought me a new bike so as to show his support for the Cultural Revolution. Being a dreamer himself, he believed, or at least hoped, that the Cultural Revolution would purify the Communist Party and save the revolution.)

When we rang the bells, we rang them in unison, for a long time. It was not to warn people to get out of our way. It was to attract their attention. Or maybe we just wanted to listen to the sound. The sound flew up, crystal clear and full of joy, like a flock of white doves circling in the blue sky. At the time, little did I know that this was the first stir of a great storm that would soon engulf the entire country.

On August 18, 1966, I saw Chairman Mao for the first time. The night before, we set off from 101 on foot a little after midnight and arrived at Tian'anmen Square before daybreak. In the dark we waited anxiously. Will Chairman Mao come? was the question in everybody's mind. Under a starry sky, we sang.

"Lifting our heads we see the stars of Beidou [the Big Dipper], lowering our heads we are longing for Mao Zedong, longing for Mao Zedong . . . "

We poured our emotions into the song. Chairman Mao who loved the people would surely hear it, for it came from the bottom of our hearts.

Perhaps he did. At five o'clock, before sunrise, like a miracle he walked out of Tian'anmen onto the square and shook hands with people around him. The square turned into a jubilant ocean. Everybody was shouting "Long live Chairman Mao!" Around me girls were crying; boys were crying too. With hot tears streaming down my face, I could not see Chairman Mao clearly. He had ascended the rostrum. He was too high, or rather, the stands for Red Guard representatives were too low.

Earnestly we chanted: "We-want-to-see-Chair-man-Mao!" He heard us! He walked over to the corner of Tian'anmen and waved at us. Now I could see him clearly. He was wearing a green army uniform and a red armband, just like all of us. My blood was boiling inside me. I jumped and shouted and cried in unison with a million people in the square. At that moment, I forgot myself; all barriers that existed between me and others broke down. I felt like a drop of water that finally joined the mighty raging ocean. I would never be lonely again.

The night after, we celebrated the event at 101. Everybody joined the folk dance called *yangge* around bonfires. No one was shy. No one was self-conscious. By then, we had been up and awake for more than forty hours, but somehow I was still bursting with energy. Others seemed that way too. After dancing a couple of hours, I biked all the way home to share the happiness with my parents. By this time, they no longer minded that I woke them up at three o'clock in the morning. In fact, they had urged me to wake them up whenever I got home so that they could hear the latest news from me about the revolution.

Seeing Chairman Mao added new fuel to the flame of our revolutionary zeal. The next day, my fellow Red Guards and I held a meeting to discuss our next move. Obviously if we loved Chairman Mao, just shouting slogans was not enough. We must do something. But what could we do? By mid-August the teachers at 101 had been criticized and some were detained in "cow sheds." Even the old school principal, Wang Yizhi, had been "pulled down from the horse" because of her connection with Liu Shaoqi, the biggest capitalist-roader in the Party. On campus, little was left for us to rebel against. Therefore, many Red Guards had walked out of schools to break "four olds" (old ideas, old culture, old customs and old habits) in the city.

This was what we should do. Only first we had to pinpoint some "four olds." I suggested that we go to a nearby restaurant to get rid of some old practices. Everybody said: "Good! Let's do it!" So we jumped onto our bikes and rushed out like a gust of wind.

Seeing a group of Red Guards swarming in, everybody in the restaurant tensed up. In August, people began to fear Red Guards who summoned the wind, raised the storm, and spread terror all over China. Small talk ceased. All eyes were fastened on us.

I stepped forward and began ritualistically: "Our great leader Chairman Mao teaches us, 'Corruption and waste are very great crimes.'" After that, I improvised: "Comrades! In today's world there are still many people who live in poverty and have nothing to eat. So we should not waste food. Nor should we behave like bourgeois ladies and gentlemen who expect to be waited on by others in a restaurant. From now on, people who want to eat in this restaurant must follow new rules: One, go to the window to get your own food. Two, carry it to the table yourselves. Three, wash your own dishes. Four, you must finish the food you ordered. Otherwise you may not leave the restaurant!"

While I said this, I saw some people change color and sweat broke out on their foreheads. They had ordered too much food. Now they had to finish it under the watchful eyes of a group of Red Guards. This was not an enviable situation. But nobody in the restaurant protested. Contradicting a Red Guard was asking for big trouble. It was like playing with thunderbolts and dynamite. So people just lowered their heads and swallowed the food as fast as they could. Some of them might develop indigestion afterwards, but I believed it was their own fault. By showing off their wealth at a restaurant, they wasted the blood and sweat of the peasants. Now they got caught and lost face. This should teach them a lesson!

While my comrades and I were breaking "four olds" at restaurants, other Red Guards were raiding people's homes all over the city. News of victory poured in: Red Guards discovered guns, bullets, old deeds, gold bars, foreign currency, yellow books and magazines (pornography) . . . Hearing this, people in my group became restless. But somehow I was not eager to raid homes, and I did not ask myself why. "We are busy making revolution at restaurants, aren't we?"

Then one day an old woman stopped us in the street and insisted that we go with her to break some "four olds" in the home of a big capitalist. None of us could say No to this request. So she led us to the home of a prominent overseas Chinese, where the "four olds" turned out to be flowers.

The courtyard we entered was spacious. A green oasis of cool shade, drifting fragrance, and delicate beauty: tree peonies and bamboo were planted next to Tai Lake rocks. Orchids and chrysanthemums grew along a winding path inlaid with cobblestones. A trellis of wisteria stood next to a corridor. Goldfish swam under water lilies in antique vats . . .

Strange! Why does this place look familiar? I am sure I've never been here before. Could it be I've seen it in a dream? . . .

Suddenly the answer dawned on me: *this place looks just like Nainai's home. Nainai's home must have been raided. Maybe several times by now. Is she still there? Did they kick her out? Is she all right? And what happened to the beautiful flowers she and Third Aunt planted? . . . No use thinking about such things! I can't help her anyway. She is a capitalist. I am a Red Guard. I have nothing to do with her!*

The question in front of me now is what to do with these flowers. Smash them! Uproot them! Trample them to the ground! Flowers, plants, goldfish, birds, these are all bourgeois stuff. The new world has no place for them. My fellow Red Guards have already started. I mustn't fall behind.

So I lifted up a flowerpot and dropped it against a Tai Lake rock. Bang! The sound was startling. *Don't be afraid. The first step is always the most difficult.* Bang! Bang! *Actually it isn't so terrible. Now I've started, I can go on and on. To tell the truth, I even begin to enjoy breaking flowerpots! Who would have thought of that? . . .*

After a while, we were all out of breath. So we ordered the family to get rid of the remaining flowers in three days, pledging that we'd come back to check on them. Then we left. Behind us was a world of broken pots, spilled soil, fallen petals, and bare roots. Another victory of Mao Zedong thought.

On my way home, surprise caught up with me. I was stopped by a group of Red Guards whom I did not know. They told me that my long braids were also bourgeois stuff. Hearing this, I looked around and saw Red Guards stand on both sides of the street with scissors in their hands. Anyone who had long or curly hair would be stopped by them, their hair cut off on the spot in front of jeering kids. Suddenly I felt my cheeks burning. To have my hair cut off in the street was to lose face. So I pleaded with them, vowing that I would cut my braids as soon as I got home. They let me go. For the time being, I coiled my braids on top of my head and covered them with my army cap.

Fearing that other surprises might be in store for me in the street, I went straight home. There I found Aunty in dismay. It turned out that she too had seen Red Guards cutting long hair in the street. So she did not dare leave home these couple of days and we were about to run out of groceries.

"What shall I do?" she asked me. "If I cut my hair, won't I look like an old devil, with short white hair sticking up all over my head?" Her troubled look reminded me that since her childhood, Aunty always had long hair. Before she was married, it was a thick, long braid. Then a bun, for a married woman, which looked so elegant on the back of her head. Even in Switzerland, she had never changed her hairstyle. But now neither she nor I had any choice. If we did not want to lose face in the street, we'd better do it ourselves at home.

While Aunty and I were cutting each other's hair, my parents were burning things in the bathroom. The idea was the same: to save face and avoid trouble, better destroy all the "four olds" we had before others found them out. So they picked out a number of Chinese books, burned them together with all the letters they had kept and some old photographs. The ash was flushed down the toilet. Repair the house before it rains. That was wise. No one could tell whose home would be raided next. Better be prepared for the worst.

Now suddenly it seemed everybody in my family had trouble, including Lian, who was eleven. His problem was our cat, Little Tiger. Lian found him three years ago playing hide and seek in a lumber yard. Then he was a newborn kitten. So little that he did not even know how to drink milk. Aunty taught us how to feed him. Put milk in a soup-spoon. Tilt it to make the milk flow slowly through the depression in the middle of the handle. Put the tip of the handle into the kitten's tiny mouth. He tasted the milk. He liked it. He began to drink it. By and by the kitten grew into a big yellow cat with black stripes. On his forehead, three horizontal lines formed the Chinese character *wang*, which means king. We called him Little Tiger because in China the tiger is king of all animals.

Little Tiger's life was in danger now, for pets were considered bourgeois too. This morning Lian had received an ultimatum from kids who were our neighbors. It said we had to get rid of Little Tiger in three days or else they would come and take revolutionary action. This time we could not solve the problem by doing it ourselves. Little Tiger was a member of our family. We had to think of a way to save his life.

Aunty suggested that we hide him in a bag, take him out to a faraway place, and let him go. He would become a wild cat. Good idea. Only I did not want to do this. What would people say if they found that I, a Red Guard, was hiding a cat in my bag? So I told Lian to do it and went back to school. Since the Cultural Revolution started, I had a bed in the student dormitory and spent most of the nights there.

A few days later when I came back home, Aunty told me what had happened to Little Tiger. (Lian himself wouldn't talk about it.) When Lian took him out, he was spotted by the boys who had given him the ultimatum. Noticing something was moving in his bag, they guessed it was the cat. They grabbed the bag, swung it round, and hit it hard against a brick wall. "Miao!" Little Tiger mewed wildly. The boys laughed. It was fun. They continued to hit him against the wall. Lian started to cry and he begged them to stop. Nobody listened to him. Little Tiger's blood stained the canvas bag, leaving dark marks on the brick wall. But he was still alive. Only his mewing became weak and pitiable. Too bad a cat had nine lives! It only prolonged his suffering and gave the boys more pleasure. Bang! Bang! Little Tiger was silent. Dead at last. Lian ran back and cried in Aunty's arms for a long time.

A week after our cat was killed by the boys, a neighbor whom I called Guma killed herself. On that day, I happened to be home. I heard a commotion outside and looked. Many people were standing in front of our building. When I went out, I saw clearly that Guma was hanging from a pipe in the bathroom. Another gruesome sight I could not wipe from my memory.

Why did she kill herself? Nobody knew the answer. Before she died, she was a typist at the college. A quiet little woman. She had no enemies; no historical problems. Nobody had struggled against her. So people assumed that she killed herself for her husband's sake.

The love story between her and her husband must have been quite dramatic. Mother said a writer had interviewed them because he wanted to write a book about it. Guma's husband, whom I called Guzhang, was a professor in the French department. I used to like him a lot because of his refined, gentle manner and the many interesting books he owned. Recently, however, it became known that Guzhang had serious historical problems. In his youth he had studied in France and joined the Communist Party there. Later somehow he dropped out of the Party and turned away from politics. Because of this, he was accused of being a renegade. A renegade he seemed to me, like one who was a coward in revolutionary novels and movies. The following story would prove my point.

After Guma killed herself, Guzhang wanted to commit suicide too. He went to the nearby Summer Palace and jumped into the lake. But the place he jumped was too shallow. After a while he climbed out, saying the water was too cold. When people at the college heard this story, he became a laughingstock. Even Aunty remarked: "You may know people for a long time and still you don't know their hearts. Who should have thought that Guma, a woman so gentle and quiet, was so resolute, while Guzhang, a big man, did not have half her courage."

These words seemed sinister. To tell the truth, I was alarmed by them. Just a couple of days before a nanny had killed herself at the nearby University of Agriculture. The old woman was a proletarian pure and simple. So why did she kill herself?

Her death was caused by a new chapter in the breaking "four olds" campaign. The idea was actually similar to mine: in the past bourgeois ladies and gentlemen were waited on hand and foot by the working people. In the new society such practices should be abolished. The working people would no longer serve and be exploited by bourgeois ladies and gentlemen. Thus the new rule said those who were labeled bourgeois ladies and gentlemen were not allowed to use nannies. As for those who were not labeled bourgeois ladies and gentlemen, they were not allowed to use nannies either. Because if they used nannies, it was proof enough that they were bourgeois ladies and gentlemen, and bourgeois ladies and gentlemen were not allowed to use nannies. Thus according to the new rule, no family was allowed to use nannies.

As a result, the old woman killed herself, because she lost her job and had no children to support her. Though she had saved some money for her old age, another new rule had it all frozen in the bank.

Aunty was in exactly the same situation. When she first came to work for us, she was forty-six. Then her son died. Now she was sixty-two, an old woman by traditional standards. Right now all her savings were frozen in the bank. Whether someday she might get them back or not, and if yes when, was anybody's guess. Now the deadline set by the Red Guards of the college for all the nannies to leave was drawing near. Recently Aunty made me uneasy. I was frightened by her eyes. They were so remote, as if they were in a different world. I could not get in touch with them. Then she made that strange comment about being resolute. Could she mean . . . ?

On the evening before Aunty left (fortunately she had kept her old home in the city, to which now she could return), Father gathered our whole family together. Solemnly he made a pledge to her. He said that he would continue to support her financially for as long as she lived. Although for the time being she had to leave, she would always be a member of our family. She needn't worry about her old age.

That was, in my opinion, the exact right thing to say at the right moment. Even today when I look back on it, I am proud of Father for what he said on that hot summer evening thirty years ago. By then tens of thousands of nannies were being driven out of their employers' homes in Beijing, and who knows how many in the whole country. But few people had the kindness and generosity to say what Father said.

Aunty said nothing in return. But she was moved. From then on, she took our family to be her own. Instead of a burden, she became a pillar for our family through one storm after another. She did not quit until all her strength was used up.

14

Red Guards Had No Sex

After Aunty left, I returned home even less often. Home was no longer the safe haven I once loved to hide in. Now it had become a nest of troubles, making me feel frustrated and vulnerable. So why not stay away from it? The things one's eyes do not see will not disturb one's heart.

Starting in late August 1966, Red Guards were beginning to travel to all parts of China free of charge. Our task was to spread the idea of the Cultural Revolution. We were seeds of fire. Chairman Mao was the spring wind. The trains and buses were waiting for us. The only thing I needed to do was to make up my mind about a target place.

I thought Guangzhou was a good idea, a semitropical city. Coconut trees stood tall, waving their fronds on the banks of the Pearl River. More than a hundred years ago, Lin Zexu, Emperor Daoguang's high commissioner, had confiscated opium from foreigners and destroyed it here. Later seventy-two revolutionary martyrs had rebelled against the Qing empire and laid down their lives for a dream of a republic. But for me, Guangzhou's attraction lay primarily in its geographic location: it was the southern tip of China, far away from Beijing. After I made revolution there, I could take my time and tour many other places on my way back.

My mind made up, I asked my fellow Red Guards where they wanted to go. "Shanghai." "Hunan." "Sichuan." "Heilongjiang." One girl said she was going to Tibet and it took her a month to reach Lhasa. Another went to Yunnan and reached the border of Vietnam. In the end it turned out that nearly thirty Red Guards from 101 wanted to go to Guangzhou. We formed a combat team.

Overnight we obtained our train tickets. The next day we were ready to set off. No one in our team had any luggage. All I took for this expedition of over two thousand miles were the little red book, a fountain pen, a notebook, a couple of undergarments, a hand towel, a toothbrush, toothpaste, and thirty yuan that Father gave me. A grass-green canvas bag was large enough to hold all of these.

We were not tourists. Our trip was not for fun and comfort. We were soldiers going out to war against an old world. In fact many of us thought at the time that this trip would be a turning point in our lives, the beginning of our careers as "professional revolutionary experts."

From now on, we no longer need envy our parents for their heroic deeds in revolutionary wars and feel sorry because we were born too late. Like the forerunners we admired, now we are going to places where forces of darkness still reign and dangers lurk. We will enlighten and organize the masses, dig out hidden enemies, shed our blood, and sacrifice our lives for the final victory of the Cultural Revolution.

Our train left Beijing in the evening. As we were given hard-sleeper tickets, we slept through the night. The next morning, I woke up at dawn. Too excited to go back to sleep. I sat down next to a window and put my left arm on the windowsill. The cool morning air rushed in and plucked at my Red Guard's armband, turning it into a small ball of fire. After a while I took off my cap and let the wind blow through my hair.

By this time I had cut my hair very short. About two inches on top of my head and shorter underneath. Yet I was not the most radical female Red Guard at 101. I knew that a couple of girls had shaved their heads, and they were very proud of it. I envied their courage, but I could not bring myself to do such a thing.

Besides my hair, my face had been blackened by the sun. My limbs were firm and nimble. After riding the bike all over Beijing for two months, I had lost fat and grown muscles. My clothes had a sour smell of sweat day and night. My fingernails sheltered much dirt. When I took off my sneakers, my feet gave out a stench that was worse than that of the boys. *I know Mother and Aunty would be very upset if they saw me like this. But I like it this way!*

A while later a boy and a girl who were about ten came over and I gave them some candies. They called me "Uncle Red Guard." Even their mother, who sat down on the opposite seat, did not seem to notice that I was not an "uncle." This was a nice surprise! I did not correct their mistake. Somehow I really liked the kids (who were only four or five years younger than me) calling me "Uncle Red Guard."

Then the loudspeaker announced that breakfast was ready. Three Red Guards in our group volunteered to go to the dining car to get box meals for everybody. Later when we asked them how much we owed them, they said: "Forget it. Money is not important. Private ownership mentality is on its way out. Our money is yours. Your money is ours. We are comrades-in-arms. We are of the same family." This idea appealed to all of us. So from then on we took turns to buy meals for the whole team.

Between meals there wasn't much for us to do except watch the landscape. The trip was long, over forty hours before we could reach Guangzhou. After a while we all got a bit bored. So we decided to make a revolution on the train.

The idea was to inquire into the family background and class status of all passengers in sleeping cars and make those who were not workers, poor and lower-middle peasants, or soldiers give up their beds to those who were in hard-seat cars. Once we made this plan, we carried it out. No need to waste our time asking permission from anyone. Chairman Mao was our commander. We were his "little red devils." He put power in our hands. We were responsible only to him.

So in less than an hour we purified the sleeping cars. Well, almost. It turned out that nearly half the passengers had problems in either one or both categories. We told them to leave. They obeyed. All of them except a group of five young men and women who were from Shanghai.

As these people failed to see the significance of our revolutionary act, we tried to reason with them.

"Workers, poor, and lower-middle peasants are masters of our country. So they should travel as masters, not as second-class or third-class citizens. Moreover, on this train, you see, some of them are old. Some are suffering from illnesses. Some have small children. You people are young and healthy. Is it right that you let them sit on those hard seats for two nights in a row while you sleep on these comfortable beds?"

"Well," one of them talked back, "frankly I don't see anything wrong in that. If they want, they too can buy tickets for sleeping cars and have beds here. But they don't want to spend the money. They prefer to go hard seats. If that's their choice, you respect their choice. As for us, we have spent our money on the more expensive tickets, we are entitled to travel more comfortably. Our right is guaranteed by law. And law is sacred!" Thus a debate started between us in a sleeping car that was already half empty. Debate was what we Red Guards had been doing these two months. We all loved to debate.

"You said 'law is sacred.' That is not right!" I retorted. Point of needle against sharp blade. "Not all laws are sacred. We should do a class analysis first. If the laws are made by capitalists and landlords to protect their property and interests, they are not sacred to the revolutionary people! We ought to violate them! We need to abolish them! That is what revolution is all about! Otherwise how can old orders be toppled? How can workers and peasants ever stand up? Where would new China have come from? How can we liberate humankind? . . . "

The debate went on along this line. I thought our argument was very convincing. If it failed to enlighten our opponents, it was because they lacked proletarian feelings. After all, they were all from petty bourgeois families. Now they had run out of things to say. Yet they refused to budge. After a few minutes of tense silence, one of them burst out.

"If you say giving up beds to workers and poor peasants is a revolutionary act, not a punishment, why don't you do it yourselves? Why do you order other people to do it? You are even younger than us! You don't really need the beds either. Red Guards should have the deepest proletarian feelings for the workers and peasants. Red Guards should set examples for others. Give up your beds first!"

Hearing this, we all became indignant. *What impudence! Now these people are not debating. They are attacking us! Is this class revenge? We must heighten our vigilance! Who has heard of such a thing: Red Guards get kicked out by a bunch of bastards from bourgeois families? Of course we won't let them have their way! We can't give in on a matter of principle!*

Just as my comrades and I were about to counterattack, the train pulled into a big station. Wuhan or Changsha, I don't remember exactly which. When the carriage doors opened, it became clear that in the hard-seat cars as well, Red Guards were making a revolution. They too had checked out the passengers' class status and rounded up a group of capitalists, landlords, and other bad elements. Now they were driving these class enemies off the train.

The "snake demons and cow ghosts" were all old men and women, driven out of Beijing by the revolutionary masses. All had been severely beaten on the train. As they walked past our window on the platform, one old woman especially caught my attention. She had what the Chinese called "looks of good fortune," which means she was rather heavy. Now her weight and her bound feet gave her a great deal of difficulty as she walked. Her hair was completely white. From her head blood poured down like a stream. It fell on her white shirt. The shirt was a mess. Although she looked ready to drop to the ground at any moment, a female Red Guard about my age was still thrashing her on the head with an iron-buckled army belt.

I could not watch such a scene. Yet I could not turn my eyes away from it. In my heart of hearts I really pitied the old woman and wished that I could do something to save her, although rationally I believed that violence was both inevitable and necessary to a great revolution. "This poor old woman," I thought, "she's on her last legs. She will probably not be able to make it. Her family in Beijing and her relatives in the countryside will never find out what happened to her. Actually it is better that they never find out! That female Red Guard is really something!"

Finally the bell rang and the train started to move. I heaved a sigh of relief and turned to face our opponents once again. But to my great surprise, I found that they had all disappeared. They must have sneaked out of the sleeping car after they saw what happened on the platform. So the victory belonged to us, as it always did. But this time it was not so sweet. We lost our chance to win the debate. And debate was a great way to kill time.

Today as I write about this incident, I am amazed by how honest people were in 1966. On that train who would know if they lied about their family background and class status? Most of them were traveling alone. There was no way for us to verify what they said. And we did not even intend to. We simply took their word for it. Yet so many people told us the truth, and we punished them for it. Ten years down the road such an incident would be unthinkable. By that time, almost all Chinese had learned to tell a few lies. We could lie with confidence. We could lie with passion. At first it was to protect ourselves. Then we got used to it. Today millions of people in China are cheating one another, telling big and small lies without blushing, to gain something, to brag, or just to make fools of others. Who is to blame for this degeneration of our moral character? The Chinese Communist Party? The Western influence? But what about us? What about me? It pains me to think about what I have done to the younger generation who cannot believe that once upon a time people had been so foolishly honest in China . . .

When we arrived at Guangzhou, we stationed ourselves temporarily at a middle school. We decided that as "professional revolutionary experts" we should spend a few days investigating the situation before we mobilized the people. So by day we went out in small groups to middle schools, universities, and various work units to read *dazibao* and talk to people.

In early September, Guangzhou was still as hot and humid as a huge steamer. The local people were all wearing shorts and T-shirts. Most of them had no shoes on. Even so they'd much prefer to sit in the shade and fan themselves with round palm-leaf fans. Old people drank Noon Tea, a very bitter herb tea, and the kids ate red bean ice to drive the fire out of their bodies.

When we went out, however, we always put on the complete outfit of a Red Guard: army uniforms with long sleeves and long pants, caps on our heads, belts around our waists, armbands, army sneakers, canvas bags, and little red books. The local people looked at us with amazement as well as sympathy. Sweat rained down our foreheads and soaked our clothes. But we would not wear skirts, blouses, and sandals. Anything that would make girls look like girls was bourgeois. We covered up our bodies so completely that I almost forgot I was a girl. I was a Red Guard. Others were Red Guards too. And that was it.

Thanks to the outfit, once I almost fainted on the sports ground of a middle school, where I talked to a thousand people about what had happened recently in Beijing. In those days we were all such vehement speakers that we could easily go on for hours, talking about class struggles, line struggles, struggles inside the Party and outside the Party. Elaborate on historical lessons. Analyze the revolutionary situation in and outside the country. Discuss policies and strategies. Stir the audience till they shed tears and ground their teeth. On that day my speech lasted more than three hours. Afterwards the audience had many questions.

"Is it right to beat people?"

"Are all books feudal, capitalist, and revisionist except Chairman Mao's works? Should we burn all of them?"

"Are all cadres capitalist-roaders?"

And so on.

It was past three o'clock in the afternoon. The sun was a big ball of fire. No. It was a huge bag of hot, long needles as a Chinese folktale describes it. The needles attacked my head. Suddenly my ears started ringing. Things turned yellow and green in front of my eyes. I was short of breath. Dizzy. I had to sit down before I finished my answer to avoid making a scene in front of all those people.

At night we all returned to our base. We slept in the same classroom, boys and girls, young men and young women. The oldest among us were eighteen, the youngest fourteen. Female Red Guards on one side and male Red Guards on the other. No screen, no sheets, nothing was put up to separate us. It was not necessary. At night we did not take off our clothes. We did not have sex or even think about it.

Sex was bourgeois. No doubt about it! In my mind, it was something very dirty and ugly. It was also extremely dangerous. In the books I read and the movies I saw, only the bad guys were interested in sex. Revolutionaries had nothing to do with it. When revolutionaries fell in love, they loved with their hearts. They didn't even touch hands.

Of course at the time it never occurred to me to ask: if our revolutionary parents had nothing to do with sex, where did we come from? In fact, I was too ignorant about human reproduction even to raise such a question. The subject had never been taught at school. Nor was it ever discussed at home. So I did not know what the word "sex" really meant. But I knew from Aunty's stories, the books I read, and the news that it had caused women to commit suicide and men to be executed or locked up in prison for ten, fifteen, twenty years. Recently it had also caused many officials to fall from people's esteem. So I sincerely wished I'd never have anything to do with it, just as we Red Guards should not smoke or drink alcohol.

At that time I thought my conviction accorded with Chairman Mao's teaching that a revolutionary should be "a pure person, a noble person, a virtuous person, a person who is free of vulgar desires, a person who is valuable to the people." These shining words came from his famous essay "Serve the People," which we had memorized. Only years later did I realize that such an attitude toward sex in a woman had another name, an ancient one. It was chastity, my dear Aunty's name. "Guard thy body like a piece of jade." This notion undoubtedly belonged to the "four olds." Yet somehow instead of breaking it, my fellow Red Guards and I had defended it as if it were a sacred teaching of Chairman Mao. What happened on the fifth night of our sojourn in Guangzhou might be understood in this light.

On that night, two female Red Guards who were senior students did not come back until after nine o'clock. We were beginning to worry about them. Then we saw them return with a "captive," who was a big, stout man in his thirties. They explained to us why they had "arrested" this man.

In the afternoon the two Red Guards got lost in the city. Because of the directions this man gave them, they ended up in an abandoned cathedral in the suburbs. In twilight the two young women wandered about the ruin, trying to figure out what went wrong and how to get back to the city. Around them the weeds were tall and the trees were casting long shadows. The wind rustled and insects chirped. Suddenly they heard a commotion behind them. It turned out that a group of local people had seized a man.

It was the same man who had given them the wrong directions; then he followed them all the way to the cathedral. The female Red Guards did not notice him, but the local people, whose revolutionary vigilance had been heightened, became suspicious. They knew that rape had been committed on this site.

Hearing this, I was shocked. Rape! In my mind, it was a crime almost as bad as murder. So we interrogated him. What he said about his name, age, and profession has escaped me completely. We must have inquired into his family background and class status too. Probably he did not belong to the Five Red Categories (workers, poor and lower-middle peasants, revolutionary cadres, revolutionary servicemen, revolutionary martyrs), or else what happened that night might not have happened. In my memory even his face is fuzzy, like a picture out of focus. The only thing I remember clearly is the pair of white cotton shorts he had on that night.

To our angry question of why he had tricked our two comrades into the deserted cathedral, he could not gave a satisfactory explanation. That convinced us that he had harbored evil intentions toward our class sisters. We closed in on him. Hands on hips. Fingers pointed at the tip of his nose. Some were already unbuckling their belts. Our questions became sharp.

"So do you hate Red Guards? Tell us the truth! Or else we'll smash your dog head!"

"Yes. I hate the Red Guards."

"Then do you hate the Cultural Revolution too? Do you want to sabotage the Cultural Revolution?"

"Yes. Yes. I hate . . . I want to sabotage . . . "

"Are you a class enemy?"

"Yes. I am a class enemy."

"Are you a Nationalist agent?"

"Yes. I'm an agent. I came from Taiwan."

"Do you hope the Nationalists come back?"

"Yes. I do . . . "

"Do you have guns?"

"Oh yes. I have guns. I have grenades too. I even have a machine gun."

"And a transmitter-receiver to contact Taiwan?"

"Sure. I have a transmitter-receiver."

"Where did you hide these?"

"I buried them in my backyard. You come with me. I'll take you there. You can dig them out."

As the interrogation went on, the man confessed that he had committed all the crimes we could think of. The words that dropped out of his mouth turned into facts in our minds. And these "facts" fueled our hatred toward him. He was no longer a suspect. He had become a criminal, a real class enemy. We started to beat him.

The next thing he did was a real shock to all of us. In a shower of fists, kicks, curses, and thrashes, he suddenly straightened up and pulled his white cotton shorts down. He had no underwear on. So there was his thing, his penis. Large and black. It stuck out from a clump of black hair. To me it seemed erect, nodding its head at all of us.

I couldn't help staring at it. I was dumbfounded. I was embarrassed. I was furious. My hands were cold and my cheeks were on fire. For a few seconds none of us moved. We were petrified. Then the dike burst. Torrents of water rushed out. All the female Red Guards ran out of the classroom. We stayed in the corridor. The male Red Guards charged forward. On their way they picked up long bamboo sticks to hit him.

We all hated him! I could not tell who hated him more. The female Red Guards hated him because he had insulted all of us. The male Red Guards hated him too, because he was a scum of their sex. By exposing himself, he had exposed all of them. They were stripped. They were shamed. This time they beat him hard. No mercy on him. He did not deserve it. He was a bad egg!

The sticks fell like rain. In a few minutes, the man dropped to the ground. The sticks stood in midair. Then someone pulled his shorts back up. After that we streamed back into the classroom. We looked. He did not move. He did not breathe. This man was dead!

We stared at one another, in dismay. *How can a man die so easily? It's unbelievable! Now we are in trouble. Big trouble! We'd better call the public security bureau immediately. This man was a class enemy anyway! Right? We recorded his confession. Of course he did not sign it. That might be a problem. But everyone in our team is a witness. We all heard him confess to these terrible crimes.*

So we braced ourselves and called the municipal public security bureau (the police) of Guangzhou. We told them that a man had just died here. In fact, he had been beaten to death by us. We begged them to send someone here to investigate the case. "Please come as quickly as possible!" Our voices were shaky as we pleaded.

At the other end, the policemen demanded to know who we were. So we told them that we were Red Guards from Beijing. Hearing this, their voices suddenly became warm and cordial. They said that they were *zaofanpai*, the rebellious faction, who had seized power at the public security bureau. They trusted Red Guards who came from where Chairman Mao was and they firmly supported our revolutionary act. Therefore they believed that there was no need to investigate this case any further. The case was closed. They would call up the crematorium and ask them to remove the corpse.

Hearing this, we all felt greatly relieved. Who could believe that we were let off the hook so easily? In fact, it was too easy. We began to feel uncomfortable. Thus we tried to persuade the policemen that at least they should send someone here to record the case. "No. It is not necessary." That was their answer. So that was it.

For the rest of the night, I could not sleep. Not because I was afraid of the ghost. The way I was brought up, I did not believe that there were such things as ghosts. It was my thoughts that disturbed me and kept me awake.

What a pity this man died! But really he was so stupid! If he had said no to all our questions, I'm sure he would have been alive. Maybe the answer would make some of us angry and he'd get beaten. In that case, well, he'd just have to stand it stoically. If he could bear the pain and show us he had courage, even if others wouldn't, I know I'd have put in a word for him and somehow saved his life. Red Guards all admire heroes. My comrades are not unreasonable. But this man, he was anything but a hero! He was such a coward! What a pity he understood nothing about us Red Guards!

Besides, even if he'd said yes to our questions, if he hadn't done that abhorrent thing, pulling down his shorts and . . . he would not have been beaten to death. At least not so fast. So in the final analysis, everything he said and did was wrong! It was his own fault he was beaten to death. He was so sordid! So disgusting! A real rapist and counterrevolutionary, he deserved what he got, every bit of it!

So after we killed this man in the evening, I killed him once more at night, in my mind. I killed him because I had to, or else I would not be able to sleep. When I passed my death sentence on him in the court of my heart, I forgot the fact that I never believed his confession. None of us did. That was why we never bothered to go to the address he gave us to check out the backyard. The policemen at the public security bureau did not even ask us about his address. Perhaps they too assumed that he was a liar.

The next morning, we moved out of the middle school to Shengwei, a big yard in which the provincial Party committee of Guangdong was located. This big yard, like the one I grew up in, was guarded by armed Liberation Army soldiers. The soldiers, however, would only stop "masters of the country" at the gate. "The servants of the people" came in and out on four wheels, saluted by the guards. We were Red Guards from Beijing; when we insisted that we station ourselves here to spread the fire of the Cultural Revolution, eventually the soldiers were told to let us enter and exit as we wished.

So we moved in. We put up at a place called *bingshi* (the ice room), where we could buy red bean ice any time of the day. After we settled down, we went out to see the big yard. It was rather nice with a large lake surrounded by blooming jasmine trees. Thousands of tiny snow-white flowers. The breeze here was fresh and cool, laden with fragrance, while the air outside was hot and suffocating, carrying a hundred city smells and noises. Here it was quiet, like a Shangri-la. But that was why we came. We came to break the bourgeois peace and stir up a red storm right at the headquarters.

From the investigations we made we concluded that the atmosphere in Guangdong province was not right. Everywhere we went, there was no smell of gunpowder and no battle cries of the Cultural Revolution. Only the soft singing of Yue opera and the bone-melting Guangdong music. Restaurants and markets were still full of people, eating, drinking, chitchatting, and shopping around. Numerous privately owned stores were doing good business all over the city. Capitalism was thriving here. In our opinion, the root of the problem was Zhao Ziyang, the first secretary of the Communist Party committee of Guangdong province. We decided that we would "grant him an interview" and try to persuade him that things should not go on like this in Guangdong.

Soon a meeting was arranged between Zhao and representatives of Red Guards from Beijing. Throughout the meeting Zhao was bombarded by questions and criticism, for others shared our opinion about the class struggle situation in Guangdong. Soon drops of sweat began to show on his forehead, despite big electric fans running at top speed in the conference room. He took out a handkerchief and wiped them. At that meeting, Zhao was extremely cautious. He talked very slowly. His attitude was patient and amiable. "Red Guard young generals," he called us from time to time. But that doesn't mean that he was going to take our advice. In fact, he resisted us and refused to give in on any of the issues under discussion. That frustrated and irritated us. Eventually the meeting ended with no results.

At the end of the meeting, I was convinced that Zhao Ziyang was no good and beyond help. He was one of the worst high-level Party officials who was determined to champion capitalism in China. A big red umbrella covering all the bloodsuckers and parasites in Guangdong! (Little did I foresee that twenty-three years later sitting in front of a TV, I would consider him one of the best Chinese leaders who did not want to kill people at Tian'anmen to save the rule of the Party.) *All right then. Since Zhao Ziyang refuses to change the ways he "leads" the Cultural Revolution in Guangdong, we will take that leadership away from him and do things our way! We do not need his permission, nor his cooperation. Let him be the Jade Emperor sitting up on high for the time being. We will be the monkey and turn his heaven upside down. Let's see who has real power.*

So we sat down and drafted an order, which demanded that all privately owned shops and restaurants in Guangzhou City go out of business on that very day; those who dared ignore our order would be responsible for all the consequences. Next, we took the article to a printing factory. The officials there did not dare interfere and the workers supported our revolutionary act. They put other jobs aside and printed out ten thousand copies of our order.

After that, we called the transportation team in the big yard for a vehicle. A jeep soon arrived. We loaded the leaflets onto the jeep and drove through the entire city. The leaflets flew out from the back of the jeep, falling like snowflakes. People in the street fought with one another to grab them. Children ran after us. Many of them. Their bare feet drummed the street. Their hands stretched out. "Gei-zang-wo! Gei-zang-wo! (Give one to me!)" they shouted eagerly in chorus. The news spread like wildfire. On busy streets, at shopping centers, blocks were set up. Local Red Guards, loudspeakers in hands, read our order in Cantonese dialect. That was also part of our plan.

We returned to our base after dark, feeling really good about ourselves. Now revolution had been made. No more hotbeds of capital-

ism in Guangzhou. Socialism won . . . But just as we were congratulating ourselves, a group of cadres filed in with big portfolios under their
arms. They said that they came from the municipal government: since
late afternoon it had been surrounded by hundreds of shop owners who
demanded that their privately owned shops be taken over by the state.

"Good! Then the state should take them over."

"But it's not so simple. The city doesn't have the money to take over
these businesses. You see, if these privately owned shops were taken
over by the state, the shop owners and their assistants would all become state employees. In the future, no matter whether their shops make
money or not, the city has to pay them fixed wages, plus health insurance, welfare, benefits, old-age pensions, provide housing and child care
for them . . . That is why the owners of these shops are eager to have
their shops taken over by the state. That means from now on they'd all
have iron rice bowls . . . "

This was something we had not thought of. But we were unwilling
to call the whole thing off, or else our revolution would be aborted. So
we talked with these officials into the small hours. On our side, we lec-
tured them on the danger of capitalist restoration and the great significance of the Cultural Revolution, telling them not to let economic concerns cloud over political ones. They, on the other hand, showed us
statistics and calculated the costs that would be incurred by such a
change. Our rhetoric soared in the sky. Their argument crawled on the
ground. Our speeches never converged.

Yet before daybreak somehow they managed to persuade us that the
time was not ripe yet for such a drastic move. Or maybe we were not
persuaded, but we gave in because we were so exhausted that our minds
shut down. We no longer cared about the order we had given. Anyway
we had dealt capitalism a fatal blow and the bloodsuckers should know
that their days were numbered. Besides, we had not expected that the
adults, government officials, and those shop owners would take us so
seriously. The mere fact that the officials thought we had authority and
came to negotiate with us gave us satisfaction. So in the end we agreed
that we would not enforce the order immediately, which actually meant
that we would never enforce it.

Although we were unable to wipe out the privately owned enterprises
in Guangzhou, we did set Zhao Ziyang's backyard on fire. Some cadres
here got our message about the Cultural Revolution. They were inspired.
They turned themselves into rebels. Others remained in the old camp

and were called *baohuangpai* (loyalists). Colleagues argued and fought against colleagues. Old friends fell out. Couples debated at night, for they had joined different teams. Kids rebelled against their parents. Red Guards blew the wind and spread the fire. The big yard boiled up like a huge pot of porridge.

Our influence reached to as far as Zhao Ziyang's home. His children, a boy and a girl who were both in elementary school, came over to us. They said that they wanted to rebel against their father. They offered to take us to their home to ambush their old man. We declined their offer and told them to teach us some Cantonese instead. So they taught us how to count from one to ten. We became good friends. Zhao's children were naive. They trusted us. We liked them. In spite of their father. Or maybe because of their father. After all, we were of the same roots. Our parents had all been revolutionary cadres. Only recently some of them had become capitalist-roaders.

While children were naive, adults could be really mean and base when their vested interests were in jeopardy. This we found out from a *dazibao* that accused us Red Guards from Beijing of smoking, drinking, stealing public property, and sleeping together, which meant having sex. Shameless fabrications pure and simple! The last charge was especially vicious. In China this was the most effective weapon to ruin a person's reputation, making him or her, especially her, as odious as dog shit.

Needless to say, we were all infuriated. If we could get hold of this rumormonger, we would bombard him with cannonballs and fry him in boiling oil, shoot ten thousand arrows through him, and smash his dog head . . . But the *dazibao* was anonymous. At the end, it merely said "several revolutionary people." We did not know whose dog head to smash. Even so, we could not afford to ignore it. Our reputation might be ruined by these lies. In this big yard, few knew us personally but many would read this *dazibao*. This was the first time I realized that *dazibao* did not always reveal the truth. It could tell lies and spread rumors too! It might be used by people to make a revolution. It might also be used by some to make personal attacks. Often it was impossible for readers to tell which was which. It could do irreversible damage to innocent people.

So we wrote a *dazibao* overnight to refute the charges. This *dazibao* I remember quite clearly. At the time, I felt it was absolutely convincing. Today, however, its logic really escapes me. Our main argument was this: since we were all Red Guards whose families belonged to the "five red categories," naturally we were endowed with all the good qualities: We had profound class feelings toward Chairman Mao. We hated class enemies. We were determined to carry the Cultural Revolution through . . . By the same token, we were immune from all bad habits such as smoking, drinking, stealing, and having sex. Those who had attacked Red Guards anonymously with such malicious slanders must be harboring dark motives. Revolutionary people should heighten their vigilance and be aware of those who were pulling strings behind the scenes. This, we concluded, was a new and desperate move made by the capitalist-roaders. We vowed that we would leave no stone unturned to get to the bottom of this matter.

Perhaps the threat we made worried the higher-level officials. Soon afterwards, we were invited to talk with Wu Zhipu, deputy Party secretary of central southern China, who was Zhao Ziyang's superior. This old man was even more patient and amiable than Zhao Ziyang. For hours he listened to our criticism of Zhao. Then he offered to arrange another meeting for us to "help Zhao Ziyang face to face."

"No. We have no time to help him. We have more important things to do." I do not remember what those important things were. Looking back on it, I think by that time I was really fed up with political struggle that was very different from what I had imagined. It was not just theories and manifestos, inspiration, debate, and noble sacrifice. It was a fight for power, ugly and ruthless. Enough was enough. Before September was over we decided to leave Guangzhou.

By the time we left Guangzhou, my fellow Red Guards and I were all in bad shape. In my case, I lost my voice completely. No matter how hard I tried, no sound would come out of my throat. It was a weird experience. I guess it was the result of too many excited speeches and debates, battling others with Chairman Mao's quotations at the top of my voice. Perhaps too little sleep and irregular meals had something to do with it too. Sometimes we would not sleep for two or three nights. Sometimes just a single meal or no meal for a whole day.

In fact, I consider myself very lucky to be alive. Shortly before we left Guangzhou, one night, a group of Red Guards, I among them, walked along Zhongshan Street. It was well after midnight. The city was asleep. The street was dim. I was exhausted. My feet were like rocks. I fell behind. Another girl named Wuliang, who was only fourteen, was with me. After a while, we literally fell asleep in the middle of the street.

Other Red Guards went ahead for a mile or so. When they realized that we were missing, they came back to look for us. Fortunately they found us before we got run over by a car or a truck. Otherwise we would have become martyrs, and martyrs of this sort were later judged to be big fools who sacrificed their lives for a wrong cause. Now history has pretty much forgotten them. I'd much prefer to be alive so that I can write this book.

15

Semi-transparent Nights

If I could fall asleep in the middle of a street far away from home in 1966, how could I suffer from insomnia the next year when I was back home? It seems unthinkable. But this was indeed what happened. After I was in bed three or four hours but sleep was still playing hide and seek with me, I would reason with myself.

Last year, that was last year. Now is now. Last year Red Guards were Chairman Mao's brave young generals, charging the enemy line ahead of millions. There was so much to do and never enough time. If a day had forty-eight hours, we still had no time to sleep. Now there's nothing for us to do. A real turnaround, one hundred and eighty degrees. "Things always change into their opposites." Chairman Mao is right. Old revolutionaries have become capitalist-roaders. Old Red Guards are now fighting against the Cultural Revolution, for the sake of their parents. Not all of them. But many are like that. Shame on them! Nowadays we are expected to become middle school students again. "Make a revolution by resuming classes," Chairman Mao said. But what classes are there for us to go to? The teachers have all learned their lessons: those who do nothing make no mistakes. So no one can accuse them of "treating students as their enemies" later on.

Enemies . . .

"Who are our enemies? Who are our friends? This is the most important issue for a revolution."

Revolution . . . Was the second trip I made in 1966 for revolution or was it for sightseeing? Well, the truth is, originally I went to Mount Hua, the gorgeous Taoist mountain in central China, for sightseeing. But later I made a revolution there anyway. All because of those old Taoists. If they hadn't provoked me, I might not have . . . They thought they were smart, using the Red Guards' own tactics to deal with a Red Guard. The questionnaire they made me fill out on top of the mountain, that was definitely a big mistake.

How many questions was I supposed to answer? Sixty? More? The class status of my parents, paternal and maternal grandparents, uncles, and aunts. Their names, ages, professions, work units, and political affiliations. If any of them had joined reactionary organizations, had other historical problems, or had overseas connections . . . It went on and on. Damn it! Just for one night's stay in their temple, for a room with no fire in December. The quilt they gave me was so cold and damp—I shivered in it all night. The chill penetrated my bones. Outside the window, mountain wind boomed. Huge pine trees were rumbling. Overnight ten thousand tons of northwest wind must have rolled over the mountain peaks.

Unable to sleep a wink, I ground my teeth and cursed the Taoists in my head: Who do you think you are? Officials setting up a file for me or police in public security bureau? How dared you ask me, a Red Guard, those humiliating questions about my grandparents and relatives in the name of class struggle, instead of me asking you? Humph. Let's see. Five hundred Red Guards in the middle school of Huayin county. That should be enough for a raid of the temples. Mobilize them. Have them set off at midnight. Ten miles to the top of the mountain. Surprise attack by dawn. Search the temples for evidences of espionage and other counterrevolutionary activities. Break up the superstition. Now that's a good plan!

Three days later, the plan was carried out. Though no evidence of espionage was found, it was still a great victory of Mao Zedong thought. All the Taoists—spiritual opiummongers and parasites—were taken down the mountain by the local Red Guards. That night I slept in the abbot's big bed. It was warm and comfortable. The quilt had a crimson silk cover and was filled with new cotton. In the room, a faint smell of incense lingered. Charcoal glowed in the dark, in an ancient brass brazier. Eternal Spring in the midst of ice and snow. Riding a crane over the five lakes and four oceans. Green pine trees on mountain peaks. Five-colored clouds. Harmony of yin and yang. Sweet dreams . . .

Sleep! I must get some sleep. Before five thirty. Don't think about five thirty! Makes me nervous all over. Relax. Count numbers. One, two, three . . . sixteen. I am sixteen years old.

I turned sixteen at Zunyi in Guizhou province. I celebrated my birthday with one fruit drop. It cost one cent. I had only one cent left by then. In November I left Beijing with five other Red Guards. We split up after we visited Shaoshan, Chairman Mao's birthplace. "The east is red. The sun rises . . . " Stop thinking about that song! It drives me crazy! Everybody in our group had a plan of her own. No one was willing to compromise. So "Good-bye! See you back in Beijing!"

The day after my birthday, I got up at daybreak. Marched out of Zunyi City by myself. Straw sandals, leg wrappings, and a bamboo hat were the latest additions to my Red Guard's outfit. By then the walking tour was in fashion. I wanted to try it too. The route I chose for myself was part of the legendary Long March called Loushan Pass.

In 1935 the Chinese Red Army had fought for its survival here, had crossed Chishui River four times. It was chased, ambushed, intercepted, surrounded by the Nationalist troops. Outnumbered. Tired and hungry, thousands of Red Army men and women died. Their graves stood on mountain slopes on both sides of the road. Some had names. More were simply marked as "Nameless Martyr's Grave."

Standing in front of the graves, I heard each soldier tell me a heroic story: Bullets flew like locusts. Battle cries filled the valley. The sun turned black. The river was red. The pain and despair were fathomless. The love and dreams remained in the green mountains . . . I was deeply moved. I felt that I owed everything to these men and women, forerunners who did not live to see a new China. "So from now on, I must live as if these revolutionary martyrs were living inside me. I will change my name. *Rae,* be it Switzerland or Auspicious, is no good. Henceforth, I will call myself *hongjun!* I will forget my old self and be a new person! The sun and the moon, mountains and rivers, please bear me witness."

Hongjun—Red Army. That was the name I used on my second trip. It was what they called me, those Red Guards from Yunnan, the southwest border of China. We met on the road. We talked. In a couple of hours we got to know one another quite well. We became good friends. (In those days, none of us had heard of the idea of "privacy." So it was perfectly natural that we asked one another all kinds of personal questions. No one felt guilty. No one was offended. All answered the questions truthfully.)

The fifteen Yunnan Red Guards, I found out, were children of silicon miners. Their hometown was Gejiu. The team leader was a seventeen-year-old young man. He was tall and handsome. Others were younger. The youngest girls among them were only thirteen.

"Small in years, not small in aspirations." My new friends told me that their plan was to walk from Yunnan to Beijing to see Chairman Mao. First, they would walk the entire route of the Long March to

Yan'an. Afterwards, they would take the road Chairman Mao had taken during the Liberation War from Yan'an to Beijing. That was a very ambitious plan. What they talked about was a journey of more than two thousand miles, on foot!

"It doesn't matter. We can walk. Every step we take, we are a bit closer to Chairman Mao! If we cannot reach Beijing this year, next year we will certainly be there! We are all determined!"

A girl of fourteen said this to me with a Yunnan accent that was indescribably soft and gentle, but her resolution was unmistakable. "We will walk a hundred li a day [about thirty miles]. Seven days a week. We'll reach Beijing by March."

Good idea! I thought. Let me try it too. After all, I am older than most of the girls here. If they can do it, I can do it too. Let this be a test of my willpower.

A hundred li a day, on that steep mountain road, that was much easier said than done. In the afternoon I began to realize how useless I was. A real armchair revolutionary! No matter how hard I tried, I just could not keep up with my new friends. So they grabbed my bag, which was filled with pamphlets, works by Chairman Mao. (I had planned to give them out to peasants on the way. Then I realized that most of the peasants were illiterate.) Later they took my bedroll and carried that for me too. Even so I still slowed them down. So after a while I insisted violently that we split up and they go ahead.

Then it grew dark. Mountains turned into huge black shadows. Stars were all over the sky. There was no moon. The road sank into darkness. No village was in sight. No dogs barked. I was still some ten li away from my destination. I felt like crying. Not that I was afraid of ghosts or bad people. It was a sense of utter helplessness. "Would Hongjun cry? No! Hongjun would only shed blood. No tears!

"Chairman Mao teaches us, 'Be determined. Do not fear sacrifice. Overcome ten thousand difficulties to strive for victory . . .'"

In those years, millions of Chinese had recited this quotation in difficult situations to boost their morale. Saying it aloud, suddenly I saw lights shine out in front of me. Like a miracle! Dim and flickering at first. Bright and clear later. The lights came near. Oil lanterns lit up the faces of three male Yunnan Red Guards, including the team leader. They told me that they had long since reached the village that was our destination and waited for me. Then it got dark. There was still no trace of me. They decided to come back to meet me.

They walked me to the Red Guard reception center in the village. There the girls had gotten everything ready for me: steaming hot water in a wooden basin. A stool placed next to it. They insisted that I soak my feet first, which they said was the most important thing for people who traveled on foot. After that, they put rice, vegetables, and drinking water onto the table. Sheets and pillows, they had borrowed for me from the reception center. The bed was ready for me to sleep in. By then, it was almost midnight. All the girls had walked a hundred li on that day and the three boys who went back to meet me nearly a hundred and twenty. They must have been exhausted. Yet they stayed up to help me. Their act touched my heart.

Afterwards I never forget that once upon a time on winding mountain roads tens of thousands of Red Guards walked to the north, sharing a dream. On this road, strangers were not strangers. People truly cared about one another. Looking back on it, I know I was part of it; yet the memory seems unreal. China has changed. So have I.

The next day, we walked another hundred li. I was walking on big blisters. I clenched my teeth and endured the pain. This time, however, I did not insist that the Yunnan Red Guards go ahead, knowing that they would come back to meet me anyway. So we walked together and arrived at our destination long after dark.

On the third day, a strange thing happened to me. No matter how hard I tried, I just could not get up from bed. Willpower or Chairman Mao's quotations. Nothing worked. The legs were not mine! I was very embarrassed. The Yunnan Red Guards, needless to say, did not leave me behind. Thus we stayed at Tongzi county, not for one but for three days. That made me feel bad. This time I really slowed them down.

So on the fourth day, I told the Yunnan Red Guards that I was going to take the train to Chongqing in Sichuan province. I made the decision partly because I needed money. Although taking a walking tour I could get food and lodging for free from Red Guard reception centers, I'd much prefer to have some cash in my pockets. My parents could wire me money only if I got to a big city.

My new friends walked me to the train station. Seeing them stand in front of my window on the platform, I was rather ashamed of myself. In the meantime, I also felt superior to them: *As a Red Guard from Beijing, I have more important things to do elsewhere! Thus I cannot afford the time to walk halfway across China like them. We are not the same.*

Before the train left, I gave them my address and telephone number in Beijing. I believed that next spring I would see them again. But I was wrong. Next spring, a classmate of mine came back from Yan'an. He told me he met a group of Red Guards from Yunnan there. By then Red Guards were no longer allowed to travel even on foot. The Yunnan Red Guards were sent home. Before they left, however, they asked him to bring a bamboo hat to me.

"They said it was yours. They told me please make sure that you get it."

"Where is it?"

"Oh, it was in bad shape. Really worn out. The rain had soaked it. It was almost black. And it was torn at many places along the edge. I didn't think you'd want it. I threw it away on the bus."

That was the hat I left behind when we parted at Tongzi county. The Yunnan Red Guards carried it all the way to Yan'an! They completed their Long March, a journey of over a thousand miles. Millions of steps along those endless mountain roads. Rain and snow. Sunrise and sundown. The bamboo hat was a witness of all these. It was also a token of our friendship. When I told my classmate the history of this extraordinary hat, he felt terribly sorry for what he had done. But it was too late. I felt sorry too. Not so much for the hat but for my friends. Knowing how much they had wanted to come to Beijing and see Chairman Mao. Their dreams did not come true. They must have been very sad and disappointed when they were made to go home.

Those Yunnan Red Guards, when we met last year, they thought I knew a great deal. They admired me for it. Last year a Red Guard from Beijing was somebody! All looked up to us. From old cadres to young students, I thought I knew a lot of things too. But really—what do I know? Now I'm not sure I know anything. Ever since I came back from the second trip, I have fallen into five miles of dense fog.

At the beginning of the Cultural Revolution, Red Guards fought against the revisionist educational line, capitalist-roaders, and lists of "four olds." Now Red Guards are fighting against Red Guards. April Third Faction, April Fourth Faction, Liandong Faction. All take sides. Comrades-in-arms of yesterday are mortal enemies now. Hatred takes the place of the love we had for one another.

Wu, my classmate, and I are no longer on speaking terms. Before the Cultural Revolution, we had been bosom friends. We used to study for exams in a quiet peach garden called Dongbei Yiyuan. Other girls dared

*not go there because it was a cemetery. We also walked in drizzling rain
around lotus ponds to create poems for each other . . . After the Cultural Revolution broke out and we shared family histories, we loved
each other as class sisters. But later she joined Liandong and I the Maoist
Commune that belongs to April Third Faction. Mutual contempt grew
between us with each passing day.*

*Wu despises me. I know it. She thinks I'm too naive to understand
upper-level struggles: Jiang Qing's ignoble history, Lin Biao's personal
ambition, Zhou Enlai's opportunism, and so on and so forth. Such topics they never get tired of talking about behind closed doors. I suppose
if I agreed with her, I wouldn't be naive. But does she really think I'm
so naive that I can't see the hidden motives behind the high-sounding
arguments made by her and others like her, all of them high-ranking
cadres' children? Don't believe them for a minute when they talk about
liberating humankind. When the Cultural Revolution touches their
vested interests, they betray the revolution to defend their parents. They
care nothing about the people! Only their privileges! They care nothing about China either, except it used to be their paradise! They are selfish and hypocritical! Even so they still think they're superior to the whole
world. I simply cannot stand them!*

But at least if Wu and I do not like each other, we show it with white
eyes, not rude words. Elsewhere revolutionary people are fighting revolutionary people with bricks and sticks. Some even use rifles and machine guns. Recently a Red Guard from 101 was killed by a machine
gun in Jiangxi province. Caught in an ambush, he died in a truck with
many others. He was only sixteen.

He belonged to our organization. At his funeral, which I attended,
many Red Guards vowed to go to Jiangxi to take the martyr's place.
While they talked, I kept my silence. *Shame on me! But I really don't
want to die like that!*

Da-Da-Da-Da-Da-Da-Da—

*In total darkness, suddenly my chest is punctured by a string of bul-
lets. Each one is screaming pain and chaos. Blood gushes out. Like water from a broken fire hose. I cannot breathe. I try not to scream. People in panic trample me down. Their boots open up my wounds. I can
still feel the pain, though my heart has stopped beating. Who killed me?
Why . . . I'll never find out . . .*

*Am I a coward? Will I become a renegade? . . . Renegades betray their
comrades under torture . . . Who are my comrades? Who are my ene-*

mies? . . . No use thinking about such things! The windmill turns round and round. Don Quixote . . . I can't figure anything out when my brain is in this shape. What time is it? Oh, no. Don't look at the clock! Don't listen to it either! The ticking will grow louder and louder. I hate that sound!

Take a deep breath. As if I'm going to dive into the ocean. Calm down. Water overcomes fire. Fire overcomes metal . . . Fire smolders in my heart night after night . . . Red candle sheds tears . . . Try a different posture. Put both hands under the pillow. Sometimes that works.

The night has grown light again. Almost transparent. Strange. In the past I always thought night was dark and opaque. Now I know I was wrong. Through the thin blue curtains, a faint light flows into my room. I am at the bottom of an ocean. Warm currents, cold currents, eddies, and reefs. My thoughts drift in all directions. Memories rise and fall. Pearls glisten. Sharks cast dark shadows as they swim by.

My room, in the past it was warm and cozy. Now it feels so empty. Little Tiger is dead. Still remember the cat's warmth and weight on my quilt. How could children be so cruel? Lovely angels. Flowers of the motherland. Rascals! Little beasts! Wish I could seize them. Slap their faces till their teeth fall out. Kick their butts. Thrash them with my belt until they beg for mercy. That'd teach them a lesson and vent my nameless fire. I am so angry. At them. At myself. I'm so useless I can't even save a cat!

Aunty is gone too. Nothing I can do about that either. I wonder if she's asleep or awake at this hour? In that old house where she lived with her husband, son, and daughter. Old memories stored everywhere. In drawers and trunks. Under the bed and over the mosquito net. Like spiderwebs, they catch the insects of drowsiness. In Aunty's stories, when these invisible insects fly into people's noses, they fall asleep . . . Sleep! Are there spiderwebs in my room too?

I ought to go and see Aunty tomorrow. She will be so glad. Rush out to buy meat and vegetables. Chop. Chop. Stir-fry. My favorite dishes will come out of her wok one after another. "Eat this! Eat that! Eat more!" A big happy smile on her face. Loneliness still lingers in her eyes. She dares not come back to visit us. The neighbors might report her and get us into trouble. I should visit her more often.

Last time I visited her . . . The thought bites like a scorpion. I can't tell anyone about it. I feel as if I've stolen something. But actually everything in that suitcase was ours! Mother's diamond wedding ring, a gold necklace, Father's German cameras, a few cherished books and records of classical music, a new Swiss watch, stuff like that. The suitcase I took to Aunty's place—it's much safer there. No one would think of raiding the home of an old woman who had been poor in the old society. Aunty was trusted by her neighborhood committee. She offered to keep the suitcase for us. But the problem was how to get it there.

Father and Mother looked at me. They said nothing. I knew what they meant. Only I could do it. I hated to do it! I did it anyway. In the street, on the bus, all eyes seemed suspicious. Everybody was watching me and the suitcase. "The eyes of the revolutionary people are bright as snow, sharp as knives." They poked holes into me. I was a paper tiger. On the outside, I was armed to the teeth, a ferocious Red Guard. But inside I was a big bag of miserable doubts and fear.

I knew what I did was wrong. Uncle Li's daughter was not so self-ish. She exposed her parents. Reported everything to the Red Guards in her father's college: the things her parents said at night, the places where they hid their treasured belongings . . .

"Place righteousness above family loyalty." That was what she did. "Drop rocks on those who have fallen into a well." That was also what she did. What she did was actually what her father had taught her to do over the years. "Believe the Party more than anyone else. Be loyal to it no matter what happens. Love Chairman Mao more than your parents . . . "

Uncle Li was Party secretary of the college before he was "pulled down from the horse." An expert in political and thought work. I think it was his fault that his daughter betrayed her family. Now he and his wife hate her more than anyone else. They should be proud of her! I admire her for her courage, knowing I'll never be able to do such a thing. I'm a hypocrite. I have to admit it. But I would rather be a hypocrite than a fool!

Chairman Mao and my parents, who do I love more? Hmmm. This is a tough question. Honestly, I think I love Chairman Mao more than my parents. For example, if Chairman Mao, my parents, and I were sit-ting in an airplane about to crash and we only had one parachute, I'd definitely give it to Chairman Mao. Let my parents and myself be blown to pieces in a gigantic ball of fire. We'd all be glad. Or suppose we were on a sinking boat in the middle of an ocean with only one life jacket, I'd put it on Chairman Mao. My parents and I would go down to the stom-achs of the sharks, with a proud smile. But now Chairman Mao is safe

in the big yard called Zhongnanhai, while my parents are in trouble.
I've got to help them too. They are not against Chairman Mao and his
revolutionary line. In fact, they got themselves into trouble because they
took the idea of the Cultural Revolution seriously.

Last year Father and Mother had no enemies. Students liked them.
Colleagues were friendly, partly because my parents did not compete
with them for promotion, housing, and other things. "Vigorously with-
draw from the rapids"—that was Father's philosophy. Mother accepted
it, although somewhat reluctantly. Because of this, many of Father's old
friends who became capitalist-roaders last year said he was truly wise.

Wise? Humph! Not when he and Mother criticized the leaders of their
college at the beginning of the Cultural Revolution. Doing that, they
got categorized as rebels. Half the people at the college became their
mortal enemies. For these people, nothing short of our blood being
drained and our bodies cut into ten thousand pieces would satisfy them.

To reach their goal, those colleagues of my parents dug up old dirt
and created new rumors. Formed special-case groups. The members
went to places all over China to investigate my parents. It made no difference whether they were in power or not. If not capitalist-roaders,
people could still be made into "black hands" (wirepullers), renegades,
counterrevolutionaries, foreign spies . . . Many caps are handy.

One fact that gave us comfort was that my parents had no historical problems. Mother was a progressive student in Yanjing University
before Liberation. Father was really lucky that he got sent to Yan'an
instead of back to Beijing to do underground work. As an underground
worker, one may lose touch with the Party or get arrested. In those cases,
how could he prove he wasn't a renegade or a Nationalist spy? And if
he couldn't convince others he was innocent, he'd be assumed guilty.
That's why many of Father's old friends were in trouble. Some were
arrested, had to face the method of *bi gong xin* (compulsion-confession-
credence).

Yan'an was a much safer place. Many people knew Father. They
could testify that he had never left the liberated area. Never lost touch
with the Party. Never got arrested . . . *How can one find a bone in an*
egg? But wait! If people use the method of bi gong xin, *they can find*
anything they want in an egg: bullets, daggers, guns, transmitter-
receivers . . . You name it.

Yan'an, who says it was safer? Knowing too many people has already
caused Father big troubles. In Yan'an, Ye Jianying was his boss. Wang

Guangmei was his colleague and Furen fellow graduate. Wu Xiuquan had introduced Mother to him. The list goes on and on. Never mind that Father and Mother weren't in touch with any of them after they became VIPs. Members of special-case groups for these people came, magnifying glass in hand, looking for clues to historical problems.

Tell them the truth? Some of them just got mad as hell. Banging on the table. Stamping on the floor. A thin closed door could not prevent Lian and me from overhearing what went on inside Father's room. Father was amiable and patient. His interrogators' voices loud and furious. "We warn you! Give us straight answers! Try to shield renegades and capitalist-roaders, you will come to no good end! Mind your dog head!" Bang! Bang!

So much pressure gets put on Father to lie about his old comrades. Mount Tai is light compared with it. What will Father do? He is determined.

"I have to tell the truth," he told me. "I cannot make things up for them. Fuzzy evidence, irresponsible answers given under such circumstances will kill people! Destroy their families! I cannot do that. I am a Communist Party member. I have to be responsible to the Party. But if I insist on telling the truth, I may have to pay a price. You may have to pay a price too. A big price, Rae. Do you understand?"

Yes, I do! Even so, you are still my hero, Father. I admire your courage and integrity. But will others tell the truth about you too? When the Red Guards from your college put pressure on them, what will they say? If they tell half-truths or make up stories to please these people and save their own skin, we are finished. A huge ax is hanging over our heads by a single silk thread. It may fall any day, at any moment. I dread the moment. I am waiting for it. Day and night.

Red Guards come. In a large number. Bang! Bang! Bang! The noise wakes up everybody. "Open the door!" "Hurry up!" "Hurry up!" Try to stay calm. Fear will only make things worse. The door opens. A crowd swarms in. Belts are unbuckled. Ropes and handcuffs. Search warrant? No need for it. Somebody has confessed something. The law no longer protects us. Pull the drawers out. Open the trunks. Throw everything on the floor. They arrest Father. They arrest me. Take us to a prison van. The kind we see in movies, vans used by the Nationalists before Liberation. "Farewell, Mother! Farewell, my dear fellow countrymen! Don't weep! Lift up your heads! Darkness will soon be over! . . . "

Darkness. I'm submerged in it. The dungeon is pitch-black. Smell of blood. Am I blind? Torture . . . All kinds of it. It's too much for me to bear. A body of flesh and blood. Yet I must endure it all so my comrades will be safe.

"*I have to tell the truth! I cannot make things up . . .*"

"*I'll never tell you the secret! I won't betray my comrades!*"

They torture me in front of Father. They torture Father . . . I torture . . . Father . . . I'm losing consciousness. I'm blind. I'm falling from a mountaintop into an abyss. Light as a feather. Whirling down. Unsettling air flows. Dizziness . . . Sleep . . .

"The east is red. The sun rises. China . . . Mao Zedong . . . "

Oh. Miserable! Just as I was about to fall asleep, this damn song starts. At five thirty! Every day. Seven days a week . . . Never gives anybody a break . . . I hate this song now! I used to love it . . . Things change into their opposites . . . Red Guards. Class enemies . . . I wonder if any counterrevolutionary can match me in hating this song. It's not music. It's torture! Pouring out of a loudspeaker in a pine tree just outside my bedroom window. It drives me crazy! Are there bedrooms in this college that don't have loudspeakers blaring into them? Guess not.

At daybreak, the whole college was drowned in this deafening music. Teachers, students, workers, their families, all were forced to wake up. Other colleges and universities in Beijing were pretty much the same. When "the east is red," everybody had to get up except a few leaders, such as Chairman Mao himself.

The broadcast, once it started, would not stop for at least two hours. The network news followed the song. Then local news, all kinds of announcements, declarations, orders, ultimatums, selected *dazibao* . . . It went on and on.

Cover my head with the quilt. Put it under the pillow. Nothing worked. The sound drilled into my ears, turning my brain into a battlefield where the persistent sound waves and my drowsiness fought a bloody battle. Such a headache. Fire burning in my heart. My sanity was wearing thin.

"Down with so and so!"

"Smash the dog head of so and so!"

Wish I could smash that cursed loudspeaker! Trample it flat. Kick it over the wall. It'd be silent then. Lying there like an abandoned chamberpot rotting away in a ditch . . .

"Working class. Seize the power!"

"Revolutionary people . . . Heighten your vigilance!"

"Guard against . . . sabotage . . . class enemies . . . "

If they catch me smashing the loudspeaker, I know they'll seize me. An active counterrevolutionary. Caught red-handed. Public trial rallies. Parades. Execution . . . Who cares? After that, ping! All would be quiet. A dead person hears no songs. Eternal sleep will be mine. How sweet!

The Red Guard commander in this college, why did he of all people commit suicide? It was a mystery. No one knew the answer. Some said he had very bad insomnia. It must have driven him crazy. So he, an intelligent young man of twenty-one who commanded a thousand invincible Red Guards in this college, jumped off the roof of the main building on campus. On a gorgeous morning. In front of a staring crowd. He leaped up into a rosy sky and came down in a perfect diving posture, as if he were competing for an Olympic gold medal. The posture he kept until he touched the concrete sidewalk seventy feet below. Everybody who saw it said it was incredible.

He broke his arms. He broke his head. He broke his neck and spine. Blood drowned him from the inside. But he did not die immediately. He gasped and groaned. Sweat of pain poured out of his body. They rushed him to a hospital, where he died a couple of hours later. It must have been hell in those two hours, before he got his sleep at last.

I'm willing to sell my soul to the devil himself if he can teach me how to silence that loudspeaker. Loose contact? A wire broken from the inside? Pull the magnet out? . . . How to climb up that tree? When is the best time to do it? After midnight, when there is no moon? "Set fire in high wind. Murder when the moon is black." My great-grandfather and grandfather. Capitalists and vampires. Teach me your bloody tricks!

A thousand ideas spun in my head. Many were crazy. All were futile. Luckily I still had some common sense left in me so I did not put these ideas into practice. Two hours later, the broadcast would break through the defense line of my drowsiness. I got up. Head heavy and feet light. Eyes sour as vinegar. Another day ruined before it began.

16

"The Hero, Once Departed, Will Never Come Back"

Insomnia tormented me for a year and a half. By June 1968 I couldn't take it anymore. I must do something about it, I said. This something was to volunteer to go to a farm in the northeast, at a place known as the Great Northern Wilderness.

I use the word "volunteer" because unlike those who graduated from middle schools in the following years, in 1968 we still had a choice: those who did not want to leave Beijing could stay. But the jobs awaiting them were not glorious: mending shoes, fixing bikes, cleaning streets, selling soybean milk and fried dough, things like that. And the co-workers in such work units were mostly illiterate old men and women, the typical "petty city dwellers." Up to the eyes in gossip from morning till night. Chicken feathers and garlic skins. Storms in a teacup . . . This was the future I had dreaded. I thought I said good-bye to it when I was accepted by 101. Who would have thought that five years later, it turned up again as the only alternative I had other than going to the Great Northern Wilderness.

So I volunteered to go to the Great Northern Wilderness. In my mind it was a mysterious and exciting place. Vast stretch of virgin land. Boundless pine forest on snowy mountains. Log cabins. Campfires. Hunting and skiing. Wild animals. Hidden enemies. Spies sneaked across the border from the Soviet Union at night. Combat of life and death . . .

Death? I can take it! Better die as a hero than live through those endless nights. Recently I'm afraid my illness is getting worse. It drives me crazy. These days my parents get on my nerves. Lian and Yue both irritate me. I don't belong to this home anymore. I'm wasting my time here. I should leave. The sooner the better.

I embarked on the journey on July 15, 1968. A day I will never forget. Everybody in my family went to Beijing train station to see me off.

Father, Mother, Lian, and Yue came from the western suburb. Aunty from her own home in the city. Several classmates of mine came too. Wu, of course, was not among them. I don't remember who these classmates were except two girls who were from workers' families. Their parents, who were more practical than ours, had persuaded them to stay in Beijing.

On that day, the train was filled to capacity by young people like me. Probably over a thousand. All were going to the Great Northern Wilderness. The platform next to our train was even more crowded, swarming with family members, friends, classmates. As the time for the train to leave drew near, some began to cry. Among my classmates, the two girls who were going to stay in Beijing were crying their eyes out.

What do they think they're doing? Are they crying because they can't bear to part with me? This I can hardly believe. They are making a scene in front of all these people. Why? Maybe they're really crying for themselves? Think of the mediocrity in store for them. The missed adventures and opportunities for heroism. Anyway I don't like them to weep for me. I don't like them to weep for themselves in front of me either. It is embarrassing. I don't know how to respond to this.

So I turned my eyes away from them to look at the sky. It was a bright sunny day. Not a trace of cloud. Numerous red flags were flying in the air. Drums and gongs were making such a din that I could hardly hear anybody. But that was just fine. I did not want to hear anybody.

In a split second, I was far away, in a different world. A scene spread out in front of my eyes, one that took place more than two thousand years ago.

> The wind is howling *hsiao-hsiao;*
> the water of Yi River is cold.
> The hero, once departed, will never come back.

The great hero Jing Ke was singing on the bank of Yi River. He had just left the capital of Yan state, which was located near where Beijing is today. Among those who went to see him off were the crown prince of Yan state and Jing Ke's good friend Gao Jianli. They were all wearing white robes, the color of mourning. They knew that Jing Ke would not come back from the expedition. He was going to Xianyang to assassinate the mighty king of Qin state, a notorious tyrant in Chinese history.

On the riverbank, the reed catkins were as white as snow. The wind was wild. Gao Jianli struck up the lute. Jing Ke improvised the song. Tears streamed down from the eyes of the company. Jing Ke was the only one who did not cry. After he finished the song, he mounted the carriage and drove off. He never looked back.

This story I read in *Shiji* before the Cultural Revolution. It left me with a deep impression. *Like Jing Ke, I won't come back either, once I depart. In history Jing Ke sacrificed his life in an attempt to rescue the people from the tyranny of Qin. His body was chopped to pieces by the ferocious bodyguards of the king, who later conquered the entire country and called himself Qin Shi Huangdi. Today our sacrifice is made for a much greater cause: we will build a society that is unprecedented in human history. Unlike all other societies in which there were upper and lower classes—as Mencius said, "Those who work with their minds govern people. Those who work with their bodies are governed by people"—in our society, educated city youths will go to the countryside voluntarily so that children of peasants will have opportunities to attend universities. Eventually the gap between cities and rural areas will disappear. Probably not in our generation. In that sense, we are the losers. But being a loser of this type is an honor. History will remember our generation, as it does the Long March soldiers.*

The bell rang. My thoughts were cut short. Last three minutes. The train was ready to leave. Aunty could not hold it any longer. So far she had been trying to put on a smiling face for me to remember in the years to come. Now her face began to crack in spite of her effort to control it. Tears streamed from her eyes. Silent torrential tears. Leaning against Lian's shoulders, suddenly she looked so old, so helpless. She stretched out one hand toward me, as if she wanted to grab me from the train, at the last moment . . .

With a jerk, the train started to move. Suddenly my heroic heart melted. Tears rushed into my eyes. Around me everybody was crying. On the platform, people ran alongside the train, holding hands. The train gathered speed; hands parted. I wiped the tears from my face. The tears my family and classmates did not see.

(Mother wept at that moment too. Later she confessed this to me in a letter. She would not let anyone see her tears either. "Like mother, like daughter." She was right when she adapted this saying from "like father, like son" to describe us. Mother was a woman who tried to hide her emotions. Me too.)

The train was pulling out of Beijing, my hometown. The gray bungalows receded from my sight, along with willow trees, date trees, ancient tower gates, and city moat . . . All were so familiar as if they were parts of my body, parts of my soul. After today, I might never set my eyes on them again. The thought saddened me.

In the future, I knew if I should regret my decision and want to come back, it would be impossible. Like Jing Ke, I had embarked on a journey from which there was no return. The moment I canceled my Beijing *hukou* (legal residency), I had sealed my fate by giving up the biggest privilege a Chinese could enjoy in those years. Henceforth I would be a rural resident, a peasant. My place was in Hulin county, Heilongjiang province. Years later, after I die, my children and grandchildren would continue to live there. The government saw to it that peasants (over 80 percent of Chinese population) stayed in the countryside so that the state needn't take care of them as it did the urban people.

When I left Beijing, I was aware yet not really aware of the consequences, for I did not think carefully about it. To me as well as to many others, this felt like another free trip that we took at the beginning of the Cultural Revolution. Singing and laughter soon returned to our carriage. Everyone seemed happy. Only I was a little absent-minded. My thoughts turned back to the conversations I had with my parents the day before.

First, Father called me into his room.

"Rae. Going to the countryside is a revolutionary act. Your mother and I firmly support you!" he said. *A declaration of his political stand first of all. Sometimes he does talk like an official.*

"In fact, soon we will follow your example and go to the countryside too. We don't know where and when yet. But it has been decided that our college will move to a rural place. It will become a May Seventh Cadre school."

Hearing this, my heart sank. *Too bad! In that case I will lose my base in Beijing. In the future I can't even come back for a short home visit. Uprooted! That is what I feel. But of course I can't tell him that.*

"Going to May Seventh Cadre school is also a revolutionary act. I firmly support you too."

"Good!" Father said. "So in the future we will all become peasants. So much the better for us! Workers and peasants are honest and frank, unlike scholars who are hypocritical and scheming. Many 'have two faces and three knives!' While they flatter you to your face, they stab you in the back. I am fed up with them!" *Wait a minute! Father. You and Mother are scholars too. Aren't you? But of course I understand what you mean. You two are different. You are not like them!*

"Now listen to me very carefully, Rae," Father continued. "You must remember this: according to my experience in the past, the Party is always correct! Chairman Mao is always correct! You must have faith in the Party and Chairman Mao under all kinds of circumstances. That way you will not make political mistakes. You will not get into trouble . . . "

"Yes. Yes. I know, Father. You don't have to tell me that."

But there was something else on his mind. I sensed it. He paused, hesitating. I waited. He looked at the door. It was shut. No one else was home anyway. Yet he lowered his voice as he explained.

"Right now I'm in a lot of trouble. You know. The special-case group is trying very hard to find evidence against me. After you leave, things may get worse. I may get locked up in a cow shed. I may even get arrested. Anything can happen. We ought to prepare for the worst. In the future if someone goes to your farm and tells you your father is a renegade, a spy, or a counterrevolutionary, don't you believe them! I will tell you the truth myself: in my entire history, I was only punished by the Party once. That was when we were in Switzerland, I had an affair with a woman. She was a Chinese. Not a foreigner. I won't tell you her name. It happened around the time Lian was born. A demerit was recorded against me. After that, the woman and I broke up. It was a stain on my history. Only this much was true. Other things people might tell you are all lies. I want you to know and remember this."

Poor Father! In the past he kept up such prestige in front of us three children. Like other fathers in China, he was an authority figure. If he didn't feel danger was imminent, I'm sure he'd never tell me this. Who ever heard of a parent talking about sex with his children? "I had an affair with a woman." How embarrassing! No wonder he chose a time when no one else was home to talk to me. Or did Mother know so she took my brothers out deliberately?

When Mother came back, she talked to me too. That was rare. In my family usually it was Father who did the talking. Mother merely supported him. This time, however, Mother had something of her own to tell me. She came into my room, sat on my bed next to me. First she took off her Swiss watch and gave it to me.

"When you see this watch, it is as if you saw my face. Take good care of it."

"Yes! I promise!" (In 1968, even among students at 101, few had wristwatches made in China. A Swiss watch for a seventeen-year-old was even more unusual.)

Then Mother said: "I know you have grown up and you have been away from home, but this time it is different. You will be away from us for a very long time. I want you to remember this: in the future if something happens and you don't want to let others know about it, you can tell it to me. You promise me: if you need help you will let me know."

"All right. I promise. But don't you worry. I can take care of myself. Really!"

The talks lingered in my mind for a while. Then they were behind me too. Scattered like the white smoke over the mountains and lakes we had passed. In three days we arrived at the Great Northern Wilderness. At the headquarters of Farm 850, we were picked up by tractors from different production teams. About fifty of us were assigned to the third team. The team was located in a village called Cold Spring, about twenty miles northwest of the farm headquarters.

We set off. It did not take me long to realize that contrary to my expectations there were no mountains and forests in this area. The Great Northern Wilderness was a huge swamp. Part of it had been turned into farmland. From afar the wheat fields were golden; the soybean fields emerald green. The rest was still virgin land, overgrown with grass that was half yellow, half green. The grass was long and slender, up to my waist. It swayed in the wind. Our tractor sailed through it. Wild geese flew up.

Suddenly everybody in the tractor felt like singing. So we all sang at the top of our lungs. Some had nightingale voices. Some had broken gong voices. *It doesn't matter. This is the Great Northern Wilderness, not Beijing. No one will laugh at us. No need to be bashful.* Our songs rose up to the sky that was so high, so wide. The color of it was almost violet, not light blue. It was very deep and exquisite, and I'd never seen anything like it anywhere else. The sun was shining in the east. A storm hung like a dark curtain in the west. Our new home was so beautiful! I fell in love with it already.

The village we arrived at, however, looked rather drab. No trees. No flowers. No vegetable gardens. Just a number of bungalows spread out like a square battle formation. The dining hall was a bit taller. It stood in the front like a leader. The other bungalows were identical, like a number of foot soldiers. Each bungalow was about eighty feet long, fifteen feet wide. It contained four units. Four doors and four windows opened to the south. No doors or windows on any other sides, because of the severe weather in this region.

Every family in this village got one unit. It made no difference if this was a family of two or a family of six. All were given one unit: a single room and a passageway. The passageway was narrow and dark, as there was no window in it. It served as the kitchen as well as an intermediate zone between the room and the outside. Coming in from the outside, people had to walk through it to the northern end where another door led to the room.

Unlike the passageway, the room had sunshine from a window. The precious sunshine was made to fall on the *kang,* a bed made of large earthen bricks, which took up the entire southern half of the room. The *kang* was actually part of the chimney. When people cooked over the stove in the passageway, the smoke and surplus heat went through the *kang* first, making it nice and warm to sleep on. In fact, the local families not only slept on the *kang,* they did almost everything on it. When they had guests, all were cordially invited to sit on the *kang* to keep warm.

For such an apartment without electricity or running water, a local family paid one yuan and a half for rent each month (the equivalent of U.S.$0.75 at the time). The rent was the same for all families. The income was pretty much the same too. But class struggle continued to exist under socialist conditions. Remembering this teaching from Chairman Mao, the Beijing youths, most of us ex-Red Guards from revolutionary cadres' families, decided that we should inquire into the class struggle situation in the village. Find out who were landlords, rich peasants, counterrevolutionaries, and other bad elements. These class enemies we must guard against. The poor peasants (that is, people who were poor before land reform), on the other hand, were our teachers. We must learn from them.

I got to know the poor peasants soon. In this village some fifty families belonged to this class. At first, strange to say, they impressed me as quite different from what they should be. My ideas of what they should be came from the newspapers and the few poor peasants who had come to 101 to talk about their hard lives in the old society. They made me believe that poor peasants were very keen on class struggle. Not the poor peasants here! When these people talked to us, they never mentioned "class struggle," "guard against capitalist restoration," "continue the revolution under proletarian dictatorship," "thought reform," and so on. Some occasionally talked about their gratitude to the Party and Chairman Mao, but even that was rare.

Most of the time they were just extraordinarily kind to us. They made sure that our clothes were warm and we had our hats on in the winter. They urged us to sun our bedding frequently so that we would not catch rheumatism, an ailment widespread in this cold and damp region. They taught us to use wula grass to stuff our boots so as to keep our feet warm. They reminded us that we mustn't exert ourselves too much before we got used to farmwork. On things of this nature they talked to us day in and day out.

Above all, I was touched by their generosity. Each time they got something special to eat, mushrooms or dried lilies they had gathered from the plain, noodles and dumplings they made at home, they shared them with us. In those years, the local people hardly had anything good for themselves and their kids to eat. Their chickens and geese had been confiscated in a campaign called Cut the Tails of Capitalism. Their private garden plots had been taken away for the same reason, and the plots soon went to waste.

In winter some villagers went out to hunt. In summer they tried to fish. Most of the time they came back empty-handed. By the late sixties in that area, not much wildlife was left. It was hard for me to imagine that only a decade before people in this area had made the famous ballad:

Hit a roe deer with a stick.
Catch fish with a ladle.
Pheasants fly into the cauldron . . .

Nonetheless if the villagers had some luck, got a pheasant or a wild duck, they always sent their kids to fetch some of us from our dormitories. *They don't have to do this! Why are they so kind to us? They know as well as we do there's no way we can repay them.* When I asked the villagers, they all gave the same answer.

"You Beijing students are used to comfort. You had such good lives in the city. Now you come here, so far away from home, doing this hard labor in the fields. Nothing good to eat. Bitten by those poisonous mosquitoes in the swamp. Aiya! Look at the big swellings on your legs! And the chilblains on your fingers! Your parents' hearts would ache if they should see this! How badly their hearts would ache!"

Such talk I heard over and over again. It made me wonder. *Is this the bourgeois fallacy of humanity we've criticized? The one about universal human feelings? If I ran across this kind of talk at the beginning of the Cultural Revolution, I wouldn't hesitate to put such a label on it and condemn it because, in my opinion, it overlooked class struggle. And now real peasants, poor peasants, are also talking like this! According to Chairman Mao, they are our teachers. If they feel this way and say such things, then such things must be all right! Who am I to judge them? I am here to learn from them!*

Thus thinking I breathed a deep sigh of relief. To tell the truth, I was truly glad that poor peasants here turned out this way rather than being keen on class struggle. Now I could relax and make myself at home on a big, warm *kang*. Eat whatever people offered me and listen to their stories. Even the stories they told me had a different flavor from the ones I read in newspapers, such as the story that happened right here in this village, about two men, one woman, and a wristwatch.

Back in 1958, a hundred thousand demobilized soldiers came to the Great Northern Wilderness to reclaim the swamp. Among them were two men who were best friends. Both were from Shandong province, where men were famous for their courage and brotherly love. In the past these two veterans had fought side by side in Korea. Now they both worked as tractor drivers at Cold Spring. One man was a few years older. He was married. Soon after he arrived here, his wife joined him from their native village. The younger man was still single.

Then one night while the older man worked on a night shift, an accident happened. His wife died at home from coal gas. Each year in northern China many people die from coal gas fumes. The husband was heartbroken, for he loved his wife very much. He felt especially bad when he thought that in the past his wife had asked him for a wristwatch, not once or twice, but many times. Yet until she died they had not saved enough money to buy one for her. (At the time a good Chinese wristwatch cost over a hundred yuan—a big luxury for a farmworker, whose monthly wages were either thirty-two or thirty-six yuan. Few in the village could afford watches.) Now his wife had died. The man decided to give her a good wristwatch as a parting gift.

So he borrowed money, bought the watch, and put it on the wrist of his dead wife while nobody was watching. Later she was put into a coffin with a pillow and a quilt. As it was the dead of winter, the ground was frozen solid several feet deep, and people in this region were unable to bury their dead until spring. The co-workers of the husband nailed down the lid of the coffin, carried it to a place called Little Southern Hill about a mile south of the village, and left it there for the time being.

That night the younger man came to console his "older brother" and the two drank *baijiu* together (strong liquor distilled from fermented wheat or sorghum). After they finished a bottle or two, the older man opened his heart to his best friend. He poured out his grief by tears and by words, and these led eventually to the wristwatch. Afterwards he fell asleep. But the young man could not close his eyes. It turned out that he too wanted a wristwatch but did not have enough money to buy one. So he thought of taking the watch from the coffin. But immediately he blamed himself: his "brother" had trusted him with a secret. Now he was thinking of stealing from him. How could he be so base? . . .

Thus for half a night, the young man tossed and turned on the *kang*. After midnight, he made up his mind. He got up, took a few tools, and went straight to Little Southern Hill. As he worked on the coffin, he pleaded to the dead woman inside.

"Sister-in-law! Please forgive me! You are dead already. What use do you have for a wristwatch? Please let me have it. I really need it. I will burn paper money for you. Lots and lots of it. You might be able to use it in the nether world . . . "

Thus saying, he opened up the coffin. There he saw the woman. Her face was as white as a sheet of paper. But her eyes were wide open! Suddenly she sat up in the coffin! She stretched out her arm. In her hand, there was the wristwatch, glistening in the cold moonlight.

"Here's the watch. Take it!" she said.

The young man was so frightened that he passed out on the spot. The woman ran back to the village. In fact, she had not really died the day before, as people believed. There was no doctor in the village and she just looked as if she were dead. But the fresh air at Little Southern Hill gradually revived her as she lay in the coffin. Then the young man came. Lucky for her! For otherwise she would have been frozen to death that night. It was forty degrees below zero out there.

When she got home, she woke up her husband and told him what had happened. The husband quickly ran to Little Southern Hill, where he found the "brother" still lying on the ground. He carried him back.

The young man, when he woke up, was terribly ashamed of himself. He apologized to the couple and begged them to forgive him. He called himself all kinds of names. But the couple only thanked him. They insisted that the young man accept the watch as a token of their gratitude. The young man refused flatly, blushing until his neck was the color of pig liver. But in the end, he had to obey his "older brother" and he accepted the watch. Henceforth they continued to be best friends and lived happily ever after.

Although people here loved to tell this story, when I asked them if they had met these people, they said no. "The first group of veterans left after Farm 850 was established. They went out to the frontier to set up new farms." After they left, new people came. They were the brothers, sisters, cousins, fellow villagers of the veterans. They came from all over China, the heavily populated areas in particular, such as Shandong and Sichuan.

When the newcomers arrived, they became farmworkers. That meant they were no longer ordinary peasants but state employees who would earn thirty-two yuan a month no matter what. An iron rice bowl! This made them so happy that they stayed, despite the bitterly cold winters, the fierce mosquitoes, the rheumatism, the fatal local disease called Hulin fever . . . The iron rice bowl was more important than all of these put together.

But was the iron rice bowl really made of iron? The answer was "not really." Under certain circumstances, the iron rice bowl could be broken, or maybe I should say taken away.

I say this because in 1959 when famine hit China, all female farmworkers in the Great Northern Wilderness were ordered to quit their jobs so as to "alleviate the burden of the country." At that time they were told that as soon as the crisis was over, they would be taken back on the payroll. So they consented. Nobody had a choice anyway, that is, if she was a woman. Next year the famine continued. Then by and by the situation got better, but the women were never taken back. (It turned out that they were considered a burden by the leaders and the famine was just a good opportunity to dump them.) So the women's status eventually changed from state employees to *jiashu* (dependents). As "dependents" they were hired as temporary workers. They continued to do the same work, but their wages dropped to 28 yuan a month. In addition they lost free health care, paid sick and maternity leave, old age pensions, and any hope for a pay raise. As a result, the women (their number totaled more than a hundred thousand in the region) were very angry at the local leaders when we arrived.

Aside from the women, another group of people called *mangliu* (unplanned influxes) had status lower than that of a regular farmworker. These were peasants who fled their native places during the famine. When they first came to the Great Northern Wilderness, they were hired as temporary laborers. They earned minimum daily wages that were even lower than the women's. But even so, they were grateful. At least they were not starving. That was enough.

A couple of years later, the famine was over and the *mangliu* were able to obtain their *hukou* from their native places. The male *mangliu* were taken on as farmworkers and the female ones became "dependents." They too settled down here. About one-third of the families at Cold Spring were originally *mangliu*.

Huar, whose name means flower, was from such a family. She was a year younger than me, sixteen when we first met, but was already an excellent farmhand. Strong and dexterous, she bent down to cut wheat with a sharp small sickle. From right to left, from right to left . . . The motion was rhythmic and effortless. Like a gust of wind. At first it seemed impossible for any of us to keep up with her.

In three months, however, I got my body into much better shape. So when it was time to cut soybeans, I clenched my teeth and followed her step after step. In four hours we reached the end of a very long ridge almost at the same time. Huar smiled at me as she straightened her back and wiped the sweat from her forehead. I managed a smile even though my back felt as if it had broken into eighteen pieces. From then on, we worked side by side in the fields. We became good friends.

As a friend, I visited Huar at home quite frequently. I liked everybody in her family. Her father, Old Ji, was a first-rate farmhand and a skilled stonemason. Her mother, whom I called Ji Daniang, was illiterate but extremely kind. They were both poor peasants in the old society. Her younger brother was just a child at the time.

Later I heard from the villagers that Old Ji used to be the Party secretary in his native village in Shandong province. I could not believe this! Party membership in 1968 was a great honor. I had dreamed about it many times, but I knew that I was not good enough. As for Party secretary—wow, that was the number-one leader in the village! How could this Old Ji give all that up to be a *mangliu* in the Great Northern Wilderness? Why would anyone want to do such a thing?

So I asked Huar. At first, she did not want to answer my questions. But I insisted and since we were friends she told me eventually that during the famine many people in her native village starved to death. These included her grandmother, a little aunt, and her cousins. They died after they had eaten all the seeds for the next spring, and the old dog, and the little cat. They peeled off tree bark and ate it. The trees died. They dug up grass roots and ate them too. After that, those who were still alive fled the area, despite orders from the higher-ups that they should not do so. Party secretary as well as ordinary peasants, anyone who wanted to live had to "flee the famine." So they came to the Great Northern Wilderness where they had things to eat.

This was even more difficult for me to believe! Actually it made me lose sleep. For up till then I had never doubted what the Party told us in government documents and official newspapers: "During the famine not a single person died of starvation in China. This itself is a great victory . . . " My parents and others who lived in Beijing believed it too. But now I was told that many people starved to death in Huar's native village, including members of her own family! Somebody had to be lying. Was it the Party or Huar? I did not dare press the question any further.

Yet somehow in my heart of hearts I knew that Huar did not lie to me. Her parents were not landlords, but poor peasants. Chairman Mao said: "Educated youths go to the countryside to receive reeducation from the poor and lower-middle peasants, this is very necessary." So this was what I learned from them: the Party had told us a big lie!

There was another story Huar did not want to tell me at first. "Don't go to Little Southern Hill by yourself at night. There is a ghost out there," she said to me once.

"A ghost? How come?"

"A young man died and was buried there. People say he haunts the place."

"Really? What does he do?"

"Oh, forget it! My parents told me never to talk about him."

I could see she was scared. That made me even more curious. So I begged her to tell me about him.

"No! I am afraid of the ghost!"

"Come on! There is no such thing as ghosts! Just tell me who he was."

"But talking about a ghost is bad luck. It'll come to you because you talked about it."

"Don't worry. Since it's me who asked you to talk about it, it will come to me. If it ever comes. All right? Now you can tell me about him."

"Well. He was a criminal. A Rightist or a burglar, I'm not sure which. A few years ago there were many of them in this area. We called them *lao gai fan* (reform-through-labor criminals). The guards did not let us get close to them."

"Yes. Yes. Then what?"

"Well. In the corn field one day in summer, this young man made the guards angry. Talked back to them or did not do the job right, something like that. So they tied him up, hands and feet, and left him to burn in the sun at the far end of the field to punish him. The other *lao gai fan* had lunch. Then they worked their way back, weeding the field. When they finished the long ridge, the sun set. They came back to the village to have supper. The guards came back too, watching the criminals. They forgot the young man completely.

"The next morning, the guards remembered him when they counted the criminals and found that he was missing. They went back to where they had left him to check up on him. They found him there all right. But he was dead already. Bitten to death by mosquitoes during the night. He was a mess, they said. No children were allowed to go and look at him. They buried him right away. A couple of years later, they all left. Guards and *lao gai fan*. Now nobody knows exactly where they buried him. Just somewhere near Little Southern Hill. There he became a ghost and he haunts the place. Some swore they heard him cry at night. So we don't talk about him. Don't let my parents know I told you this."

A man bitten to death by mosquitoes? To those who have not been to the Great Northern Wilderness, this may sound like tales from the *Arabian Nights*. But when I heard the story, I had been there a few months. I shuddered at the thought and fell silent.

The mosquitoes in the Great Northern Wilderness were in my opinion a different species from those gentle and delicate creatures I had known in Beijing. Gigantic. Black. Savage. Bloodthirsty. They were born and bred by the millions in this huge swamp. By daytime, they were less active. But even so they had bitten me through thick blue-jean working clothes and the result was swellings the size of dried apricots that did not go away for at least a week. No wonder the local people said the mosquitoes here were poisonous.

In summer and fall, occasionally we came back from the fields late. After sunset, running and with both hands free, blue-jean clothes covering my body and a nylon scarf wrapped around my head, I still could not defend myself against the assault made by those ferocious creatures. Hundreds of them moved in the air, like patches of black clouds, chasing me. They sounded like the Japanese bombers in World War II movies.

And this young man, just think, tied hand and foot. Left on the edge of the swamp. After sunset and throughout the night. Alone. Forgotten. At the mercy of those deadly mosquitoes. Though in the past I'd fantasized about torture and painful deaths, such an idea horrifies me!

What could he do in such a situation? Roll on the ground? That would only make it worse. He'd sweat, and the smell would attract more mosquitoes. Yell? Curse? Plead? Pray? Nothing helped. All human beings had forgotten him. Heaven and earth were deaf and dumb. Perhaps the only thing he could do was to weep. Weep because of the agony. Weep because he knew he was doomed.

Before he died, perhaps he called out to those he loved? Parents? Wife? Children? Did they hear him in their dreams? Were they awakened by nightmares? Or maybe they too forgot him? Drew a clear line between themselves and a criminal, like Shenshen did to Second Uncle? No one deserves to die like that! Not even a Rightist! Not even a murderer!

So perhaps the local people are right. This man has become a ghost. Because of the great wrong that was done to him, he could not rest in peace. He continues to weep, to howl, and to haunt the place. Is he looking for a substitute? Is he trying to avenge himself? But on whom? The mosquitoes? The guards? Those who sent him here? The friends who betrayed him? The colleagues who denounced him? The family members who abandoned him? This young man was a criminal, not a hero. But like the hero, he'd embarked on a journey from which he did not return. I feel so sad. I am sorry for him . . . Bourgeois fallacy of humanity . . . A human being made of flesh and blood . . . I'd better not think about it anymore. It seems my thoughts are running out of control. Am I possessed by this ghost?

17

In a Village, Think, Feel, and Be a Peasant

Seventeen years after the campaign of educated youths going to the countryside ended, many are still bitter about it. "A big mistake," they label the campaign that lasted more than a decade and involved twenty million young people. Or they say, "A tremendous waste." I agree with them. Yet I disagree. Lao Tzu, the ancient philosopher, says: "Good fortune breeds disasters. Misfortune ushers in well-being." Sometime after I came to America, my anger toward the campaign died down and I began to feel lucky that I had been to the countryside.

I don't mean that I have much use for the skills I learned on the farm: castrating piglets, building a good *kang* or a fire wall, winnowing grains with a wooden spade, cutting soybean with a small sickle . . . But knowing that I did all these and did them well somehow gives me a safe feeling at the bottom of my heart. I do not lose sleep over my tenure evaluation, for example, because I know that I am not just a professor. I was a peasant and a worker. Today if I cannot make a living with my brain and my pen, I will support myself and my son with my muscles and bones.

In addition, the Great Northern Wilderness taught me how to live on a low budget. So nowadays I don't have to spend all my time making that extra money I won't need. This, to some extent, enabled me to do the things I really wanted to do, such as majoring in literature and writing this story. Otherwise the thought that I was alone in a foreign country where there is no iron rice bowl might have driven me to take up projects and careers that do not interest me.

I could not, of course, foresee all this in 1968. Yet I was grateful to the Great Northern Wilderness. For something else. It cured my insomnia. Two months after I arrived on Farm 850, I could take a nap when there were only five minutes left before the lunch break was over, in a small dormitory room where nine other people were doing all kinds of things: listening to radios, washing clothes, talking, singing, sharpening sickles on whetstones . . . In the wink of an eye, I was asleep. It was nothing short of a miracle, and hard physical labor was the only medicine I took. A big dose of it.

During summer in the Great Northern Wilderness, the day was very long. Daybreak was at three o'clock. Lunch at eleven. (In China, everyone everywhere uses Beijing time. So in the northeast people eat lunch at eleven and in the northwest, depending on where they are, at two or three.) Sunset was after eight. During the wheat harvest, we got up at five o'clock each day, seven days a week. An hour later we were already working in the fields. Lunch break was short. To save time they often carried the food out and we ate at the end of the field. After lunch, we continued to work till shortly before sunset.

After supper, if some work had piled up on the threshing ground, we would rush it in the evening. First we had to light huge bonfires along the windward edge of the threshing ground and throw wet grass on top of them to produce volumes of thick smoke to drive away the mosquitoes. Then the whole village came out and worked till almost midnight.

Thanks to such a rigorous schedule, my problem was soon reversed. Falling asleep was easy but getting up in the morning required a great deal of willpower. No complaints from me. Everybody on the farm had a hard time getting up in the morning. I considered myself perfectly normal.

While I was cured of insomnia, a young woman who slept next to me was captured by a strange illness. One night we found that she was "dream-wandering." At first we did not think it was serious. We were a little alarmed, simply because we had heard a story in which a sleepwalker chops up people's heads in the middle of the night saying, "The watermelons in this field are ripe." That was pretty much all we knew about this disease. Would Cao, this roommate of ours, do this to us? Of course, she did not.

When Cao was told that she had walked in her sleep, she sat down on our big bed, was silent for a while, then her tears fell. It was sad to see her cry like that. I wished I could do something to help her. Ever since we were assigned to sleep next to each other, she had been very kind to me, like a tolerant older sister. I liked her and I trusted her, partly because she was from the same big yard where I grew up. On top of that, she was from 101 too. But unlike my other schoolmates, she was not aggressive at all. Now I could see that she was scared, more so than all of us.

On the farm there was no doctor who knew how to deal with this illness. So the leaders resorted to an old trick: they transferred her to a production team that was very far from ours. Maybe they wished that in the move she would be able to leave the illness behind like a piece of old clothing? But the idea did not work. By the time the soybean harvest was over, we heard that Cao's condition had worsened. So four of us jumped into a tractor and we drove in the snow for a whole day to see her.

When we entered Cao's dormitory room, we saw her sitting alone in a dark corner. Her face turned to the wall. We called her. She did not move. We called her again. Eventually she turned round. In less than three months, she had become all skin and bones. Worse still, at first she did not seem to recognize any of us. After a while, she burst out: "I confess! I have opposed Chairman Mao! I am guilty! I deserve to die! I deserve ten thousand deaths! . . . "

What talk is this? What nonsense! She must have lost her mind! Out here, she has no friends, no schoolmates. Everybody is a stranger. She's ill and she's got that kind of illness! Why did the leaders . . . Frustrated and frightened, we began to cry. Cao was the only one who did not cry. She stared at us. Her eyes were very large, very strange. They were neither glad nor sad. The next day we left. Then we wrote to her parents. Later we heard that her parents came and took her back to their May Seventh Cadre school in Shandong province. This instance proved that the Great Northern Wilderness was not for everybody. Only those who were strong, mentally and physically, could survive it.

Cao and those like her who perished here were, in my opinion, a minority. We were the majority. We were the mainstream. As the slogan put it, "Growing healthily in the wide world of the countryside." I knew I was. No doubt about it. Yet I was not so healthy, because of a new problem: in the first three or four months, I was unable to eat a breakfast large enough to keep me going for a whole morning.

In my family we had always gone to bed late, gotten up late, and had little or no breakfast. Only after I got to the farm did I realize how important breakfast was. That is, if I did not eat at least two big steamed buns in the morning, by nine o'clock I was very hungry. After ten, I was like a tractor running out of fuel. My hands and feet turned icy cold on a hot summer day. *Xuhan* (sweat of weakness) soaked my clothes. Sometimes I suddenly felt dizzy and was short of breath. In that case I had to sit down and hold my head between my knees for awhile to keep from fainting.

I knew and dreaded the consequences, but after I forced myself out of bed at five I had no appetite. The steamed bun went round and round in my mouth. It simply would not go down my throat. In the meantime, others had finished two or three, and some even four big buns. For this I hated my own body, which would not listen to reason! I swore to conquer it. REFORM! *I must reform myself into a new being. Just to think and feel like a peasant—that's not enough. I want to BE a real peasant!*

So in the next few months I battled against my own body. Pushed it to the limit and went beyond. When I was exhausted, imagining myself to be a wheelbarrow helped a bit. *"As long as the wheelbarrow does not fall apart, push it! Press on!" Which hero said this? It doesn't matter who said it. It makes sense. If my bones haven't fallen apart, if I still have one ounce of strength left in my body, if I'm still breathing, I will keep up with the others. I won't fall behind!*

So I went on working, as fast as I could. All this while a big voice cried out from the bottom of my heart: How I wish I could drop to the ground this very instant! Drop like a sack of wheat! Stay there for ever and ever! Never get up again! Physical labor had indeed purified my mind. It drove all my thoughts away except this one. *But this thought is wrong! I mustn't indulge in it! It's bad for the morale.*

What was good for the morale? I told myself, This is the test, the trial, the firing line. If I can hold out, I am the winner and the hero. If I collapse, I am no good. A pile of dog shit! Chairman Mao teaches us: "Be determined . . . " Aunty said a person must have *zhiqi* . . . And what did the peasants in this village say? "A person's strength is different from all other things. It won't be used up. The more you use it, the more it grows out of you." These words gave me hope. I persisted. By and by, new strength grew out of me. The peasants were right!

Other educated youths must have gone through a similar process, whatever sayings they might have used to keep up their spirit. When we first got to the village, four of us could hardly move a sack of wheat that weighed two hundred pounds. The next year most of us could carry it alone, on our shoulders, and walk one or two planks to load it onto a truck or pour the contents into a grain bin.

The work on the farm was hard. The best way I know to describe it is the saying, "Drops of sweat fall to the ground, each breaks into eight pieces." For such work, our pay was thirty-two yuan a month—"three hundred and twenty big dimes," as some Beijing youths put it jokingly. I didn't know how others felt about this. In my case, I felt great! On my own at long last! Truly independent! The pride I felt deep down in my heart was beyond words.

When I received my first month's pay, according to Chinese convention, I sent ten yuan to my parents and ten yuan to Aunty. (The twelve yuan I had left was for food. On the farm all educated youths, male and female, paid twelve yuan a month for whatever we could eat at the dining hall.) The letters from my parents and Aunty made me feel they were even more proud of me than I was.

As for independence, on the farm the young women were truly independent. Same work, same pay the men got. Most of us did not feel inferior to men in any way at all. Whatever job they could do, we could do too. In fact, we always did it better.

Cutting soybean was probably the most physically demanding work on the farm. We did it only when the fields were drenched with rain and the machines had to stay out. Trudging through mud up to a foot deep, small sickles in our hands, we cut soybeans on ridges that were over a mile long. Under such circumstances, the whole village would come out to "storm" the soybean fields. Everyone worked side by side. Men, women, old, young. It was a marathon race. By the day's end, those who carried off the palm were always some "iron girls."

At first, the men tried to compete with us. After a while they gave up the attempt and pretended that they did not care. Nobody could beat Old Feng, a student from Shanghai. The men nicknamed her "rubber back," because she never stopped to stretch her back no matter how long the ridge was. Her willpower was incredible! After her, there were Huar and several other formidable "iron girls." Who ever heard of "iron boys" in those years anywhere? In China only "iron girls" created miracles and were admired by all.

The older women, the *jiashu* (dependents), were a very different story. They lagged far behind everybody and did not seem to care what people might say. This caused more contempt for them. "Those stinking dependents are shameless!" the local men remarked with a sneer. "Stinking dependents" they called the women, right to their faces! Just think, these were their husbands, brothers, and family friends!

When we first heard the men say "stinking dependents," we were shocked. (In China, to call a kid a stinking so-and-so is all right and even endearing. But to call an adult stinking is very unusual and is certainly an insult.) *After all, aren't most of these women poor peasants too? "Half the sky," according to Chairman Mao? Theoretically the revolution depends on them as well. Men aren't the only heroes of the country . . .*

Yet somehow little by little our ears got used to the phrase. After a while even we began to call the women "stinking dependents" behind their backs. Half fun. Half serious. After all, we did not invent the phrase. We learned it from the male villagers. To me, there was some truth in this phrase. Though the women were not dependents, many of them did stink. Their clothes were dirty. Their hair was a mess, and they did not seem to wash or comb it very often. Close by, some of them smelled of onion, garlic, kerosene, or baby's urine. Some had yellow teeth and awful morning breath . . . But were we educated youths less stinking than the "stinking dependents"? The answer was no. A few weeks after we arrived at the village, we began to smell bad too.

Our clothes might still be newer, but they were just as dirty. Washing clothes in the village was a big deal. First we had to draw water from a well at the center of the village. Then carry the water back with buckets and a carrying pole. Pour this icy cold water into a big tin basin. Wash the clothes by hand. Then rinse them. More water was needed. Later wring them out and dry them on a line. All this took time and energy, of which little was left after we came back from the fields.

So we invented a method to deal with the problem. When we saw that our clothes were dirty, we took them off and hid them under our beds. Later the clean clothes we put on became even dirtier than those we had put away. So we put the cleaner ones back on. This cycle continued for some three months. It saved us the trouble of washing clothes.

In the meantime, none of us had taken a bath. We simply did not know how we might do so in a village where there was neither a public bathhouse nor a private bathroom. Then in October, one evening people in our dormitory found strange creatures in the seams of our clothes. They were white and small, but their bellies were rather big. They crawled slowly and laid shiny eggs. "What on earth are these?" At first we were puzzled, scratching ourselves all over. Then somebody cried out: "Lice!" That made our hair stand on end and gooseflesh creep all over our bodies. "How disgusting! It's terrible! What should we do? What should we do?"

Finally it was the "stinking dependents" who came to our rescue. "Don't be afraid! We'll help you! Let's get rid of them." So they came to our dorm, gathered our clothes and sheets, took them to their own homes, and boiled them in big woks. After that we learned to take baths in big tin basins in the middle of our dorm room. Under nine pairs of eyes. That was all right. No need to be shy. In a village, this was the only way to take a bath and we all took turns to do it.

"In Rome, do as the Romans do." The "Romans" in the Great Northern Wilderness, I soon found, had ways that were very different from those in Beijing. For instance, people here did not like those who were too polite. When I dropped in on a family and they were having dinner, if they asked me to join them, I should simply sit down, pick up a pair of chopsticks, and eat. Eat as much as I could. That was the right thing to do. Show your host and hostess how much you liked their food. "Show. Don't tell." The local family would be very pleased.

Back in Beijing, I was taught otherwise. If I went to somebody's home and they were having dinner, I should apologize and leave as soon as possible. If I was invited beforehand, I could go. To be a good guest, I should praise the food but eat sparingly. Never eat like a hungry wolf. Never reach the chopsticks to a dish across the table. Never touch the last bit of food in any plate . . . Such good manners in Beijing had all turned into bad ones here.

Besides food, there was *baijiu*. If the villagers offered me liquor, I ought to drink it. Those who could drink *baijiu* were popular with the local people. They took this as a sign of respect and trust. On the other hand, if an educated youth could not drink, the villagers would not force him or her to do so. *Baijiu* was a luxury on the farm, at the price of one yuan a bottle. People here would hate to see this good stuff wasted.

In fact, the educated youths did not need the villagers to force us to drink. In a few months, we all learned to love *baijiu*. Young women as well as young men. Probably it was because of the weather, which was extremely cold half of the year and humid the rest of it. And of course we all missed home and our lives on the farm were not easy, although at first nobody wanted to admit this. Instead we all said that we loved the Great Northern Wilderness and we were determined to put down roots here.

Baijiu was not supposed to go alone. The Chinese always ate plenty of food to accompany it. In this area, the best food to go with *baijiu* was dog meat. Something I had never touched before. On the farm, no other meat was available. So the villagers ate their dogs. When they invited me, sure! Dip the meat in dark soy sauce and munch it with lots of raw garlic. Gulp down the *baijiu*. Three cups. Four cups. *Ganbei* (bottoms up)! These things tasted great! The truth was, after a strict diet of steamed buns and boiled turnips with no oil, no meat for several months, I would have eaten rats, had they been offered to me.

Thus on the farm, by and by I changed. Like Huar and the local girls,

I talked loudly, laughed wildly, and sang at the top of my voice. I liked this life-style! Everyday we got up with the sun. Everyday we worked up a good sweat in the fields. The sunshine and the wind made us healthy. Physical labor made us strong. Drizzling rain and snow no longer bothered us while we were working in the fields. Dust and dirt were no big deal. Even the mosquitoes I could put up with. But the lack of cultural activities in the village still bothered me. It was hard for other educated youths as well.

Especially when winter came, the nights were long. After four o'clock it was pitch-black outside. Water froze as soon as it dropped to the ground. In the village, there was no TV, no movies, no library, no ping-pong, no chess, no poker . . . Besides the marathon political study meetings, there was nothing for us to do after supper. Many local families would just blow out the lamps (to save oil) and go straight to bed.

"Is there anything we could do to change this situation? The poor peasants here have been so kind to us. Maybe we could repay them with an evening of performances?" That was a good idea. In Beijing we had all learned some songs, dances, and parts of revolutionary Peking operas. We decided to put these together and show them to the villagers.

Our show turned out to be an unprecedented event in the history of Cold Spring village. On that evening all houses in the village were literally empty except for the dining hall, which was filled to capacity. Thanks to some tractor drivers who had driven to the farm headquarters the day before and borrowed a generator, the dining hall was lit by electric lamps. Many villagers came an hour earlier with stools to occupy better seating positions.

Our performances were amateur, as one may expect. Some forgot their lines and stood on the stage scratching their heads. Some burst out laughing in the middle of their acts. When this happened, the audience burst out laughing with the performer in a good-natured way. No ironic cheers, as some old Peking opera fans would give. Our audience was extremely supportive. The kids' eyes opened wide and shone like little lamps. Old men and women were so carried away that their mouths hung open during the show. After each performance, cheers and applause for a long time . . .

Watching this, suddenly I remembered *Pride and Prejudice*, the play Father and his comrades had staged in a mountain village in 1943. *He said it was a big hit. Now I understand why. Since then a quarter of a century has passed and New China has been founded. Many campaigns*

*were waged. But the poor peasants here are still living in a cultural
desert. Many of them had never seen a live performance before tonight.
We must do more to change this situation. Maybe we can stage a play
too? Of course it won't be* Pride and Prejudice *but a revolutionary one!*

So when we met the next time, I suggested that we put on a spoken
drama named *The Younger Generation*. This was an ambitious proposal, but my fellow educated youths liked it. Thus we began by se-
lecting actors and actresses.

The play's hero is a young college graduate named Xiao Jiye. He
volunteers to prospect for minerals in a remote border area. There during an accident he risks his life to save a teammate. As a result, one of
his legs is badly injured and the doctor is going to cut it off. But the
limbs of a revolutionary hero, of course, should not be amputated. So
in the end the doctors find a way to save his leg and he returns to the
border.

This role, everybody agreed, should be played by Zhou, a young man
from Beijing. He was handsome, of course. But more important he was
warm and enthusiastic, always eager to help others. Thus in our minds,
he was a Xiao Jiye incarnate. No better choice was possible.

Another important character in this play is Lin Yusheng. He is a senior student in college. Unlike the hero, he is afraid of the hardships in
the border area. He wants to stay in the city after graduation. Later, of
course, he changes his mind, after he finds out that his parents are both
revolutionary martyrs. He, too, volunteers to go to the border.

The ideal person for this role, we thought, was Wen, a classmate of
ours at 101 who always got As. His parents were college professors
and Wen himself looked scholarly. A pair of glasses with a white plas-
tic frame. In those years saying someone was scholarly, however, was
not a compliment. It implied that the person was weak, hesitant, and
useless. Thus when we suggested that Wen consider taking up this role,
he was annoyed. "Why me? Am I like him in your opinion?" he protested. But his "brothers" from 101 were glad he had been chosen. Later
they talked him into accepting it. (Eight of them at the time were sharing a dorm room. Buzzing around, they called themselves "eight happy
big flies.")

A female character is also important in this play. Her name is Lin
Lan. She is Lin Yusheng's younger sister, a passionate revolutionary
youth. For this character, I had Huar in mind. But at first my idea met
with resistance from some Beijing youths.

"What? Huar? Are you serious? She has not even finished fifth grade! Are you sure she can memorize all the lines and act on the stage?"

What they said was true. When Huar was twelve, her parents made her quit school to take care of her little brother. The same thing happened to many girls in this village. Girls or boys, few of them could continue beyond sixth grade anyway. The nearest junior middle school was ten miles away. Even so, I believed that Huar could play this leading role. I knew she was dying for such a chance, even though she would not admit it.

Huar loved to sing and act. In the past she had entertained us in the fields by imitating different people. At one moment, she was a coughing grandpa whom we all knew quite well. The next, she became a fuming "stinking dependent" who had quarreled with another on the thrashing ground the day before. In my mind, she was bright and observant, a born actress waiting to be discovered.

Nowadays girls with this kind of talent can make money by imitating Hong Kong and Taiwan stars on stage. Back in 1968, Huar thought herself the luckiest person in the world when she got the role in our play. For this I had to use the argument that since we were here to unite with the poor peasants, our cast should include at least one of them. Moreover, I promised that I would tutor Huar myself.

So I helped Huar get the lines. Then a dress rehearsal. Then we were ready to present the play. Another big event in the village. When the show started, however, the educated youths such as Zhou and Wen were merely reciting the lines they had memorized. The show lacked spirit. I was worried.

Then Huar walked onto the stage. From the start, she was Lin Lan body and soul. A gust of spring wind. A thunderstorm. When she rushed across the stage and asked Lin Yusheng: "Brother! Do you know, soon Xiao Jiye's leg will be cut off?" her voice cracked and she burst into tears. Everybody was moved. At that instant, other actors and actresses entered their roles. Henceforth emotions surged in people's hearts and tears flowed freely. The play was a success, even in my judgment. Moreover, everybody agreed that it was Huar who sparked the cast to it.

Huar's success meant a great deal to me, not because I had been right and others wrong about her. I was proud of all of us educated youths, for our sacrifice was worth it. In the past even though I had volunteered to come here, I somehow still thought that the kids in the countryside were less gifted than those who grew up in big cities. What a stupid mistake! I was glad, however, to find I had been wrong.

From then on I dreamed that someday Huar would be studying at Beijing Film Academy or the Liberation Army Art College. After four years' rigorous training, she would become a brilliant star, shining on the stage or the silver screen. To get her ready for this day, I decided that I would tutor her in Chinese and make her memorize some Tang dynasty poems I had learned by heart.

Huar was not the only bright kid I met at Cold Spring. Little Tang was another. He was the only son of Old Tang and his wife. When Little Tang was four years old, the villagers told me, his parents had locked him at home by himself while they went out to work. (In the village many parents had to do this, for unlike the work units in cities, the village had no day care center.) Then one day, Little Tang found a box of matches. He played with them and set the cotton quilts on fire. Black smoke rose from the *kang* and filled the room. He tried to escape, but the door was locked. He cried for help. But no one was around. No one could hear him through the sealed double-pane window anyway.

This little boy, however, did not panic. He ran into the kitchen, found a poker from near the stove. Then he ran back into the room, climbed onto the *kang;* he smashed a windowpane, then another. He did this against the repeated warnings of his parents. As a result, he survived. "Those who survive big disasters have good fortune in store for them." People in the village used to quote this saying to end Little Tang's story.

Four years later the same disaster struck the two little boys of Old Wang and his wife. Both children were suffocated to death, one at the age of five and the other three. We witnessed the tragedy with our own eyes. By this time Little Tang was already a second grader. Sometimes he and other kids would come to our dormitory and ask for a "wit game."

"All right. There were seven birds in a tree. A hunter came and shot down one. Now how many birds are still in the tree?"

"Six!" "Five!" other kids yelled. Little Tang looked at me with a knowing smile as if he was telling me that he had seen through my trick. Then he proudly announced: "None!" That was, of course, the correct answer.

I also had a bunch of funny riddles. One of them goes: "It looks like a lantern from afar, but seen from close by it has many holes." This riddle had baffled everybody in the village, educated youths as well as the villagers. But when Little Tang heard it, he immediately said: "Oh yeah? It's a worn-out, no good, ought to be thrown away, broken lantern!"

Everybody laughed, suddenly seeing the light. Since then, I had paid special attention to this bright little boy.

To my disappointment, however, Little Tang soon got himself into trouble. In the beginning, his teacher at the village school disliked him, saying the kid was disrespectful. But according to other villagers, the teacher was no good. He got the job not because he was qualified, but as a favor from the political instructor. So when the boy asked him too many questions, he was embarrassed and shame led to anger. Later this teacher detected a counterrevolutionary slogan within Little Tang's scribbling in a notebook. He reported this to the political instructor Zhao. Zhao in his turn reported this to the farm headquarters. Soon policemen arrived at our village from the public security bureau of Hulin county to investigate the case.

On their arrival, the policemen detained Little Tang and questioned him day and night. Old Tang and his wife were detained and questioned too, because they were suspected to be the abettors. As they both denied the charge, the investigation went further. Meanwhile, the counterrevolutionary slogan was kept a secret. No one was allowed to see it. As if the leaders thought that once we set our eyes on this slogan, our faith in communism and the Party would collapse. What trust they had in us!

"Beat the grass to startle the snake." "Follow the vine to get to the melons." As time went by, everybody in the village grew nervous. "Who knows what the little boy might say when he is interrogated like that? What if he says . . . ?"

Even we, the educated youths, became uneasy, not because we wanted to "share weal and woe with the poor and lower-middle peasants" in this case, but because we weren't on such good terms with the political instructor, Zhao. We feared that he might bear a grudge against us and use his influence (as he represented the local Party organization) to get some of us implicated.

To tell the truth, we were partly to blame for the tension that existed between Zhao and us. When we first came to Cold Spring, we had cherished some very unrealistic notions about the political instructor. Actually it wasn't our fault either. The notion had been put into our heads by the movies we saw and the books we read. In such literature, the political instructor is always portrayed as a loving and caring older brother to the soldiers. Warm as a ball of fire. Gentle as the spring breeze. He always knows what the soldiers think and how they feel, and he guides them with timely advice and well-meaning criticism. When there is danger, he gives the chance of life to the soldiers and takes death himself . . . In short, he is a great, perfect hero, shining and noble, tall and handsome. Not a bit like Zhao, our political instructor here!

Zhao was in his early forties when we met him. He was short, his complexion sallow. His face was long and thin, like a squash. He had small, sharp eyes, though. He especially liked to watch people from the side or from behind, when they were not paying attention to him. If this wasn't enough to make us feel uncomfortable, there was more: he was distant and did not open his mouth easily. Nor did he ever smile. He kept up his prestige in a village where he was the number-one leader.

But perhaps it was wrong to judge a person by his appearance? Some people were more reserved than others. If Zhao did not come to us, maybe we should go to him and break the ice? Perhaps that was the idea a group of Beijing youths had, when they went to visit him at home one evening.

First they met Zhao's wife at the door. Not a trace of smile on the face of "the first lady" either. She looked as if these educated youths had borrowed money from her and never paid her back. She simply told them to go in, while she herself went away. What a decent hostess!

Once inside, the youths saw that Zhao was lying on the *kang*, enjoying his cigarette after dinner. He propped one leg up and crossed the other on top of it. When he saw the youths come in, he made no attempt to sit up. Nor did he even lift his eyelids. Through his nose, he uttered an impatient "What's up?"

The members of the group were very embarrassed. They did not know if they should sit down or continue to stand. Should they leave or stay? "We have come to report our thoughts to you . . . political instructor . . . We want to seek your help . . . " they stammered, all the while standing awkwardly in the middle of the room.

"Spea—k." Zhao's voice was dry and cold. His eyes were on the ceiling. Smoke came out of his nose, puff after puff. Still not the slightest gesture for the youths to sit down.

By this time these educated youths from Beijing were outraged by the reception and had lost their zeal to report thoughts. So they made it very short, said good-bye, and got out. On their way back, they were speechless with anger and disbelief. Once inside the dormitory, the volcano erupted.

"Fuck! That Zhao! What does he think he is, to dare treat us like that? Number-one man in the village? Parents official? To put on such airs! Of all the high-ranking officials in the central government, I never met one who was so arrogant!"

"Agreed. He thinks he's a big shot! Actually he's a small radish! He's a nobody! A mere 24th-grade cadre! Next to the lowest rank! Even the person who guards the gate of our big yard in Beijing is three scales higher than him! What's he so proud of?"

This last remark was made by one of the "eight happy big flies." Except Wen, the other "flies" were all from high-ranking cadres' families. Somehow this comment caught on in Cold Spring village, like the child's remark about the emperor in Andersen's fairy tale: "But the emperor has no clothes." At first it went round among the educated youths and we all had a good laugh. Later somehow it leaked out and the villagers heard it. Gladly they whispered it into one another's ears, saying that it was not him or her but the Beijing youths who said that. Then someone who belonged to Zhao's inner circle heard it and reported it to Zhao. That was why we were uneasy.

I hope Zhao is not too offended by this remark. After all, he is the number-one leader and we are the real small radishes here. The power is in his hands. Whatever he thinks, I can't tell from his face, which is forever overcast. Thought report? What a stupid idea! As if these people still did not have enough of it at 101! Serves them right—Zhao treated them like dirt and they lost face! Then they said this thing about Zhao's rank, which is true. That makes it even worse! "When you hit a person, do not hit him on the face. When you poke fun at someone, do not touch the sore spot." The ancient wisdom should not be neglected. Now if Zhao takes this amiss, we are all in for a lot of trouble. We'd better be very careful.

18

"The Tree May Wish to Stand Still, but the Wind Will Not Subside"

Although I thought it unwise for my fellow educated youths to provoke Zhao, it didn't mean I liked him. He was, in my opinion, a typical "local emperor." He treated the peasants in "his" village like dirt under his feet. So perhaps he didn't mean to be particularly rude to the Beijing youths the other day. He was just his normal self. Many villagers resented the way he treated them as well. But they did not dare show it. Only after we gained their trust did they tell us behind closed doors some of the things Zhao and his few trusted fellows did.

Over eight years Zhao had placed his trusted fellows in key positions at Cold Spring village. These included the person in charge of the tractor crews, the village accountant, the manager of the dining hall, the head of the pig farm, the head of the horse farm, the person in charge of the thrashing ground, the statistician, the agrotechnician, and the village schoolteachers. After that, the village became his family domain. The cadres who were assigned to work here would either join their coalition or find their lives so difficult that sooner or later they would want to leave. The ordinary farmworkers and "dependents" had nowhere to go. So they had to kowtow to Zhao. "If you dare offend him, he will give you small shoes to wear."

"Small shoes? What kind of small shoes?"

"Many different kinds. For instance, the jobs that are harder and dirtier. Or the same job but just at night or some other inconvenient time. You ask for a sick leave or private business leave, he'll either reject it or delay it until you don't need it anymore. The firewood given to your family might happen to be the dampest; the potatoes the smallest . . . Numerous little things like that and you are 'the dumb person tasting the bitter herb *huanglian* who can't complain.' You'll never get a promotion. But that's not all. It can be worse. Look at Old Tang and his wife, the two lower-middle peasants who were out of favor with Zhao!"

As for those who belonged to Zhao's inner circle, the villagers did not know exactly what favors they obtained from him. One thing everybody knew, however, was that during the famine (1959 to 1962) the families of these people were well fed, while others in the village were hungry all the time. During the next campaign, called the Four Cleanups (1964), cadres were sent down here to check the accounts. They found that over the years a great deal was missing from the village dining hall and storehouse: flour, soybeans, cooking oil, sugar . . . Chen, the manager of the dining hall, was held responsible. Some villagers said that back in 1960 they had seen him visit the Zhaos at night carrying things on his back. No wonder when Chen was punished, Zhao had him switch places with the head of the pig farm, who became the manager of the dining hall. That was all.

After I heard such stories from the villagers and saw with my own eyes how arrogant Zhao was, I wondered if there was anything we might do about this situation. *If this were in 1966, all would be simple. Mobilize the peasants. Expose Zhao. Overthrow him as a capitalist-roader and seize power. But that was then and now our status is different. We are no longer Red Guards. We are educated youths who came here to reform ourselves. Zhao, on the other hand, represents the local Party organization. Yet he is a local emperor! When we see him abuse his power, should we look the other way and pretend to know nothing? Otherwise what could we do? The* shangfang *sword—which the emperor in olden days gave his trusted commissioners to execute corrupt local officials before they reported the cases to him—is no longer in our hands. In fact, we are as powerless as the villagers. Under such circumstances, we cannot fight and win against Zhao. The idea is crazy. Forget it!*

Thus thinking, I decided to stay out of the conflict between Zhao and the villagers. But my decision made no difference. I got involved anyway. Chairman Mao was right when he said, "The tree may wish to stand still, but the wind will not subside." By this metaphor he meant that class struggle was unavoidable despite people's desire to shun it.

One day toward the end of October, Zhao suddenly sent for me. *Why does he want to see me? This is strange. Very strange! What's he up to? I'd better be careful!*

I went to see him at home. This time he was quite polite. Asked me to sit down. Then he sat down too. *Ha! He should have done this last time, when those Beijing youths visited him. He would not have lost face.*

"You have been here for more than three months. The work on the farm is very hard. Isn't it?" he asked.

"Well. I'm used to it now. I'm getting there."

"Besides physical labor, what other problems do you have?"

"I don't really have any problems. The poor and lower-middle peasants here are very kind to us. But thanks for your concern anyway."

"What about your thoughts? Do you have any questions, or any doubts? If you tell me, maybe I can help you. You know?"

Why! Zhao is definitely a different person today. What is he trying to do? Maybe he realized he made a mistake with the educated youths and now he wants to make it up? But to me? I'm not among those who wanted to report thoughts to him.

"I read Chairman Mao's works every day. They answer all my questions. But in the future if I run into problems I can't solve, I'll seek help from you."

"Do you have any complaints you want to make about the leaders here? Chairman Mao says, 'Say everything that is on your mind. And when you do so, say it without reserve.' You might as well make a clean breast of it in front of me."

"Well. I think right now the most important thing for me is to reform myself and get a reeducation from the poor and lower-middle peasants. I don't want to complain about the leaders."

At this point it seemed that Zhao had run out of things to say to me. He was silent for a while. Then suddenly he spoke.

"If you have no complaints about our work here, why do you say you're a labor worker?"

"A labor worker?" This was a bolt from the blue. I was startled and shaken. "I can't recall I ever said that." *Of course not! How could I say such a thing? Labor worker refers to the Chinese who were captured and forced to do hard labor by the Japanese during the occupation. Many of them died because of the diabolic conditions . . .*

"You said you did not say it? But you wrote it down! Black characters on a sheet of white paper! Do you want to deny it?"

His small eyes were watching me sideways. Sharp as nails. They seemed to be drilling holes into my body and soul.

"Where did I write it? When did I write it?" My voice trembled.

"You think about it yourself!"

"I can't recall anything like that."

"In that form you filled out a few days ago. You wrote that your occupation was labor worker!"

That form! Damn it! Could it be true? I really can't remember what

I wrote. Didn't think it was important. I should have double-checked! How stupid that I didn't!

"I meant to write farmworker (*nonggong*), not labor worker (*laogang*). It must be a slip of the pen. May I see the form, please?"

"No. It has been sent to the farm headquarters. At this moment it may be at the public security bureau of Hulin county."

My heart sank. I knew I was in trouble. Very big trouble! I didn't know what to say.

"Now I want you to think very carefully. Probe into the depth of your soul. Ask yourself if you are dissatisfied with reality and if you resent the Party for sending you to the countryside . . . "

"But I volunteered to come here! I love the Party and Chairman Mao! I'm from a revolutionary cadre's family! . . . "

As I said this, I was trembling all over. It seemed the room temperature had suddenly dropped to forty degrees below zero. The chill got into my bones. I had to bite my lip to stop my teeth from chattering.

"Revolutionary cadre's family? Humph! Let me tell you this: from now on, for everybody from Beijing, family background will depend not only on the status of your parents before Liberation but also on that of your grandparents on both sides. For instance, if you have a grandparent who was a landlord before Liberation, your family background will be changed to landlord. On the other hand, if your grandparents were poor peasants, but your father or mother was a landlord, you will still be considered the child of a landlord."

This was another heavy blow! The ground under my feet was crumbling. Suddenly I felt an urge to cry. *But I mustn't cry in front of Zhao! I mustn't let him see I'm afraid. If I'm done for, then I'm done for. But I won't give him any more bullets to shoot me down.* So I remained silent. After a while, Zhao went on.

"You go back and think about the roots of your problem, which by the way, we do not think is a slip of the pen! Write a self-criticism. You know the Party's policy has always been to show leniency to those who confess and severity to those who try to resist."

Thus the talk ended and I got out. I was in a funny state. My hands and feet were icy cold and my cheeks were burning. With glazed eyes, I saw a bottomless abyss open up in front of me. I was standing on the brink of it.

In the past I had seen and heard about people who became counterrevolutionaries in the wink of an eye because they had made a slip of the tongue or a slip of the pen or whatever. Little Tang was the latest example. Before him, there was Zhang, a Beijing youth who came to Cold Spring in 1964. After the Cultural Revolution broke out, one day he took an encyclopedia from a deserted library at the farm headquarters. In it he found the anthem of the Nationalist Party. He hummed it. Others told him to stop. He was too proud to obey. So he argued with them instead, saying that when the Nationalist Party was first founded by Sun Yat-sen it was a revolutionary party, therefore the song was once a revolutionary song. Because of this, he was labeled an active counterrevolutionary. His rights were stripped away. He was banned from all political activities. His wages dropped to 15 yuan a month. Since then he had been doing penal labor under surveillance by the revolutionary people.

Now am I going to be like him? If so, that'll be the end of me. And worse still, I'll drag my whole family down. My parents will be implicated. Lian and Yue's future will be ruined. And Aunty? I will break her dear old heart! We'll all be finished. That is exactly what Zhao wants. The poisonous snake!

"Kill a chicken to warn monkeys," so goes an old saying. If he can make a counterrevolutionary out of me, the other young people from Beijing will be subdued. No one dares challenge him anymore. He'll break our backbone, bring us to our knees. This group of proud ex-Beijing Red Guards, who acted as Chairman Mao's commissioners and raised red storms all over China. What a threat we must be to him and his little empire. Even if nobody ever said anything about his rank, he'd have lost sleep over us . . .

At the age of seventeen, I was not so ignorant about politics. I knew that I had been made into an example. Now my fate depended to a large extent on how others would take this. If they would see it the same way as I did, all was not lost yet. Or else, I was doomed.

Thus thinking I got back to the dormitory. As soon as I came in, I threw myself on our big bed and cried my eyes out. My roommates were alarmed. They asked why and I told them what had happened. They took it very seriously. Soon a small group of Beijing youths gathered in our room. This was the think-tank, so to speak. The assembly concluded that Zhao had launched an offensive. The target was not just me, but all of us. If we let him get an inch, next time he'd take a yard. Lucky for me that my fellow educated youths were not so ignorant about politics either.

In fact, many of them were especially exasperated when they heard that Zhao was trying to change our family backgrounds by adding the class status of our grandparents. That was the Achilles' heel for many high-ranking officials' children.

"According to Zhao's theory, Chairman Mao's children would be from a rich peasant's family, and if Premier Zhou Enlai had children, they would be considered children of a capitalist! How absurd! This ingenious invention of Zhao's will get black and white all mixed up!"

So my fellow Beijing youths took united action. They talked and protested to all leaders in the village, demanding clear-cut answers about the nature of my mistake and a clarification of their stand on our family backgrounds. And if the leaders failed to respond in a timely fashion, the Beijing youths threatened to take the issues to higher authorities.

In a few days, Zhao backed down. At the next meeting he announced that the mistake I made was a slip of the pen, not intentional. As for our family backgrounds, they would remain unchanged. Aside from our solidarity, what explained the victory was a new political campaign that was gathering force on the horizon at the moment. Under such circumstances, Zhao did not want to make new enemies, knowing that he had gotten enough old ones to deal with in the village.

So I was lucky. Really lucky! What a narrow escape! Actually I knew it was not luck but my fellow Beijing youths I ought to thank. As for the villagers, throughout the incident they remained silent like a mountain. I was not sure of their stand until a couple of weeks later.

By that time, the farm headquarters issued a document requiring all its subordinate production teams to choose an activist who studied Chairman Mao's works well. This person would attend a meeting and then talk about his or her success story at various places. Moreover, the document said that the activist must be elected by anonymous votes. Thus the whole village gathered in the dining hall. One person, one vote. Cadres, farmworkers, "dependents," and educated youths, all were the same. The names of several candidates were written on a blackboard. My name was among them.

In a while, all had cast their votes. Subsequently two people were chosen to "sing" them, while another marked the results on the blackboard. With each vote, he would add a stroke to the Chinese character *zheng* under the person's name. *Zheng* is a square character of five strokes, which means upright and aboveboard.

As soon as this started, I heard my name "sung" again and again.

By and by the dining hall grew quiet. Chitchatting subsided. All pricked up their ears. Something was going on. People's eyes began to shine in the dark. I got so many votes! My name echoed in the hall. It was like a gust of spring wind, whispering a secret message. Those who were present got the message, whether they liked it or not. The ice started to melt and the earth began to thaw. Many hearts blossomed. A few drooped. In the end, I had a landslide victory, which was a silent show of force by the villagers against Zhao and his group. His days as the local emperor were numbered.

Sure enough, during the next campaign, whatever it was, I don't even remember the name, Zhao was dragged down from his throne. Lost his official position and for the next three years it was his turn to labor under surveillance by the revolutionary people. One of his crimes was the persecution of educated youths and another, sabotage to the movement of students going to the countryside.

While others in the village were struggling against Zhao, I was touring places along the beautiful Wusuli River, talking about my success story and being treated as a hero. Was I glad that things turned out this way? Of course I was! Did I want to be chosen by history or destiny to play such a hero again? Never!

Actually throughout the incident I knew that I was no hero. The way I saw it, I was a helpless puppet. A puppet has no thoughts and feelings though, while I knew the dangers full well. I was scared to death. If riding a roller coaster is scary, such a political game in China is ten times worse. For on a roller coaster at least I know which way I am heading and chances are I'll get off it safe and sound. In a political struggle, there's no such guarantee. Over the years many people were crushed and their families fell apart. The truth is, by that time I was really tired of political struggles. I vowed that in the future I would try even harder to stay away from them. Always double-check every single word I wrote. Black characters on a white sheet of paper. It was no laughing matter!

Despite my determination to wash my hands of political struggles, as soon as I returned to Cold Spring village, I realized that I could not quit yet. A revolution half done would be more deadly for the revolutionary people than no revolution at all. This was but commonsense knowledge to all of us. After we overthrew Zhao, we must proceed to reckon with his influence throughout the village. His trusted fellows still remained in key positions, holding on to the power they had seized, waiting for their "boss" to make a comeback and then revenge . . . Taking these into consideration, I volunteered to the new political instructor Yan to go to the pig farm.

The purpose of this was twofold. On the one hand, I wanted to challenge myself with the hardest and dirtiest work in the village. On the other hand, work at the pig farm meant taking on Chen, who had been Zhao's right-hand man all these years. In the short run I knew I had to work under him and learn how to run the pig farm. Then sooner or later we would oust him and give the power back to the people.

Even with such well-defined plans, I just could not foresee what I would run into. When I went to the pig farm to confront Chen, I had no illusions about him. I knew that he was Zhao's henchman, bound to him by vested interests. Politically he was our enemy. Yet he was also a veteran and a poor peasant. A married man in his forties. The father of three small kids. In my opinion he was snobbish, sly, and sordid. I expected to loathe him just as many villagers did.

After I had worked on the pig farm for a few weeks, however, I found myself dreaming about him. I mean not just about him, but about the two of us, at night, making love. It happened when I worked on the night shift; sleeping alone in that small room in the middle of the pig farm, I dreamed about him night after night. Here the *kang* was hot. Chen and I had built it together. It was a very good *kang,* kept the small room as warm as spring when snowstorms shrouded the world, in the middle of the night.

Pitch-black all over. The night is fathomless. The dogs do not bark. The pigs do not stir. Without the slightest warning, suddenly the wooden door of the small room opens and there he is. My heart stops beating. I am transfixed. No use crying for help. No one off in the village will hear me.

The next moment he grabs me. He holds me in his strong arms. He is as hot as fire and I am as soft as water. His body burns around me. My strength has evaporated. I cannot break away. He presses me down onto the kang. *His weight is a heavy mountain. His bulging organ rubs me between my legs. He tears away my shirt, pulls off my underwear. I am naked. Waiting for him to come. A prisoner on the execution ground, panting and trembling with painful desire for the fatal blow.*

My little cave is flooding. Twist my body and frantically squeeze my muscles to close the door. Shut out the rapist! Keep my virgin's treasure intact! The rapist forces his way in. Big. Brutal. Blazing hot . . . No use, now, to resist him anymore. Let him do whatever he wants with me. I am deflowered. I will kill myself afterwards. But now I am in heaven. Dancing a wild dragon and phoenix dance. Such ecstasies! My body and soul are consumed. I don't care what happens to me beyond this moment . . .

If Chen had had any inkling of such dreams, he might have tried to rape me instead of Laomizi. Had he really come, what would have happened? Most likely I would have used the pair of scissors I kept hidden. Spilled either his blood or my own right there on the *kang*. But who knows? I might have lost my mind and then what happened to Laomizi would have happened to me.

In fact I suspected that Chen might not be totally ignorant of what was going on in my mind. It might be part of his scheme. A trap he laid for me as well as for the other educated youths working on the pig farm. Or maybe I overestimated him. It was not his scheme, just the nature of our jobs that worked on our minds and bodies.

On the pig farm what kinds of jobs did we do? Day after day we watched out for sows in heat, made sure the sows and boars copulated properly and the sows all got pregnant. Then in due time we delivered the piglets, found teats for all of them, and watched them suck . . .

This job was a big eye-opener for me! By watching the pigs, suddenly I understood everything about men and women. The topic of sex was taboo in China in the years when I grew up. No adult was willing to talk about it with a minor. Mother never told me anything about it. (She did not even tell me that women have menstruation. As a result, when I first had it, I was scared to death.) Nor did Aunty, Nainai, or any of my teachers—including the one who had taught us physiology and hygiene—give me any clues. The books I read and the movies I saw were of no help either. They were perfectly clean. Completely sterilized.

Yet looking back with my new insight, I realized there were clues, lots of them, in classical literature and folk songs. Such as "the clouds and rain of the river gorge," "the mast on a sailboat," "the bee tickling the flower to make honey," "two people galloping together," "the hungry horse feeding at a trough," "the dew falling into the heart of a peony" . . . The adults who knew about sex understood these metaphors. I just took them as clichés and wondered why they were so oddly irrelevant.

Then there was the question all children ask: "Where do babies come from?" In my case, later the question became "What makes a woman pregnant?" This was not just curiosity. It really worried me! What if I got pregnant because I made a stupid mistake? Ate the wrong food, stood at a wrong place, or slept on a wrong bed. For didn't one story I had read say that once upon a time a virgin girl ate a plum and that made her pregnant? Later she had a baby boy whom she named Plum Son. In another story a young woman stepped on the toe of a god's footprint. She felt a stir in her heart and at that instant she was with child. Then there was this friend of mine at 101, who told me that girls got pregnant because they let boys kiss them on the lips. Another disagreed, saying it was not a kiss but a nap in the same room that would make a girl pregnant.

Now suddenly I realized how stupid we had been. Of course each of us had our own bedroom as we grew up. In China, this was a luxury most families could not afford—a fact I became aware of only after I got to the farm. But even boys or girls less naive about sex would be affected by the jobs we did, I think. It was like watching pornographic movies day in and day out. In fact, we were not only watching, Chen made us participate in them.

From time to time he assigned us to help the breeding boars mate with the sows. As Chen was still the head of the pig farm and all jobs here were revolutionary ones, I could not say no to him. I would not say no either. That way I would have betrayed myself and given him evidence of my vulnerability. Otherwise he might try to guess what was going on in my mind, but he would never find out the answer.

So I went to do the job, and Chen often watched me from behind. I hated him for doing this to me. Yet I could not protest. He would simply say that he was supervising to make sure that the job was done properly. A trace of smile would flicker on his face. Of course it could mean a lot of different things.

The pigs got together. The boar and the sow were wild with desire. Chen and I were on guard against each other. The boar jumped onto the back of the sow. With my hand I guided its quivering and foaming genitals into the sow's vagina. I must keep my breathing under control. I mustn't blush. These things I could manage. But I could not suppress the itch I felt deep down. I could not put out the fire that suddenly shot up in my heart. I was not a rock. Nor a piece of wood. I was a healthy, strong, seventeen-year-old young woman, made of flesh and blood. In spite of my pride, in spite of my reason and the so-called good upbringing, I felt a crazy urge to mate just like the pigs, right there and then, shamelessly, with whatever man . . . *But Chen is watching me right now, ever so closely. Can he read my mind and see through my body? I mustn't let him guess the hell I am going through!*

The truth is, I never quite figured Chen out, and I doubt if he was ever sure about me. Sometimes I was almost certain he was harboring ill intentions toward us. Then the next moment I was not so sure. Sometimes I even felt he had a special esteem for me and my friend Yuan, who was also a young woman from Beijing. We were somehow his favorites, and the two of us learned a great deal from him. Aside from raising pigs, Chen trained us to be veterinarians, brick masons, and carpenters. He himself was good at all these. To be fair to him, I had to admit that he was quite bright and diligent.

Soon after we came to the pig farm, Chen began to teach us about medicines, when and how they should be used. Next he made us give shots to the pigs. That was not easy. We had to puncture the pig's thick skin with a syringe and inject the medicine in a split second, before the pig felt the pain and jumped off. But after awhile we became pretty good at it. Then he made us do small operations, such as treating pustules and hernias and castrating piglets. Among these, castrating female piglets was the most difficult. With a sharp scalpel, we had to cut through the belly of a screaming and struggling piglet at exactly the right spot. The cut could not be too deep, nor too shallow; so when we put pressure around the cut, the ovary and oviducts would pop out. These we would remove completely amid copious blood; then we had to sew up the wound stitch by stitch. Throughout the process, no anesthetic was applied.

Mistakes could be fatal. I found this out the very first time I tried my hand on this operation. Either I cut too deep or the position was a little off: as soon as my knife went down, huge amounts of blood gushed out. In a minute or two, a plump, jumping, and kicking little piglet died in my hands. Badly shaken and utterly discouraged, I told Chen I'd rather quit. But he said such accidents had happened to all vets when they first started to learn the trade. "Don't be afraid. Try another one!"

With trembling hands I took up the scalpel again. Chen stood behind me and put his right hand over mine; his hand was firm and precise. Thus he guided me through the operation. Yuan, in the meantime, was holding the piglet down with all her might. This time the operation ended in a success. We straightened up and I smiled at Chen in spite of myself. The three of us were a funny sight: we were all drenched in sweat. Three smiling faces. Bright eyes. From our hands blood dripped down as if we had just murdered someone.

Then it was Yuan's turn to learn it. Another piglet's ordeal. Gradually, however, we gained experience and our confidence grew. The operations we did became almost as neat as those done by Chen himself. With this skill alone, I heard later, I could make a decent living in a village anywhere in China.

During the next years more educated youths came from Shanghai, Tianjin, Hangzhou, Harbin, and Qiqihar. In 1969 there were more than two hundred in the village. Of these, eight or nine worked on the pig farm constantly along with several local girls. *If Chen likes to show off his skills and teach young people, why hasn't he ever tried to teach others? Why only Yuan and me? He should know we belong to a different political camp and we are here to oust him. Can he like us in spite of such knowledge, and vice versa? Is he really scheming against us? What tricks is he up to? A person is a mystery. Sometimes class analysis is not omnipotent and knowing someone's political stand does not throw much light on his or her behavior. Should I hate Chen or be grateful to him? What is the nature of our relationship?*

19

Death of a Hero: Nainai's Last Story

On the pig farm each of us was responsible for a group of pigs. These hundred pigs, I took care of them from the moment they were born. When spring came I let them out to graze. In summer I got up before four o'clock everyday. By four thirty my pigs were out on the grassland.

The morning breeze was cool and faintly fragrant. In June the Great Northern Wilderness was an ocean of wild flowers. Gold lilies were delicate and sweet. Red lilies looked waxy and sturdy. Irises purple and blue grew around shallow ponds of water. Wild peonies in full bloom were the size of small basins. In this swamp where the soil was black and water never in short supply, everything grew to a gigantic size. The scenery was so beautiful that even now I dream colorful dreams of it.

Herding a hundred pigs on this swamp was no easy job though. Unlike sheep, the pigs were headstrong and did not like to stay with the group. They constantly drifted away, disappeared into the tall grass. To keep them together, I had to run around them, four to five hours at a stretch. The morning dew soaked my pants and made them stick to my legs, hindering my movement. A chill entered my bones. My sneakers squeaked under my feet. Even cold, wet sneakers were better than dry rubber boots. Better than any extra weight on my feet when I had so many miles to run each day.

When I was not racing the pigs, I was singing. Folk songs, foreign songs, revolutionary operas . . . Others were doing the same. I could hear them from a distance. Why did we do this? I cannot speak for others. In my case, I felt that when I started to sing, the pigs stopped running and fighting. They grew calm. They listened, swinging their tails back and forth as if they were beating time for me. This convinced me that pigs were intelligent and they could enjoy music.

The first group of pigs I raised, I gave them names. One of them looked cute. He had drooping ears and a very big belly. I named him Capitalist. Another was tall and stately; his name was Prince. Natasha was named after the girl in *War and Peace*. She was pretty and frivolous. Lin Meimei was once very sick. Like the heroine in the Chinese novel *Dream of the Red Mansion,* she walked with weeping-willow steps. Her moist eyes were almost human when she lifted her head up to look at me. So I took pity on her. After Chen condemned her, I kept her in the hope that someday she would somehow overcome her nameless illness.

Believe it or not, my pigs knew their names. When I called Lin Meimei, she would come, knowing that I had something special for her. By and by I hid the medicine I thought might help her in the treat and she took it all. Chen and others on the pig farm were amazed by this. Encouraged, I tried different medicines on her. One of them worked— I wasn't sure which. Lin Meimei was cured, while her fictional counterpart died of consumption and a broken heart.

In the Great Northern Wilderness, it rained often. Sometimes the rain lasted for days and weeks. When this happened, the pigs had to stay home. They were cold, hungry, and miserable. Their feet turned the sties into huge pots of mud porridge well seasoned with pig urine, pig shit, and worms. The mud was a foot deep.

Feeding pigs under such circumstances was tough. The moment I stepped into a sty, my feet got stuck and I was surrounded by a hundred pigs. Each tried to snatch feed from the two big buckets I was carrying. I fought the pigs off with the buckets and pressed on. The yard was over a hundred feet each way. The troughs were placed in the middle of it. Struggling, I lurched across the yard like a leaky boat on a raging ocean. Sometimes I would make it to the little island. Sometimes I capsized and turned into a "mud monkey."

The mud could be washed off afterwards. Worse still was to step onto a nail sticking up in the mud from a board that had fallen from the fence. When the sows were in heat, they often knocked the boards down. Later when the boards sank, there was a 50 percent chance that the nails would point up rather than down.

Such invisible nails were a nightmare for all of us who worked on the pig farm. Once in a while we got a taste of them. No way to predict where and when, all of a sudden, a sharp nail pierced the sole of my rubber boot and plunged into the arch of my foot. Cold sweat broke out. I struggled to lift the foot from the mud; but the weight of the buckets hanging from a carrying pole on my shoulder continued to press me down. The impatient pigs added pressure by sticking their big snouts into the buckets . . .

Afterwards, others would help me squeeze the puncture wound and wash it clean. But such a wound always hurt a lot and took days to heal. Next day my foot would be swollen because of the rust on the nail and the germs in the mud. Sometimes I had to stay in bed for a few days, which was a shame for all of us in those days. Yet after half a dozen of such accidents on the pig farm, I did not get tetanus. So who can say that I was not lucky?

In October 1969 the first group of pigs I had raised were grown. One day a truck came from a city called Jiamusi. The time had come for my pigs to make their contribution to the world revolution. On that day, it had rained earlier and the pigsty was muddy. The workers who came from the cannery tried to catch my pigs. My pigs were alarmed. They ran around the yard at top speed, squealing, jumping, and kicking up mud. The workers chased them. After a while they were out of breath. Their hands and clothes were coated with mud. Cursing aloud, they came to a stop.

Seeing this, I told them to stay out of the sty. Then I called my pigs by their names. My pigs stopped running. They watched me with frightened eyes. For a moment, they hesitated. Perhaps their instinct was telling them that danger was imminent and they should not trust a human being. Then they came to me anyway. They followed me onto the planks. They walked into the truck. Lin Meimei, Natasha, Prince, Capitalist . . . all my pigs were there. The workers applauded. They thanked me. Next they shut the door and the truck drove off.

The pigsty was empty now. Somehow my heart was empty too. With an empty heart and a full stomach, I went straight to bed.

"What's the matter? Are you sick?"

"No, I'm all right."

"Is something wrong?"

"Not really."

Tell others I love my pigs and my heart is bleeding for them right now? Nobody will understand. It can only turn me into a laughingstock. How can I change people's minds, convince them that pigs aren't lazy and stupid? They're intelligent! They've got feelings! They trusted me at a critical moment, and I betrayed them! I became an accomplice in their murder! Now I regret what I did. I hate myself.

I wonder where my pigs are right now. Perhaps they are being driven into a slaughterhouse? They are screaming for me to come and rescue them. Save them from the terrible machines, which are about to strip

them of their skins, cut their flesh off their bones, chop them into a thou-
sand pieces, turn them into cans of pork . . . Contribution to the world
revolution? That doesn't help! Not at all!

Try a different approach. Since you are born as pigs, your fate is to
be raised, killed, and eaten by people. Sooner or later, this will happen.
See, nowadays in our village even the breeding boars and sows are killed
and eaten when they grow old. So perhaps it's a good thing that you
die early. You'll be reincarnated sooner. In your next life, be a bird, a
fish, even a worm, or an ant. Just don't be a pig! Anything is better than
a pig! Where did I get these ideas: fate and reincarnation? From the vil-
lagers, of course. I know it is superstition. But I already feel much better.

After that I continued to take good care of the pigs. But I would not
call them "my pigs" and give them names anymore. It was stupid of
me to let them get close to my heart. These pigs were not pets. We raised
them for the pork, the liver, the hearts, the stomachs, the ears, the
tongues, the trotters, the blood, the bones, the skin . . . Other people
were wise to believe that pigs were lazy and stupid. It was not to my
advantage that I knew better.

If my first year on the pig farm seemed exciting and eventful, in the
years that followed there was hardly anything new. In the fall the sows
got pregnant. In winter piglets were born. Throughout spring and summer we raised the piglets. In the fall they were taken away by trucks,
and the sows got pregnant again.

Caught in this ancient cycle, we tried to make a difference nonetheless. We experimented with saccharified pig feed as soon as we read
about it in the newspapers. We constructed wooden floors for the pigs
to sleep on so they were less likely to catch cold at night. With relentless effort we wiped out a contagious disease called *zhufeiyi* (pig lung
plague) that had killed hundreds of pigs each time it broke out. We made
sure that our pigs had plenty of exercise and a balanced diet. From morning till night we watched out for the slightest sign of any problems . . .
In short, we took such meticulous care of the pigs that one day I suddenly felt sad, for it occurred to me that no one cared half as much about
us as we did about the pigs. But of course this thought was ridiculous.
I drove it out of my mind in no time.

Aside from saccharified pig feed, we also made tofu. The residue went
to the pigs. Tofu came to us, day after day. Sometimes the tofu reminded
me of Buddhist monks and nuns in the olden days, who ate it out of
religious conviction. Today we ate it out of necessity. By the end of Oc-

tober we ran out of cabbages and onions. A month later, no more turnips and potatoes. From December to June, tofu was all we had: boiled tofu, stir-fried tofu, deep fried tofu, salted tofu, fermented tofu, smoked tofu, dried tofu, steamed buns stuffed with tofu filling, tofu flower soup . . . Tofu three meals a day, seven days a week. The educated youths who worked at the dining hall tried their best to change the menu. But as the saying goes, "A clever wife cannot cook a meal without rice"; they could not cook a meal without tofu. Eventually we all got so sick of it that the mere mention of the word tofu would give us heartburn.

In addition to the tofu diet, we had hard physical labor, little sleep, few holidays, no money, and no sex. (Having a boyfriend or girlfriend was strongly discouraged before 1971.) If that was not enough to qualify us as ascetic monks and nuns, we also experienced days and nights with no fire in the winter. This happened when we ran out of coal. Our room became an icebox. At night, everybody was wearing a fur hat in bed. Next morning the front part of it was white with frost. Put our sheepskin coats on top of three quilts, still we shivered all night and got cramps. Meanwhile the water vat in our room froze over and the wet towels on the line became stiff, hanging there like a bunch of frozen fish. The attempt to take them down often broke them.

Looking back on it, I think Cold Spring was like a mountain cave in which we tried to cultivate ourselves. Tormented our bodies to purify our minds. Encouraged ourselves with a splendid prospect of a paradise on earth. A day was as long as a year; a year was as prosaic as a day. For three years I persisted. If I had continued like Master Dharma who sat with his face to the wall for nine years, seeing nothing and hearing nothing from the outside world, maybe I too would have achieved something. Tao or nirvana. Madness. Who knows? But in my case, in 1971 suddenly we were told that we were up for a twenty-four-day home leave. So I was back in Beijing in August.

Aunty was the first person I wanted to see. Before I heard about the home leave, I did not realize how much I had missed her. It was like a dream come true when I rushed into her arms. At that moment, I realized how big and strong I had grown over the years, while Aunty had shrunk into a small old lady. Yet she was holding me in her arms as if I were still that helpless baby girl left in her care at Nainai's house twenty years before. It made me feel strange and awkward. It also made me feel very good.

"Aiya! My own, dear daughter has come back!" She uttered a cry on seeing me. The phrase she used, *wode qin nuer,* could mean "my own daughter" or "my dear daughter," and it could mean both. Then her tears fell. The tears melted my hero's mask. For three years I had been wearing it, day and night. *Now I am back home. I can be as soft and ridiculous as I want. No one will criticize me. No one will laugh at me. It's a wonderful feeling!* Nonetheless, I did not feel like crying with Aunty. Instead I wanted to coax a big smile from her, as she used to do with me when I was little.

So I opened the sacks I had brought back. One was filled with soybeans. Another had red and green beans, a keg of soybean oil, a bag of giant-sized potatoes, dried lilies, wild mushrooms . . . Aunty watched me with amazement, as if I were a magician. Her face started to beam. For in those days such things had all but disappeared from the shops in Beijing, along with many daily necessities such as matches, soaps, detergent, and feminine napkins.

Aunty was smiling now. When I looked at her, I could not help noticing that she was getting on in years. At the age of sixty-seven, she was looking after Lian and Yue all by herself. (If she hadn't taken them to live with her when my parents left Beijing for the countryside in 1969, my brothers would have had to go too, losing their Beijing *hukou* and ending up in some dead-end schools like the one we had at Cold Spring.) In 1971 Lian was still a teenager and Yue was eleven. They were a lot of work and endless worries for her. Aunty was exhausted. I could see it. *Now she needs me to help her. I want to help her! I promised her I'd take care of her when she grew old. But how can I do so?*

These three years, in fact, she had been taking care of me too. Before each festival, she would send me a parcel filled with goodies: chocolates, cookies, nuts, moon cakes, dried fruits . . . Each time I received the parcel, I wrote her a letter telling her that she should not do so. Yet when the next festival drew near, I looked forward to another one, and sure enough another parcel arrived, before May Day, Dragon Boat Festival, National Day, Moon Festival, my birthday, New Year, and Spring Festival, which was traditional Chinese New Year.

Before Spring Festival, almost all educated youths in our village received parcels from home. I always got two. The other was sent by my parents. Hundreds of parcels came from all over the country to the post office ten miles away. The postmaster could not possibly carry all of them. So the village dispatched horse-drawn carts to pick them up, day after day.

Aside from parcels, Aunty had sent me many letters, telling me what she did and how much she had missed me. Yet in letters there were things she could not discuss. Black characters on a white sheet of paper. It might cause trouble for both of us. On the night I came back, after Lian and Yue went to sleep, Aunty told me what was on her mind.

Recently, she said, a new campaign had started in Beijing. It was called We Also Have Two Hands: We Won't Lead Idle Lives in Cities. A housewife started it by making the above statement while she volunteered to go to the northwest. Now the leaders were using her to pressure other city dwellers who either had never worked outside their homes or had only temporary jobs to "volunteer" to go to the northwest.

Aunty was upset. I was upset too when I heard this, knowing that at her age if she were sent to the northwest, she would not be able to survive the hardship. They might as well kill her, and also the old men and women who were her neighbors. Many of them, Aunty told me, were crying at night because the prospect scared them. If she and her neighbors had to die, much better die in Beijing where their families had lived for generations. Aunty had cried too, after Lian and Yue were asleep. She was very glad that I was back so she could talk to me about this.

"But what can I do?" When I heard this, frustration almost choked me. "Nothing!" *In my family of six, the three adults have already gone to the countryside, of our own accord. But this doesn't seem to be enough. Now they want to sweep Aunty and my two brothers out of Beijing as well. So they can move in, settle down, and take over. Become permanent residents of this beautiful city—our hometown! That's going a bit too far!*

By "they" I meant the army representatives who came to Beijing by the thousands at the time. Once they got here, they used their power to move their entire families and relatives from the countryside into the city. "Seven big aunts on the father's side and eight big aunts on the mother's side," as the Beijing people put it sarcastically. As a result, I was surprised to find that by 1971 more people were living in Beijing than three years before, and among them few were the talented kids of the poor peasants we had meant to make room for.

This fact irked me, and the way I was treated here irked me even more. On buses, in stores, and in the street, people gave me white eyes and cold shoulders, as if I were a stupid country bumpkin. They made me acutely aware that my clothes were out of fashion, my face was black, my shoes were old . . . But I refused to be ashamed of myself.

Shit! If we hadn't volunteered to leave the city, how could you people have gotten in? If we don't work our tails off growing crops and raising pigs on the farm, what will you feed on except northwest wind from Siberia? How could these people be so ungrateful? But wait! In the past we students of 101 were just like them. Such arrogance. Such stupidity. Look at those ugly faces, they make me see myself in a mirror.

Aunty's old neighbors, on the other hand, were as courteous as they had always been and full of goodwill. Yet their conversation made me equally uncomfortable.

"Have you found a 'door' yet?" they would ask me in earnest as soon as we exchanged greetings, "To get yourself transferred back, you know. The Zhangs have just gotten their son back through 'family difficulty return.' The old couple said they needed a child to live with them so he could take care of them. The Wangs are trying to get their daughter back through 'sick return.' You should hurry! Ask your parents if they know someone who can help. Or ask your Third Aunt. She is a doctor, isn't she? Maybe she can get you a certificate . . . "

Hearing this time and again, it dawned on me that while we toiled in the village, the trend in Beijing had changed. Now going to the countryside was no longer an honor. It was a shame, which showed that the family lacked power and *guanxi* (connections), so their children had no other choice. For those who had power and *guanxi,* they could transfer their children back. No wonder I was held in contempt by those haughty newcomers. They considered us failures.

This discovery made me lose some sleep. *If these old Beijing residents are right, then too bad. I am trapped. My parents have no power, no guanxi. Moreover, they are in the countryside themselves so they can't even get me back through "family difficulty return." But maybe these old men and women are wrong? After all, they are "the petty city-dwellers" we despised because they have no vision. Perhaps I shouldn't put too much importance on what they said. I ought to discuss this with my parents.*

A few days later I went to see my parents and we talked. What they said was reassuring, even though there was hardly anything new and original in it. It sounded like the newspaper editorials. "Stick to it. There is a great future for you in the countryside." "Do not hesitate. The road is tortuous, but the prospects are bright." This was, and yet it was not, what I wanted to hear.

At the time my parents were living in a small village in Raoyang county, Hebei province. It seemed to me that they too were living in a mountain cave. On the map, the place was not far from Beijing. But to get there I first had a jolting ride in an old bus for seven hours. After I got off at the county seat, I had to hire a man and ride behind him on a bike for another hour. This means of transportation was called "second-rate," a term I'd never heard before.

When I arrived at the village, I found that my parents had both changed literally beyond recognition. Father looked like an old peasant who had worked in the fields all his life. A deep tan. A bony body. Crew-cut hair. Furrows in his forehead. A white T-shirt that was not white anymore, shorts, and black cloth shoes. Definitely this was not the father I remembered, who was a diplomat and a scholar! However, he was not a real peasant either. For although he was doing farmwork just as the peasants did, the government was still paying him nearly two hundred yuan a month. The real peasants in the area were making eight cents a day, that is, less than two and a half yuan a month, even if they worked thirty-one days a month. Thus at the time the peasants all owed considerable amounts of money to the production team.

Mother had changed even more. In the past, everybody said that she looked ten years younger than her age. Slim figure. Upright posture. Permed hair. Rosy cheeks. Elegant dresses matched by carefully selected accessories . . . All these were gone now. In three years, Mother had become what everyone would call a "yellow-faced crone." At the age of forty-five, she looked as if she were in her late fifties. Her back was bent and she walked with a limp. Her face looked swollen. Her lips were purple . . . I was shocked to see Mother like this.

"What has caused her to change so much over this relatively short period of time?" I could not ask this question, knowing if I did, Mother would be offended. Yet it was on my mind and I kept guessing at it: her high blood pressure, irregular menstruation, a recent operation (to remove a tumor from her leg), sprained ankles . . . *Maybe there are other illnesses that don't get diagnosed, as there's no doctor in the village? Maybe the farmwork is too hard for her—but the way she is, would she ever admit it? Maybe it's something else? What about the strain caused by the separation of our family?*

Trying to cope with the financial strain caused by moving and the family living at three different places, Mother had sold her few pieces of jewelry. The last piece she sold was her diamond wedding ring. Aunty knew and told me about this, because she had been hiding these for my mother since the beginning of the Cultural Revolution. The ring was sold for only one hundred yuan at a secondhand store. "A robbery price!" cried an indignant Aunty. But Mother sold it anyway, because she had received a letter from me in which I asked for a sheepskin coat.

Mother never mentioned the wedding ring to me in her letter, but she described in detail how she got the coat. The night before, she went to Aunty's home and slept on a few chairs. The next morning, she got up at five and took the first bus to Renmin Shangchang (people's department store) downtown. She arrived there shortly after six. Some people were already waiting outside the gate. Standing in line, Mother prayed that the store would carry a few sheepskin coats on that day and also that those who were ahead of her were trying to buy something else. For in 1968, hundreds of thousands of educated youths had gone from Beijing to the northeast, northwest, and Inner Mongolia. These were all very cold places. Suddenly everybody needed a coat, the heavier the better. As a result, sheepskin coats were sold out in Beijing.

After seven o'clock, more people arrived. The line broke up. All pressed their bodies toward the gate like sardines. At eight, the gate opened. Mother raced with others toward the back of the store where coats were sold. As she approached the section, she saw a few sheepskin coats hanging on the rack. Great! Mother rushed toward them, grabbed one that looked the heaviest, and embraced it with both arms. Others did the same. They were parents too. Each embracing a coat as if this were their beloved child who was shivering in the cold wind hundreds of miles away. After that Mother gladly put down the money, about eighty-five yuan, and returned like a general who had won a decisive battle.

If Mother had worried about me in 1968, later she worried about Lian and Yue even more. But at the May Seventh Cadre school where she and Father were "studying," the rule was very strict: no one was allowed to leave the village, unless a family member elsewhere had died. Thus Mother was unable to return and see her own father before he died in 1970.

I heard my maternal grandmother blame Mother. I visited her in Beijing after I came back from the village. "How could she be so heartless? You know how much your grandfather loved her. She was a pearl on his palm! He sent her to Zhongxi, the most expensive middle school in Shanghai, and then to Yanjing, the best university in China. He gave up his career and retired early when his company moved out to Hong

Kong in 1949, only because your mother said he should stay. After that we moved from Shanghai to Beijing just to be near her. But when he was dying, he waited for your mother to come so he could see her for the last time. One telegram. Two telegrams. Three! Your mother never showed up! Did she want to draw a clear line between her and us? She is a Party member, a cadre, and we were capitalists? When your grandfather died, his eyes were open . . . "

For two hours she went on and on, sobbing from time to time. I listened quietly, after I told her about the rule that did not make sense to her. I knew how lonely she was after my grandfather died. I was sympathetic. But still I could not love her. I could not forget that twenty years earlier she had tried to talk Nainai into dismissing Aunty to let a professional nurse from Shanghai take care of me. For that, both Aunty and I bore her a grudge. I forgave her only after she died two years later.

Nainai, on the other hand, was my savior! Because of her decision, Aunty stayed and the Shanghai nurse went back home. Nainai, I heard from Father, was still alive and she lived at the same address. In fact, I had promised Father, who could not leave the village either, that I would visit Nainai before I returned to the northeast. To tell the truth, I also missed Nainai. I had not seen her since the Cultural Revolution broke out.

Aunty was truly glad when she heard of my promise. She got herself busy immediately: cooked lotus-leaf pork and three-cup chicken, which were Nainai's favorite, bought pastry and fresh fruit. "Go see your Nainai! Go this afternoon and give her my best regards!" Aunty was still devoted to Nainai. No political campaign could change that. After she packed everything into a big basket, she almost pushed me out of her home. Thus an hour later, I stood at the gate of the compound where I grew up.

The gray brick wall looked familiar. The street number was still the same. I pushed the wooden doors open from the middle. The creaky sound rang an ancient bell. But once I was inside, I knew that nothing was the same in this compound.

The first courtyard was now extremely crowded. Three families had taken over the two bungalows that faced each other. Coal stoves, wash basins, diapers . . . Kids were running in the yard. Adults watched me with suspicion. I had become a stranger here. I was an intruder.

The second courtyard, once a beautiful garden, stung me in the eye with its ugliness. The white lilac tree and winter jasmine had disappeared. Nainai's tree peonies and Third Aunt's roses were gone. In their places stood makeshift shacks, built with broken bricks and asphalt felt. I could not tell if they were kitchens or storehouses.

A family of five was now living in Nainai's room. "Where did you move the old lady who used to live here?" I bit the question back, however, when I saw the unmistakable hostility of these people toward me. *Better not provoke the revolutionary masses here. Once I set foot in this compound, I am the granddaughter of a big capitalist. A head shorter than everybody else. Perhaps that's why I haven't been back these five years?* Thus thinking, I lowered my eyes, walked around them, and knocked on the door of Third Aunt's room.

Third Aunt looked frightened when she opened the door. Perhaps I had knocked too impatiently. Seeing it was only me, she heaved a sigh of relief and let me in. After we sat down, however, I realized that we simply could not talk in this room. The wall between this and the adjoining room, once Nainai's, was a work of art. It was elaborately carved through at many places. As a result, it was no thicker than a piece of rice paper and every word we said here would be overheard by those who lived next door.

So I simply told Third Aunt that I came to see Nainai but did not know where she was. Hearing this, Third Aunt stood up and gestured me to follow her. She took me to the storeroom, which was portioned out from our old dining room along the northern wall. On the way, she told me that because of serious diabetes, Nainai had been pretty much confined to bed these five years. Then we were at the door. Third Aunt opened it for me. I walked in. She left, closing the door gently behind her.

At first, all I could make out was a flickering candle. It made me realize that the room had no windows, and there was no lamp. When my eyes got used to the dimness, I saw Nainai. Half sitting and half lying against some pillows, she was watching me. Our eyes met. The trace of a smile lit up her face. That familiar old smile of hers!

"Nainai!"

"Little Rae. So you come. I knew you would come. Today."

"Nainai. How have you been?"

"Fine. Fine. I am all right."

But everything I saw in this room told me the contrary! The room was narrow and small. A black iron stove stood in the middle of it. The stovepipes should have been removed when spring came. But here they remained when summer was almost over. Seeing the dead stove, I felt a chill and realized that the room was damp and cold even in August. It was stuffy and smelly too. A chamberpot stood next to Nainai's bed. During the day no one was here to clean it. Third Aunt was at work. On a small table near the head of Nainai's bed stood a candle and a few steamed buns. So that was how she had her meals. Warmed up the cold buns over the candle, ate them with no vegetable, no soup, no tea. Not even a glass of hot water was available to her as far as I could see!

So for five years, they put my dear old Nainai in this rat hole! Buried alive! No day. No night. No summer. No winter. She was bedridden with diabetes. Most of the time, no one is here to help her. No one to talk to. Father and Second Uncle cannot come. One is an old revolutionary; the other a counterrevolutionary. Neither is allowed to leave the village where he was sent. Third Aunt is here. Thank heaven and thank earth! But she is a doctor, and the neighbors are so hostile. She cannot come but once or twice a day. And me? I could have come. I should have come! But I was so busy making revolution that I forgot I had a Nainai! All these years I never tried to find out what happened to her!

As if she could read my mind, Nainai said: "Rae. Listen. I've got everything I need. Don't be hard on yourself. See. Here's the *People's Daily*. I read it every day. And the rest of the time, I have this atlas. So I can look at the maps. Especially this one. This is Hunan. I grew up there. It was a beautiful place. The rivers Xiang and Yuan were pink with petals in spring. In summer, bamboos on the riverbanks were so green that the color dripped into the water. It was actually the tears of two women, Ehuang and Nuying, which dripped from the mottled bamboos.

"These women were the daughters of a wise king. They both married a great man named Shun. When he died in the south, Ehuang and Nuying cried before they threw themselves into Xiang River. Afterwards they became goddesses and the bamboos stained by their tears became mottled. Death is eternal life. Life is dying. The goddesses are dancing on the peach blossoms; they fly and twirl with the fallen leaves. When finally I am free, I'll join them on the misty Xiang River . . . "

"Nainai! What are you talking about?"

"I'm talking about Hunan. The shamans there had great power! One used to favor me. So she came and worked as my nanny for five years. At night, after others were asleep, she taught me how to open my wisdom eye so I could see things that happened far away and long ago. I practiced with her. I made progress. Then I came back to Beijing and got married. I had children. I was not in the right mood and I stopped practicing. The light in my wisdom eye went out. But nowadays I've got the power back!

"Come here. Look. Everyone has a wisdom eye. It's right here, in the middle of your forehead. This eye is upright, unlike your other eyes that are lying down. Take a deep breath. Let the *qi* go slowly down to your cinnabar field. Close your eyes. Now can you feel it?"

It seemed that I felt something indeed! A small ball of fire was burning inside my forehead. A flicking light shone in the dark. *Maybe it is just my weird imagination? So what? For so many years I have been a terrible granddaughter! This is probably my last chance to mend my ways and be good to Nainai. So today I will do anything she wishes me to do. No questions asked.*

"Good. You are getting there. Someday the power will be yours. So tell your father he needn't come. I can see him. I am with him day and night. I am with your Second Uncle too, and Little Ox, Little Dragon, Lian, Yue, and you. Especially you!

"Not only did I see you in the northeast, I could see you in your previous life also. In that life you were not a woman. You were a man, an extraordinary one. Your father taught you kung fu when you were a little boy. At the age of seven you began to learn strategy and tactics from a great master. Seven or eight years later you fought in real battles and distinguished yourself. When you turned twenty, you were already a general. Oh, no, I can't say I liked you very much in your previous life. A red-tasselled spear in your right hand, a short sword in your left, you were a furious whirlwind on the battlefield, cutting open bloody paths. Whoever stood in your way was dead in an instant.

"Yet I can't blame you. You were a loyal subject and an upright man. You cared about your soldiers, not gold and silver. You were brave and smart, even though you were illiterate. Yes! You were illiterate in your previous life! That's why you always make mistakes when you write characters. At the age of twenty-five, the emperor made you a noble and built a palace for you. You brought glory to your ancestors and wealth to your clan. Two years later, however, you were forced to kill yourself.

"In that battle your forces were greatly outnumbered. The enemy laid siege to your city. You held the city for forty-nine days, waiting for reinforcements. In the end, you had neither food nor arrows left. Most of your soldiers and male civilians had died on the city wall. Finally the gates were stormed open. Fire engulfed half the city. Smoke darkened the sky. Your soldiers were still fighting in the streets. But you knew this was the end.

"Protected by a few bodyguards, you rushed back to your palace, a short sword in hand. The sword was a priceless treasure left to you by your ancestors. Your wives came out to meet you. Seeing you appear with the sword, they thought you were going to kill them, as tradition demanded. But you said: 'Don't fear. I won't hurt you. Run or hide. Follow other men. I won't blame you. But hurry! The city's fallen. The enemy could be here any moment!' Saying this, you turned the sword and plunged it into your own chest."

At that instant, excruciating pain shot through my heart, as if a sharp sword pierced it. The metal was as cold as ice and yet it was hot. As it went in all the way to the handle, it set every cell of my body on fire. The sky turned yellow and the earth went black. Red blood? Green blood? The sword drank it like a hungry serpent . . .

Nainai nodded her head with a knowing smile. "The name of the sword was Yin Bi [drink green]. It was made for you, hundreds of years ago. It was your destiny! After you died, the sword would leave the world.

"Now let me tell you what happened after you died. Your wives did not run away. They loved you and your death broke their hearts. They threw your body into a well that was nearby, so that it would not be seized and mutilated by your enemy. The sword went down with you to the bottom of the well. By this time, your palace was surrounded. It was burning. Your wives jumped into the well. Then a building collapsed over it. The well became your grave. As a result, in this life whenever you go near a well, you have an eerie feeling. You can't help peering into it, for you sense something there at the bottom. Yet in the meantime it horrifies you and you want to run away from it."

This is exactly true! How does Nainai know it? Is there really a mysterious blood tie between us so that she can get into my mind and I into hers? For I suddenly "remembered" the well in "my palace." The mouth of it was a hexagon, made of six dark blue stone slabs. The water at the bottom was clear and deep. Nearby several cassia trees were in full bloom. A gust of wind. Tiny gold flowers fell like a fragrant shower. On my face and my body. On the pool of blood. "Loyal subject and heroic man left a fragrance for ten thousand years."

I also "remembered" the heart-piercing remorse I felt while I was dying. The moment seemed as long as a lifetime. *"Ten thousand years?"* *By then who will remember me and who cares how I died? In a moment, however, I will be no more. Buried under the nine springs. Never to see the sun again. Or feel the wind blow. The only thing I have—this body, this life—I've given it up for fame and positions. How stupid! I don't want to die! I'm still young. My body is filled with life and energy . . . Now my strength is draining away. My body is dying. Dying by my own hand! I had to do it! Now I understand how horrible it is to be killed and how horrible to kill others. But now when I understand this, all is too late! Heaven. I deserve your anger and punishment. I accept my fate. In my next life, please make me into a woman so I won't have to kill or be killed. I want to live. In peace. I want to learn to read books and love people.*

"Now you are beginning to remember," Nainai said. "Good. But don't carry it too far, or else it will hurt you. People are much better off if they can forget certain things. Because of your remorse, Heaven took pity on you. Your dying wishes were granted. As a woman, you are actually stronger than men. Do you know? It has always been that way in our Manchu families. I took care of my father and brother in the past. You will take care of yours in the future. You will help your Second Uncle too. Someday your wings will grow strong and they will carry you over great mountains and vast oceans. You will be free too."

I smiled at Nainai in spite of myself. A confident smile shining from the bottom of my heart. Nainai was smiling too. Her eyes were full of love and wisdom. Her face was pale, yet not pale. It was half transparent and half luminous. In my eyes, she was a jade bodhisattva, sitting in a dark cave. This was my last impression of Nainai.

When I came out of Nainai's room, however, I began to feel bad again. Third Aunt suggested we go to Beihai Park. There at least we could sit on a bench and talk quietly, while the crowd passed us by.

"Now you have seen it," Third Aunt said, watching my eyes, "your Nainai's head is messed up. I haven't told your father and Second Uncle about this. They can't come anyway. I will be with her when the end comes. It won't be long, judging from the level of her blood sugar and the condition of her heart and kidneys."

After a short pause, she continued: "Sometimes I wish things were all over with her. For five years, loneliness and this disease were the only things she had. Five months like that would drive me crazy! The neighbors never helped. Not only that, once an old servant of ours sent her daughter here to help Nainai and the neighbors reported them to their neighborhood committee! After that she did not dare come anymore. Those neighbors wanted your Nainai to die! You know. She made them feel guilty. Because she is the owner of this house. And they threw her out and moved in without her consent. Six families altogether. Class struggle was only an excuse."

"But did you say Nainai was out of her mind? Are you sure of it?"

"Well, you heard the stories she told. What do you think? They are weird!"

"Did she tell you a story about a sword?"

"What sword?"

"A sword called Drink Green."

"Never heard of it."

"What about a well?"

"Never heard of a well either."

Hearing this, I was relieved. And very glad. The story Nainai told me, she had not told anyone else. Not even Third Aunt. So it was a secret shared by the two of us. The story might be weird. But I loved it! It touched me in a strange way as no other story could. For that reason I really felt there was something in it. But I could not explain. Not to Third Aunt, who was a medical doctor. She believed in things she could see under a microscope: virus, bacteria, tissues, and cells. Things such as destiny, previous lives, heaven, even *qi,* she'd call them superstition. So I dropped the topic.

After I left Beijing, Nainai died in September. She died in the storeroom. No chance to see Father and Second Uncle before her eyes closed for good. Yet maybe she did see them, as she said? Maybe she saw them with her wisdom eye all the time, and she saw me too?

20

Remorse

When I returned from Beijing, somehow I had a feeling that nothing was the same at Cold Spring, as if suddenly I looked out of another pair of eyes. Or maybe the place had indeed changed in my absence, like a change of season? One morning I woke up, summer was gone and autumn had its signature on everything. Flowers had vanished from the fields. Leaves were falling. The wind carried sharp blades and the insects' chirping had a sorrowful note as if they knew the end was near.

The first news that welcomed me back was of rape and Laomizi's transfer to a remote village. Chen lost his position. Henceforth he avoided me. Maybe he was ashamed of what he had done?

Then I was appointed the head of the pig farm. I set myself and others to work. I stopped dreaming about Chen. After all, I was not in love with him. Soon I forgot him. But I could not forget Laomizi so easily. Sometimes I wondered, if I had not volunteered to work on the night shift, would she have been all right? Now her future was in jeopardy, even though nobody had thought of blaming me. Should I hold myself responsible in certain ways?

If the Laomizi incident had caused me some small disquiet, another, known as the September 13th Incident, brought on a violent storm in my mind. Looking back on it, I believe it was a turning point in the lives of many of us.

The September 13th Incident refers to the attempt made by "our most revered vice-commander in chief Lin Biao" to assassinate "our most beloved great leader Chairman Mao." It ended in Lin Biao's death in Mongolia on September 13, 1971. This incident shocked me and made me question the nature of the Cultural Revolution. Was it really an unprecedented revolution in human history led by a group of men (and a few women) with vision and exemplary moral integrity, as I had believed? Or was it a power struggle that started at the top and later permeated the whole country? If the Cultural Revolution was just a power struggle, it meant that we were deceived and used by a bunch of dishonest politicians. Lin Biao was a typical example. Who would have thought that the successor of Chairman Mao, handpicked by the great leader himself, his position guaranteed by the Party constitution, was such a scheming and murderous opportunist? If he was like that, what about others just like him who had seized power during the revolution?

As for the theories and slogans invented by such politicians—words I had taken so seriously, and followed—perhaps these were merely tools for them to gain power and defeat their political enemies. Thus Lin Biao and his followers declared, "Educated youths going to the countryside is labor reform [of criminals] in disguise." The other side who remained in power insisted: "Educated youths must go to the countryside. They have a great future there. These general guidelines will never be reversed."

After Lin Biao died, the news media continued to tell educated youths to take root in the countryside. But at Cold Spring our subscriptions to newspapers and magazines dropped to an all-time low—from nearly two hundred in 1969 to barely above ten in 1972. Yan, the political instructor, did not like this. So he held meetings and talked about the importance of subscribing to newspapers and magazines. But as long as he was not paying for them, we just kept our silence and ignored him. Who would want to waste our blood-sweat money on such empty talk and hateful lies since we could recite it all from end to beginning anyway?

One of the lies the newspapers told people was that all educated youths went to the countryside voluntarily. In fact, many hadn't. A girl who worked on the pig farm confessed this to me. She was an educated youth from Harbin, the capital city of Heilongjiang province.

In 1969 she came to Cold Spring at the age of fifteen. Because she was so thin, so small, people nicknamed her Little Monkey. Two years later she replaced Laomizi on the pig farm. When the next Chinese New Year came round, I noticed that unlike others, Little Monkey got no parcels from home. On New Year's Eve, she looked very sad. So I quietly called her aside and gave her some of the goodies I had received. This brought a trace of sad smile onto her thin face. Later that night she explained why she never received anything from home.

"There are six of us in our family. My father is a factory worker. My mother is a housewife. She is ill. Mentally ill. You know. So she can't work.

"I am the oldest child. Ever since elementary school, I've done all the housework: grocery shopping, cooking, washing and mending clothes, buying coal, taking care of my two younger brothers and a little sister. My father made some seventy yuan a month. He could not afford to hire a nanny.

"In 1969 I was going to graduate from junior middle school. My father went to our school to talk to the leaders. He explained our difficulties. He begged the leaders to let me stay. But the leaders replied that on this issue there was a nationwide policy: all older sons and daughters must go to the countryside. Only the youngest child, male or female, was allowed to stay. Period. This policy had a name. It was called Red All Over the Country's Mountains and Rivers.

"So my father came back, told me about this. We were both worried, about my mother. We feared that the news might upset her and cause a relapse. We did not tell her until the last night.

"When my mother heard the news, she was calm. She said she'd make tea-leaf eggs for me to eat on the train. Hearing this, my father and I were both relieved. The next morning, however, my mother was crazy again. Weeping and laughing and talking nonsense. Of course there were no tea-leaf eggs. And my father could not even go to the train station to see me off. So I took my bedroll and went away by myself.

"Later my father told me in his letters that when my mother recovered somewhat, she remembered her promise. She felt very sorry that she had lost her mind on the day I left home. From then on, my father said, whenever she had a relapse, she made tea-leaf eggs, using all the eggs we had at home. Then she took them to the train station and gave them to strangers who were girls of my age . . . "

At this point, Little Monkey burst into tears. It was such a sad story. It made me cry too. *What's the use of trying to be heroic? Why pretend that I stand higher than her and have a vision? Now we are all the same, the educated youths who volunteered to come and those who did not. We are trapped in this swamp! Judging from the propaganda, I can tell that some leaders in Beijing have bet their political future on this campaign being a great success, no matter what price we'll have to pay. We have become their bargaining chips in a political game. They cannot back out of it without being attacked by their opponents. Thus the policy will not be changed.*

But this is so cruel! Now I think about it, what is at stake here is the future of millions of young people in China, and our fate touches the hearts of tens of millions of parents and relatives. Who knows how many people are shedding tears like us on this New Year's Eve? But the politicians do not care, as long as their positions are safe and secure.

By this time, the farms in the Great Northern Wilderness had become Heilongjiang Production and Construction Corps. Farm 850 became Regiment 36. Army officers came. They settled down at the farm headquarters where there were electricity, houses with central heating, a hospital, a general store, an auditorium that also served as a movie theater, and a train station. Only occasionally would they come down to the village to lead a campaign.

Once an officer came to our village (which had become Company Three) to supervise the wheat harvest. For a couple of months, he made us get up at four o'clock and run around the threshing ground until we almost fainted. After that we went out to the fields to work, while he disappeared into the village. What he did there, we had no idea. As soldiers, we were not supposed to question an officer. All we knew was that he never worked side by side with us.

Another officer came in winter. Seeing that we had not finished the corn harvest, he ordered us to "storm" the corn fields at night. The attack began at twelve o'clock sharp. By then the temperature had dropped to well below zero, but the moon did not come out. Carrying heavy rattan baskets on our backs, we tried to wipe out the "enemies" in the dark. For several hours, we trudged in the snow, slipped, and fell numerous times. Finally it was dawn. When we looked back, we knew that the attack had been a miserable failure. So many "enemy sentries" were still standing on the stalks behind us. We had to do the job all over again.

Frustration and indignation were what I felt toward our "beloved kinsfolk," the People's Liberation Army officers. They knew nothing about running farms. Yet since they had the power, all had to obey them. Under their "leadership," the farms in the Great Northern Wilderness got into debt. Hundreds of millions of yuan each year that Premier Zhou had to cancel out himself. To add insult to injury, the officers were extremely arrogant. They really treated us like dirt. Compared with them, Zhao, our former political instructor, was a "small witch." Yet this time nobody dared complain. Attacking "the Great Wall," "the pillar of proletarian dictatorship"? That would qualify anyone to be an active counterrevolutionary. "Dare to be angry. Do not dare to speak." But we did speak out even though just once.

In the early spring of 1972 an accident happened on the pig farm.

Li, who was a local youth, was running the fodder grinder. This machine was dangerous, I knew it. When it ran at top speed, we had to feed corn or soybean stalks continuously into an opening that had no safety devices around it. It was the mouth of a tiger. Anything that went beyond it was bitten off and chewed up in a matter of seconds. Yet as this was the only fodder grinder we had and the pigs had to be fed, we continued to use it. In fact, on our farm, many machines were just as dangerous.

On that day, somehow Li's knit glove got tangled among soybean stalks. Before he realized it, his glove passed through the opening and so did his right hand. When he felt the pain and pulled his arm out, a split second before the machine caught the sleeve of his cotton-padded jacket, all he saw was a bare wrist with a white bone sticking out. His hand was gone! Blood gushed out from the wound.

Everybody on the pig farm was horrified by the sight. With hearts beating like drums, we rushed Li to the barefoot doctor. The doctor was visibly shaken by the sight as well. Yet she managed to bind up Li's wound and said we must rush him to the hospital. The hospital was twenty miles away at the farm headquarters. And in the village we had no cars or trucks. All we had were tractors.

The tractor drivers quickly hooked a cart to a tractor. Some twenty of us got in with Li. Educated and local workers alike. Male and female. We threw in a few quilts and coats. Then the tractor drove off.

Once outside the village, the wind became very cold. It cut our faces like so many small knives. We huddled around the wounded man, trying to use our bodies to shield him. It didn't help much. Li was shivering all over. From time to time, he groaned and tears rolled down his ashen face. The tractor crawled like a snail on a dirt road covered by ice and snow. At this speed it would take us more than three hours to get to the hospital. Probably we couldn't make it before sunset. What if after dark the tractor strayed off the road and got stuck in a snow pit?

Just as we were worried to death, someone spotted a jeep on the horizon. It was coming toward us. "Heaven has eyes!" A jeep could run so much faster and it was much warmer inside! So we all jumped out of the cart and stood in the middle of the road to intercept the jeep.

When the jeep stopped, we saw our regiment commander sitting in it. A stout man in his forties. He looked very displeased. So we explained to him that this was a real emergency: a soldier's hand had been cut off in an accident and he must be rushed to the hospital. We begged the commander to please take our tractor and let the wounded man go to the hospital in his jeep.

The regiment commander frowned deeply when he heard this. He was silent for a moment. Fearing that he might not understand the seriousness of the situation, we implored him to come out and take a look at Li's wound. I was sure that once he saw Li's agony with his own eyes, he would immediately give up his jeep for him. No doubt about it!

The regiment commander finally got out of the jeep at our repeated entreaty and looked at Li's wound. After that, however, he climbed back into the jeep and said impatiently to us: "Just take him to the hospital in the tractor. I have some urgent business. I have to go. Speak no more! Do what I said!" Then he told his driver to step on it.

The jeep sped away. We stood there in utter disbelief, in the snow thrown up in its wake. *He saw Li's wound. He saw the pain. He saw everything with his own eyes! How could he refuse our request and leave a soldier behind in such a condition? Is his heart made of iron and stone? Does he have a heart at all? "Urgent business." Humph! He cannot fool us with such an excuse! We know he has no urgent business in this part of the country. He just does not want to ride in the slow and bumpy tractor when it's so cold. And this man is our regiment commander! A "beloved kinsman!" A stranger would not be so cold-blooded!*

In a moment our rage boiled over. The rest of the journey with tears in our eyes we cursed the commander, up to eighteen generations of his ancestors and down to all his descendants.

"He is not a human being!"

"He isn't! That's for sure! He only has human skin! Deep down he has animal offal!"

"Someday heaven will strike him with five thunders!"

"When he has a son, the baby will be born without an asshole!"

All the traditional, local, and modern curses we could think of, we threw on him. The next day when we returned to the village, we were still extremely angry. So we told the other educated youths about this. But gradually my anger cooled down and I began to reflect on the incident. It brought home to me some basic facts about our situation.

Call us "corps soldiers" or "educated youths," the truth is we've been turned into peasants. Peasants are never in short supply in China. In 1960, who knows how many peasants starved to death. Millions, perhaps. Yet there were still hundreds of millions more. As peasants, our limbs are worth nothing. Our lives are worth nothing. We are "ant peo-

ple." Our lives are "ant lives." Whoever created these phrases in ancient China understood the essence of the matter.

Now what about you yourself? You hate to be treated like an ant. No respect. No sympathy. No value. But when you volunteered to go to the countryside, didn't you say you were willing to give up your privileges? You wrote in your diary, copying a hero's words, "I am willing to be a green leaf, setting off red flowers. I am willing to be a stone in the foundation, supporting the great edifice." Have you changed your mind?

Come to think of it, I'm still willing to be a green leaf. Let others get the spotlight. I don't mind living in obscurity. At least a green leaf has a patch of blue sky over it. It sees the sunshine and the moonlight. It feels the wind and the rain. This is enough for me. But I do not want to be a stone in the foundation! To be buried alive and trampled on. Carrying the dead weight of a huge building on top of me for as long as I live. No hope to get out. Darkness day and night. Silenced and petrified. This is no life! This is worse than death!

Willing or not willing, I no longer have a choice. Once I moved my hukou here, I was at the mercy of the local leaders. Equality? The word still sounds good. But if they don't care to grant it to us, what then? We and our posterity will be "people who are governed," and they "people who govern." They can treat us like dirt under their feet or like beasts. Since we are losers, we have to swallow the bitter fruit.

How stupid I was to dive into this quagmire and be so proud of what I did! Idealism, ignorance, and vanity. These cost me dearly! Next time I should look before I jump. But in my case, will there be a next time?

"One blunder leads to eternal remorse."

This traditional expression describes a woman who lost her chastity. Nothing, not even her suicide, could redeem her in the eyes of society. In 1972, somehow I was seized by the same emotion, which was as profound as an ocean. It lumped at the back of my stomach during the day; the saying cried out from the bottom of my heart when I woke up at night.

By this time I could only guess how other educated youths felt about our situation. All had said they were willing to take roots in the Great Northern Wilderness. They had said so because they had to. Anyone who did not say this would be criticized. Yet soon after the September 13th Incident, seven out of "the eight happy big flies" flew away. Wen was the only male student from 101 left behind.

Unlike Wen, the others had parents who were high-ranking officials. Even though at the time some of them were in trouble, they all seemed to have old comrades-in-arms who were willing to help. Thus at first the seven big flies left the village on home leave. Later they joined the army elsewhere. By and by their *hukou* was transferred from Regiment 36 to their new army units. A few years later, when they were demobilized, they could go back to Beijing. The policy had always been that a demobilized soldier returned to his native place.

How I envied them! Secretly, of course. The method they used was called "curving back to the city." To use it, there were two conditions one must meet. First, the person's parents must have "iron buddies" in the army who could open a back door for an old friend's child. Second, the person had better be a man. The army did not welcome women.

Too bad for me! I was not a man; nor did my parents have friends in the army. Yuan, who was my best friend at the time, was more fortunate. Her father was a high-ranking officer who had been in the Long March. But even he could not get Yuan into the army. Thus Yuan was forced to take another path that turned out to be a shortcut. It led her straight back to Beijing.

The method Yuan used involved politics that I did not quite understand at the time. Seeing that the majority of Party members at Cold Spring were still those who had been in Zhao's inner circle, Yuan first advocated the idea of rehabilitating Zhao. It immediately made her popular among the local Party members. Never mind how the ordinary villagers might have felt about this. Their opinions did not count. Yuan was clear about this from the very start.

Before long she became the first Party member recruited from educated youths. After that she worked even harder and vowed that she would stay in the Great Northern Wilderness throughout her life. With tears in her eyes and speaking in the name of all the revolutionary martyrs, she sounded so sincere that I was touched. Secretly I felt really ashamed of myself.

Later she was recommended by the local Party organization to go to college. This was done in the name of the poor peasants, even though the poor peasants had no say in this matter. Not just any college, either: she was assigned to go to Beijing Foreign Language Institute, while others were sent to local agricultural, mining, and metallurgical schools. At the time I thought Yuan was really lucky. For she had told me that when she was in middle school, her dream was to go to Beijing Foreign

Language Institute and be a diplomat in the future. Now her dream had come true.

It was only months after Yuan left the village that I learned from others that luck had nothing to do with it. Yuan and her father had the whole thing figured out. While Yuan was beating her breast and vowing to take roots in the Great Northern Wilderness, her father was busy pulling strings for her at a lot of different places. Perfect timing. Flawless tactics. A lot of *guanxi*. Everything worked out as they had planned. Hearing this, I had a hard time believing that Yuan could lie like that to me, her "best friend." Because of this, I despised her! At the same time she amazed me. By fooling me, she taught me a big lesson on "materialistic dialectics," that is, the more earnestly an educated youth swore that she would never leave the countryside, the faster she was liable to go away from it.

Knowing this in theory was no help for me, though. I just could not bring myself to lie like that. Nor would I go to the local leaders with gifts and honeyed words, much less "dedicate my body" to some of them. "Sick return"? Too bad I was healthy. Even those who were really sick, like Liu, who had rheumatic heart disease, and those who got hepatitis A or B on the farm, could not get permission to go back. "Family difficulty return"? As my parents were not in Beijing, that would not help me either.

Thus for me, the situation seemed hopeless. Some thoughts and questions that churned in my head in those days found their way into my diary:

> At the age of twenty-one I am stuck in the bog, wasting my time day after day. All opportunities are lost. Doors are shut in my face. My life has just started. Yet it is already over. Like a wild goose with broken wings, I can only watch others fly into the horizon. I am water in a shallow pond, unable to flow anywhere. All this happened to me because I had a dream. It was a beautiful dream. It was a fatal mistake. When I woke up from it, I found myself in a nightmare that had no exit. If this is my fate, why? It is not fair! What have I done to deserve it?

This passage from my diary later got me into trouble. Yan, the political instructor, thought I was brewing rebellion. Actually when I wrote this, I was wondering about *yinguo* (causes and results). For centuries people had believed that everything in every life happened for a reason, which might reach back to previous existences. Though people often failed to see the causes of their reward and punishment, heaven knew them all and hell kept detailed records of their behavior. Thus there was the saying, "The net of heaven has large mesh, but it lets nothing through."

And heaven and hell never made mistakes. So the villagers at Cold Spring believed. I found it out when thunder struck our dormitory during a storm. Out of the thirty women who lived in it, five fell to the ground. They lost consciousness. Their backs were slightly burned. They were "rushed" to the hospital, where in a few days they all recovered.

While these women were in hospital, the villagers gossiped about them. Many insisted they must have done bad things. Even though people never found them out, heaven had eyes. Thus the thunderbolt was *baoying* (retribution) from the fathomless blue. It struck the guilty ones alone. The crimes they had committed were written on their backs in a heavenly language ordinary human beings could not comprehend . . .

When I first heard this, I was outraged. This was what I would call "adding insult to injury." How could the local people be so superstitious? It was unfair and cruel for them to say such things! But there was no way to convince them. Especially a month later when they found out that one of the five victims had indeed done something bad. That is, a few days before the thunderstorm she said she was going to Hulin, the county seat. Hearing this, a friend of hers asked her to send money home for her at the post office. The family never received the money. Later the friend made inquiries and the woman confessed that instead of sending the money, she had used it and lied about it. Afterwards she paid the money back.

"See! That is what we meant! *Baoying* is always fair and just! Always! Now tell us you don't believe it!" The villagers with whom I had argued before were triumphant.

"Of course not! This was merely a coincidence!"

Even though I would never agree with the villagers on this, I guess I was influenced by them. Or maybe the belief of *yinguo* had been planted in my soul a thousand years before. It was a heritage from my ancestors. Thus in 1972, day and night my thoughts hovered around a reason that might explain why I was so unfortunate. Perhaps I had offended some Taoist deities.

In 1966, who masterminded the raid to drive the Taoists down the sacred mountain? I did. At that time, didn't the local people tell me that the deities at Mount Hua had worked miracles? If they were angry at me for depriving them of joss sticks, candles, and sacrifice from their priests and worshipers, I'm afraid I'll be doomed for many reincarnations to come.

Once my mind was on this track, there was no end to it. Old memories flooded back. In darkness, I saw vividly the Taoists with long white beards paying their last homage to the temples where they had lived for decades. They walked down the mountain road, looking back. Local Red Guards kicked them from behind. Their sorrowful eyes blamed me silently . . . *Whose eyes were those? The elderly homeowner was looking at the flowers we had crushed. Others were looking at the food they were unable to finish at the restaurants. Their faces were sweaty. Their eyes pleaded for mercy. I had no mercy in my heart. All I had were malice and self-righteousness.*

But these were not the worst memories. What about that song I ordered our teachers to sing when I was guarding the cow shed?

I am a cow ghost and a snake spirit.
I am a criminal against the people.
I am guilty. I deserve to die.
I am guilty. I deserve to die.
The people should smash me and crush me.
Smash me and crush me . . .

The singing I seemed to hear again, in the stillness of the night. The teachers' voices were trembling and faltering. The singing carried so much grief, it was more like moaning and wailing. *It should have broken my heart. Yet apparently I didn't have a heart. Proud of my status as a Red Guard, glad of the power I had over them, I ordered them to sing the song once more.*

I also remembered the day we went to put up my *dazibao* at Teacher Lin's home. The room was dark, even though it was broad daylight outside. We had just pasted the long *dazibao* not only on the walls but also over the only window as a punishment for her. Teacher Lin and her family stood in a corner. Squeezed together, they tried to get out of our way. There were five of them, if I remembered correctly: Lin, her husband (who was also a teacher at 101), two small children who were probably not in elementary school yet, and Lin's old mother. At the time they all looked very frightened. The old woman was trembling and the kids did not dare to cry . . .

On that day I saw with my own eyes that Teacher Lin's home con-

sisted of only one room. Aside from the beds, it could not even hold two desks. No living room. No bathroom. No kitchen. No running water. No central heating . . . Three generations were living together. Two teachers had to share one small desk . . . I saw these, but I paid no attention. Because on that day, my mind was set on revenge. My revenge! How could I be so selfish? Teacher Lin's life was not easy and I made it even harder. So perhaps I deserved what I got and it had nothing to do with the deities?

After some time, even that disgusting "rapist" whom we beat to death in Guangzhou came back to haunt me. *Was he really a rapist? Maybe he had the intention, but he certainly had not raped any of us. Even a convicted rapist may not get a death sentence. So what right did we have to take the law into our own hands and beat him to death? He was a man, after all. Maybe he had parents to support? Maybe he had a wife and children too? Would they ever find out what happened to him after he vanished through the chimney of the crematorium that night? Perhaps today they are still waiting for him to come back?*

Was I thinking of the beating before I fell asleep? Or was I thinking of a trip I made to Hulin in winter? I had a strange dream one night.

I was walking on a snow-covered plain. The sun had just set. I was in a hurry. I must get back to the village before dark. Then it was dark. The village was nowhere to be seen. Fortunately on that night the wind was calm and the moon was very bright. The surface of the snow had been hardened by a blizzard. Under the weight of my foot it slowly gave way with a crunch. A second later, my foot touched solid ground. Then another crunch, solid ground again. I pressed on.

I took another step. The snow gave way. But under it, there was no ground. Before I had time to react, I slammed into a hole half a person deep. Shocked and cursing mothers, I climbed out. Dusted off the snow all over me and picked up my fur hat. I started walking again. But before long, I fell into another pit.

Then it dawned on me that I had strayed off the road and gotten to Little Southern Hill. (The summer before we had dug holes here to plant apple trees. But for some reason the saplings never arrived. Then winter came. Snow filled up the holes. On the surface, all was smooth and flat. Underneath, pitfalls.) So I was not far from the village. Yet I did not dare move my feet. At the moment, I was the only person left in the world. Around me the ice and snow glittered in the moonlight like so many diamonds.

Helplessly I looked up. The moon was disappearing. A white screen came up. It was not a screen. It was dense fog and it was churning violently. The fog advanced. Suddenly, I heard a woman's voice from it. It said: "Zhang Heihei. Zhang Heihei. Zhang Heihei . . . " I woke up hearing the voice ringing in the air.

Zhang Heihei? Who was Zhang Heihei? Don't think I know anybody with such a weird name. But, wait! The name does ring a bell. Have I heard it somewhere? How come I don't remember?

The name made me uneasy. It seemed ominous. Yet I felt it was a revelation of some sort. I wanted to get to the bottom of it. So for several days, I kept the search signal flashing at the back of my mind. Then one night when I woke up at three o'clock, suddenly the rusty gate of my memory opened.

Zhang Heihei. Of course I know her! She was a schoolmate of mine. We were in the same grade, not in the same class. But how much do I really know about her? Before that night in 1966, we had never met, and afterwards I never heard about her again. We were strangers "met as drifting duckweed in a river." But that one night! How could I possibly forget?

On that night, the weather was very hot and stuffy. A thunderstorm was in the making. In a small room on campus that used to be a teacher's office, seven of us stood in a semicircle. We were a Red Guard Fighting Team. At the moment, we were interrogating a suspect who had been "arrested" by her classmates the day before. The suspect was a rather pale and thin girl of medium stature. Straight short hair. A simple white blouse and blue pants. She stood in the middle of the room. She was talking nonstop in a shrill voice.

"I am Zhang Heihei! My father is Zhang Laohei! My mother is Zhang Dahei! My younger brother is Zhang Xiaohei! We are a black family! Our home is a black den! I am the dog child of a capitalist! My father, my mother, me and my younger brother. We are all dogs! We are all black! . . . "

Hei means black, so the personal names she made up for herself and her family were Black Black, Old Black, Big Black, and Small Black.

Hearing her words, a Red Guard slowly unbuckled her belt. The iron buckle flashed in the air. It drew a curve and landed on Zhang Heihei's bare arm with a thud. The skin was cut open. Blood oozed out.

"Zhang Heihei!"

Black Black. Her voice grew louder. It sounded like a challenge to us.

"She must be a real counterrevolutionary!" I thought. "How dare she call herself Zhang Heihei?" My fellow Red Guards seemed to be thinking along the same lines. At the time China was engulfed in a turbulent red storm. Everybody was either a Red Guard, a Little Red Soldier, or a Red Rebel. Chairman Mao was our red commander in chief. We called ourselves "his little red devils." We read and quoted his little red book. Wore his red buttons on our chests. Red flags. Red armbands. Red blood. Red hearts . . . We could not tolerate anyone who was of a different color. Peach was guilty. Yellow was criminal. Black and white were definitely counterrevolutionary!

So we all unbuckled our belts. As Red Guards, we could not possibly let her get away with this. Red Guards hated class enemies. We wouldn't handle them with care! The next moment, we were thrashing her.

"Zhang Heihei!"

"Zhang Heihei!!"

"Zhang Heihei!!!"

Each time one of us hit her, she would yell "Zhang Heihei," as if it were a punctuation mark. Her voice had become so shrill, to me it was no longer a human voice. It sounded like a piece of chalk scraping against a glass blackboard. It made my hair stand on end.

Her voice was a whip, with which she drove us to beat her. For as long as she was yelling "Zhang Heihei," we could not stop. We had to beat her into submission. It was impossible to beat her into submission! We had no mercy. She had no mercy. Willpower against willpower. We gave her no break. She would not let us off the hook. After a while we were all drenched in sweat and Zhang Heihei was soaked in blood. Her face, arms, and shoulders were covered with wounds. Black, blue, purple, and red. It was a heart-startling sight!

Yet Zhang Heihei did not seem to feel the pain. Nor was she afraid of us in the least. Utterly fearless, she was like a heroine in a revolutionary movie. Actually she was no heroine. She was schizophrenic. A doctor told us this the next day. But the night before, the idea did not occur to any of us. On the previous day Zhang Heihei had been "arrested" as a suspected counterrevolutionary. Her classmates handed her over to us for a trial and we judged her guilty.

Looking back on this incident six years later, I realized that I was put on trial too that night. Am I a hero or a coward? Am I loyal to Chairman Mao or sympathetic to a class enemy? These questions I had to answer with my action, not with empty words. Other Red Guards

were watching me. I was watching others. We were witnesses and judges
for one another. I could not afford to let others see my weaknesses. Thus
the more uncomfortable and scared I felt, the harder I thrashed Zhang
Heihei.

*Uncomfortable and scared. That was how I felt. I wouldn't admit it
then. But I can admit it now. The whole thing happened like a nightmare to me. I was caught in it. No way to escape. I was matched against
others. I knew I lacked class feelings. I was hesitant. I was inferior. A
ghost lived inside me. It made my heart skip a beat when the iron buckle
of my belt hit Zhang Heihei. Later it wiped out the memory from my
mind until I wanted to remember.*

*Now I think of it, the ghost had been put into me early on by Aunty's
stories. Later it drank the music Father loved, Beethoven, Schubert,
Chopin, Mozart . . . and fed on the literature I read, Cao Xueqin, Shakespeare, Tolstoy, Hugo . . . On that night it was trying to tell me: What
you are doing is wrong! It is terrible! How can you lift up your hand
against a helpless girl who is your schoolmate? Shame on you! Are you
crazy? . . . I did not want to listen to it. I did not have the courage to
listen to it. Instead I tried to beat it into silence. So I was a coward after all. A hero should have the guts to say Stop!*

*Besides, was it just discomfort and fear I felt when I beat Zhang Hei-
hei? Nothing else? Now the judge is no other but my own conscience,
I ought to be more honest. Perhaps the beating and the blood stirred
up something deep down inside me? I was thrilled in spite of the ghost's
voice. Torture, death, agony, ecstasy, orgasm . . . In the past, I had
dreamed about these. I was obsessed. Then I had a chance to carry them
out and whatever I did was justified. The wildfire burning in my heart
had a good name: class hatred. The stronger, the better. In its name, torture and kill the class enemies. Drink their blood. Bite the flesh off their
bodies. Smash their bones. All for the good of humankind . . .*

*Now it's too late to take Nainai's warning. She was right when she
said, remembering certain things can be a scourge and forgetfulness is
often a blessing. Henceforth how can I look into the eyes of all the innocent people in the world and not see a verdict of Guilty! Guilty!
Guilty!*

Zhang Heihei! Where are you?

*I don't even know your real name! I never tried to find it out. In-
stead, I forgot you for six long years! Not again. Never again. As long
as I live, I will pray that you recover from the illness and the trauma*

we inflicted on you. If you wish, take revenge on me. Thrash me with that bloody belt for three days and three nights until there is no skin on my body left whole and no breath in my throat. I won't beg you to stop. If you tell me to cut off my right hand, I'll do it. Just stick it into that fodder grinder as Li did the other day, it'll be gone in a few seconds. Stop such morbid fantasies! They don't help. Nothing can take the blood stains from off my conscience. What's done cannot be undone! Henceforth remorse will be mine for as long as I live. When I die, I will drop to the eighteenth level of hell. I deserve all the punishments!

Friends and Others

By the time I remembered Zhang Heihei and then sank into despair, about ten educated youths from Cold Spring had left the Great Northern Wilderness for good. Without exception, these were the sons and daughters of high-ranking cadres from Beijing. After the "seven big flies" left, for a while Wen had the dormitory room all to himself. He took advantage of this privacy and studied fortune-telling. Though I wondered how serious he was about such stuff, as time went by his reputation grew. People sought him out during the day and in the evenings. Later some even came from other villages. This left him with little time to read his beloved books or to rest. Yet while he complained about the inconveniences, he seemed to really enjoy telling people their fortunes.

Those who came to see him were almost all educated youths who had no prospect of going to college or joining the army. The big question on everybody's mind was, Will I ever be able to return to my home city? If yes, when and how? But this question could not be uttered. Wen knew it anyway, because he too was an educated youth who was unable to go away.

I heard that he had a number of ingenious ways to tell a person's fortune. Sometimes he used the traditional diagrams from *I-Ching*. Sometimes he simply asked the person to draw a spontaneous picture with certain objects in it: a river, a snake, a toad, a tree, a bird . . . He also had a bunch of weird questions.

"Do you like the autumn moon or the winter sun?"

"Would you prefer a brick wall, a wooden fence, or nothing around your home?"

"Which would you like to have: a gold lock, a silver lock, or an iron lock?"

His questions varied from person to person. I was curious what questions he might put to me. When I came, however, he asked me no questions. No diagrams and picture drawing either. He only looked at me intently for a while, yet I felt that he was not looking at me. He was using his wisdom eye to detect some secret messages from the depth of my brain. Then he opened his renowned iron mouth (meaning the person always speaks bluntly) and spoke solemnly.

"You are destined to work hard throughout your life. The man you love, you will not marry. The man you marry, you don't really love. But he is not a bad man. Intelligent. Honest as well. You will have a son with him. Then a divorce. In this life, you can't depend on anyone. You have to depend on yourself. Eventually you will go back to Beijing. Then travel to faraway places. You'll see the world. Adventures, fulfillment, loneliness, anxieties, these are all in store for you. On the whole, your fate is not bad. In your old age, you'll have good health."

I smiled, so as to be polite to him. In my heart, I was talking back. *What is this? This nonsense about a husband, a son, seeing the world, and old age. Make my belly ache for a wild laugh in his face. Wen, you know nothing about my fate. I know it myself! I will not have good luck, because I don't deserve it. A person like me, foolish and complacent, cowardly and vain, morbid and grotesque, is good for nothing! This life is useless for me. It might be harmful for others. So I will end it, soon! Wait and see. You'll be aghast. I promise you this.*

In fact, on that day I was not interested in having Wen tell me my fortune. My friend Fang wanted to hear about hers. But she did not know Wen well enough. So she dragged me along, knowing that Wen and I had been schoolmates.

Fang was a girl of my age who came from Shanghai. Like me, she had studied in a top middle school before the Cultural Revolution. Her parents, however, were not cadres. They were ordinary office workers who had no power, no *guanxi*. Fang began working on the pig farm in 1969. At first, she was so quiet that she escaped everybody's attention. Besides, at the time Yuan and I were together a lot. After Yuan left, I began to realize that Fang was not only intelligent but also warmhearted and trustworthy. So we became close. Now it was her turn to be examined by Wen.

Wen told her to shuffle a set of cards. "Do it with a sincere heart. Otherwise the results won't be accurate. Shuffle them until you feel you're really satisfied. Then let me see them."

Fang shuffled the cards for a long time. I could tell she was nervous. When finally she was done, Wen laid the cards out and made his interpretations. First he talked about Fang's parents and family. Then her childhood and personality. As for her future, although I don't remember the exact words he used, what he said did not seem promising: She would have to work hard throughout her life too. *Everybody seems to get that. He can't go wrong there!* Her job was going to be hard and tedious. Yet she had no other options. At the age of twenty-five, she would marry a man who was very jealous. Though she couldn't love this man, she would continue to be his wife for the sake of their son. Loneliness was in store for her. Someday she would lose her best friend. *Now there he's got a point! But as the saying goes, "A blind cat ran into a dead mouse"—he hits it by chance.* After that, she would have no one to talk to. Although eventually she would be able to return to Shanghai, more frustration would await her there . . . Wen's iron mouth went on and on. I wished he would shut up!

"Don't you listen to him, Fang. His fortune-telling is humbug! What he said about me is completely wrong." As soon as we got out, I felt the need to reassure Fang.

Fang said nothing in reply. Later she avoided the topic. Yet she looked preoccupied not just for days but for weeks. Because of this, I suspected that she took what Wen said rather seriously. In this regard, she was not alone though. Many in the village believed Wen's words as if he were a guru of some sort. The fortune-telling eventually got him into trouble. A demerit was recorded against him, a stain on his history, and his punishment was publicized in the whole corps as a warning to others.

Old B, an educated youth from Harbin, was the one who got Wen into trouble. Once Wen said to him that he would not be able to get married until he was thirty-five. Moreover, the woman he would marry was not a virgin but a widow. When we heard this, we took it as a joke and burst out laughing. But Old B took it to heart. Afterwards others heard him murmur to himself: "What am I to do? Marry a widow at the age of thirty-five?" This behavior made him into a laughingstock in the village. People nicknamed him Old Thirty-Five. Later, Old Thirty-Five went back to Harbin for a home visit. His family took him to a doctor and the doctor suggested that he might have some mental problems. But this did not get him a "sick return" as his family had hoped. It only got Wen into trouble.

That should teach him a lesson! Sometimes he's so carried away by his fortune-telling he forgets other people's feelings. Yet in my opinion, the punishment isn't fair for Wen. After all, he didn't offer to tell people their fortunes. They came to him and begged him to do so. Unable to turn them down, he obliged. For this, he never received anything in return.

Besides, was it his fault that suddenly all educated youths in this region turned superstitious in one way or another? Wen was fascinated by fortune-telling. Others believed in what he said. I believe in Nainai's story. I also believe in the existence of heaven and its retribution. Perhaps we are indeed reformed by the peasants? But why are the peasants in China so superstitious?

In the past I thought it was because they were ignorant and the ruling class had deceived them. Now I know better. They are superstitious because they're so powerless. Constantly at the mercy of disasters, natural and manmade, they still cherish hopes. For themselves. For their posterity. The harder their lives, the more fervent their hopes. They believe in heaven, yinguo, and reincarnation, because in this life there is almost no chance for them to make it. Anyone who is put into such a position is likely to become superstitious after a while, no matter how intelligent or well educated. I'd never have understood this, if I hadn't become a peasant myself.

The educated youths were now peasants because we had rural *hukou* and no way to return to the cities. But we were not real peasants yet, because many of us would not resign ourselves to such a fate. One night, Fang and I worked together on the pig farm, delivering piglets. While we waited, we chatted. Suddenly Fang looked me in the eye.

"Rae, do you know what I want? I'll tell you the truth. I want the Sino-Russian war to break out! I want it to escalate into the third world war! Atom bombs. Hydrogen bombs. Let them fall. We might as well all die. I don't care if I am blown to pieces. But if I survive the war, maybe I'll be able to return to Shanghai. Maybe I'll return as a hero."

"I understand," I said, nodding my head. Yet I was surprised, for Fang had impressed me as a gentle and very prudent young woman. A lot of self-restraint and common sense. I never expected that such a vehement confession would pour out of her mouth. Meanwhile I was touched, for she had to trust me a great deal to tell me this. As for looking forward to the third world war—Second Uncle was labeled an active counterrevolutionary because of such a charge. Fang could get herself into a lot of trouble if she said this to the wrong person.

This short conversation started a lifelong friendship between the two of us. When people did not dare speak their minds, a few words could carry a lot of meaning. Immediately I saw that Fang and I were kindred spirits: we had come to the Great Northern Wilderness for a dream.

Now the dream was shattered, but we were forced to stay. In this village, all we could do now was to work, eat, and sleep. Year after year, we grew crops; we raised pigs. The surplus value we created (if any) was to be consumed by "those who govern the people." This kind of life was meaningless and hateful. Thus Fang looked forward to the third world war and I could not drive the idea of suicide out of my mind.

Suicide, it shouldn't be too hard. I am sure I can do it. Wish I had that short sword in Nainai's story: Drink Green. I'd pierce my heart and see my blood spray out like a scarlet fan. I'd love to die like that! But the sword is at the bottom of a well somewhere. What I'd hate most is to jump into a well. An educated youth in a nearby village did that. Another was blown to pieces right here last winter. Nobody knew exactly how. He went to ignite the explosive at daybreak so others could dig the drainage canal late. Something went wrong. It was a crazy idea to dig a canal in the dead of the winter here anyway. The earth was frozen solid like a rock.

What other options do I have? Drink poison? I've got the only key to the medicine cabinet on the pig farm. DDT, dipteryx, DDVP . . . A generous dose of any of these would send me out of this world. Or a more traditional way: I can hang myself. The main building of the pig farm is custom-made for the purpose. So many log beams. Each one long and sturdy. One, two, three, four, five . . . Forty-eight of them from one end to the other. Choose one I like. Find a thin rope. Nobody will come during the night. Plenty of time to die.

When I heard the wolves howl on the plain, I went out to meet them, but they ran away. The rats here carried a mysterious disease called Hulin fever. A few educated youths in our regiment had died of it. When I saw the rats, three black lines on their backs, I didn't bother to get out of their way. Yet somehow the disease did not want to claim me.

Some educated youths in other regiments died while they tried to put out forest fires. They ran against the wind. The wind spread the fire. When they were engulfed by a roaring mountain of flame, they cried "Long Live Chairman Mao!" and protected the Mao buttons on their chests. This way they became revolutionary martyrs.

I was no longer interested in becoming a revolutionary martyr. On the contrary, I gave much thought to becoming a traitor. Cold Spring was not far from Wusuli River, the borderline. Just a few hours' walk, I would be there.

Jump into the water in the middle of the night. Swim quietly toward

*the other shore. Maybe today is my lucky day? Farewell, homeland!
"Workers have no homeland." Who said that? Marx or Lenin? Hurry
up! The frontier guards may come at any moment. The dogs bark. Suddenly a beam of light cuts the darkness open. A shower of bullets. I'm
hit! "Come back! Come back!" "No! Never!" Whatever I did, I will
pay for it. Can't implicate others in my family. Thus I continue to swim,
carrying the pain on my back, until I kiss the bottom of the river . . .*

At this point I remembered that the other shore was only the Soviet
Union. My daydream burst like a bubble. Out of the frying pan into
the fire. Even though my life was dirt cheap, I did not want to throw it
away like that.

When I contemplated suicide, I remembered the heart-piercing remorse I felt when I listened to Nainai's story. So I put it off. *In that situation, I had no choice. The city had fallen. I had to kill myself to avoid
capture, humiliation, and death at my enemies' hands. But now, what's
the hurry? I can carry out the suicide any night, any way. In this life, I
am nobody. Whether I am alive or dead—that doesn't matter. So why
should I die today? Why not tomorrow? In the past because I was rash
and reckless I made terrible mistakes. What's done cannot be undone.
I do not want to make another fatal mistake.*

Going to the Great Northern Wilderness was a fatal mistake. If I
could cut off a hand and then be allowed to go back to Beijing to start
all over again, I would want the deal. That was how I felt at the time,
and so did my three bosom friends, Fang, Liya, and Old Song.

Liya became my friend because of Fang. The two of them had been
close ever since they were middle school students in Shanghai. Unlike
Fang, Liya was from a capitalist family, which had been wealthy before 1949. Although Liya never mentioned her parents, I guess they were
proud, like Liya herself. Among all my friends, Liya was the most talented. She could play the piano, draw, and write poems. Moreover, she
was remarkably good-looking. Bright eyes in the shape of half-moons.
Deep dimples on rosy cheeks. She liked to smile in front of people. Other
feelings she kept to herself. I was like that too: hearty laughter. Loud
voice. Never let others see the tears . . .

Thus Liya and I did not need to talk about feelings. We understood
each other. I could see through her facade and read the ambition, the
pride, as well as the complex of inferiority and remorse in her heart, as
if I were reading them in my own. Between us, words were awkward
and needless. So when Liya and I met, we talked about trivial things

only. Yet sometimes I wondered how others could fail to perceive what Liya hid behind her sunny smiles. The story of her coming to the Great Northern Wilderness was no secret. Everybody in the village knew it.

In the fall of 1968, for the first time, Shanghai was sending educated youths to the Great Northern Wilderness. The life on the northern border excited Liya and Fang's imagination. They both volunteered to come. A few days later Fang received notice of acceptance, but Liya was rejected. Because her parents were capitalists, she was not considered politically reliable enough to work in this region.

Hearing this, Liya moved out of her parents' home and wrote them letters, declaring that henceforth she would have nothing to do with them. But this was not enough. Later she wrote a *dazibao* and denounced her family publicly. But even after that she was not accepted. Then came the day when Fang and others were leaving Shanghai for the northeast, Liya came to the train station to see them off. She sneaked into the train and locked herself in a toilet for four days and three nights. Finally when the train arrived at Hulin, she came out with a letter written in her own blood, vowing that she was determined to take roots in the Great Northern Wilderness. The leaders were moved. They let her stay.

Four years down the road, Liya's prospect looked bleak. Unlike others who knew their parents loved them and would try their best to get them back, Liya had severed her relation with her family. What she did before she left Shanghai made her parents lose face. Now how could she go back on her words and ask them for help? Besides, even if her parents were willing to forgive her, they were not in a position to help.

As a result, Liya stayed at Cold Spring for more than ten years. She returned to Shanghai in 1979 with the last group of educated youths. At the time, she suffered a chronic backache without knowing that she had cancer. She died in 1993 after several operations and a lot of pain. Thus going to the Great Northern Wilderness was indeed a fatal mistake for her.

My other friend Old Song had a different problem. At the age of twenty-six, she was the oldest of all the educated youths in our village, four years older than Fang, Liya, and me. The villagers were already calling her an old maid behind her back. Her parents in Beijing were worried to death about her chances for a "lifelong big affair." As for Old Song herself, she told us she'd never get married in the Great Northern Wilderness. Old maid or whatever, she did not care.

In fact, Fang, Liya, Old Song, and I, the four of us vowed together that we would all remain single as long as we were here. I remember vividly the day that we gave our pledge. It was in August. A sunny afternoon. Earlier a heavy shower had washed the whole world crystal-clear. The four of us walked out of the village hand in hand. Wild flowers lined the road. The wheat fields that had been harvested looked like a boundless green meadow. A southern wind was on the rise. Warm and moist. It blew against our faces. It lifted our short hair. We were heading toward Little Southern Hill.

On the way we discussed our future. We decided that we would remain single and the four of us would always be best friends. That way we would continue to enjoy our twenty-four-day home visit every two years. The rest of the time, we would simply try to save up money, make plans, and look forward to the next trip. We would do this year after year until we were too old to travel, then we would die together.

Just as we were saying this, a rainbow appeared ahead of us like a miracle. *It has to be a good omen! This seven-colored bridge in heaven. Where will you lead us? Even if we won't have a future, are you trying to tell me some kind of joy is still possible? Just think. If I have forty more years to live—twenty home visits? that's four hundred eighty days—well, at least for nearly a year and a half I will be truly alive even though the rest of my life will be a toilsome living death. Not too bad! Besides, there's the rainbow and here are my friends. Such a life might still be worth living. Who knows?*

Little Southern Hill was ahead of us. It reminded me of a lecture given to us by an officer a few months earlier. He set his jaw and said: "Don't you educated youths dream of leaving the Great Northern Wilderness. You can't! When you are alive, you belong to Company Three. When you die, you will be buried at Little Southern Hill! You will never go back to the cities! Mark my words!" This was like putting salt on our wounds. He seemed to hate us so much. Why? Thinking of what he said, I decided that I would not let his prediction come true in my case. I would not commit suicide yet, for I did not want to be buried at Little Southern Hill!

Old Song and I became bosom friends literally overnight under unusual circumstances. One night after midnight, while I was working alone on the pig farm, Song came to see me. I was surprised, for in the past we had hardly spoken to each other. Although she was from Beijing also, her home was in Mentougou district, a far suburb known for its coal mines. She was from a worker's family. While still gasping for breath, she burst out.

"Hey! Yang Rae! Your diary is marvelous! I love it! I love it! Every single word in it comes from the bottom of my heart! Only I did not know how to express my feelings. You did it for me! You did it beautifully! That's great!"

I was shocked by her words.

"What? My diary? What are you talking about?"

Then it was Song's turn to be surprised.

"You don't mean you don't know yet? Come on! At least fifty people in the village have read your diary. The rest will read it tomorrow or the day after tomorrow."

"But that's impossible! My diary is under my pillow. I saw it there last night!"

"Hey! You're really naive! Let me tell you this: Yan, the political instructor, has another copy of it. As a matter of fact, right now he is mobilizing educated youths to criticize you. There'll be a rally. You'd better be prepared."

Later I found out that Old Song was one of the educated youths Yan was trying to mobilize. Thus she heard Yan read my diary the day before. I guess it did pollute her mind. Anyway, she told me everything she knew about my diary.

I'd never have thought that Gao, a girl who grew up in the same big yard, went to the same elementary and middle schools, would read my diary while I was working on the pig farm. And she reported me to the political instructor, so Yan read it too. After he read it, he asked Gao to copy parts of it. These parts Yan read to all the platoon and squad leaders, who were mostly educated youths. Old Song was among them. According to her, at that meeting after Yan finished reading my diary, there was a deep, long silence. Many looked as if they were lost in thought. As for Old Song, she said that my diary put her mind in turmoil for a whole afternoon. That night she couldn't sleep. After midnight, she jumped out of bed and came to talk to me.

After I heard this, my mind was in turmoil too. Of course I was alarmed, knowing that I was in trouble again. Meanwhile, I was awfully grateful to Old Song. I was glad to find a true friend when things were at their worst for me. Then I was very angry. I hated myself for being such a fool. *Look at all the things others did behind my back, things I was totally unaware of. Someday, someone might cut off my head from behind and I'd have no clue who did it and why.*

But I was even angrier at Gao. *Not only did she read my diary with-*

*out my permission, she sold me out to look good in the eyes of the po-
litical instructor! How could she be so base? Stab me in the back. Why?
As far as I know, I never offended her . . . And Yan, the political instructor, how could he encourage an educated youth to do such a thing?
And now, mobilize people to criticize me! He should have criticized Gao!
Given her a big lecture on honesty and propriety. But now that he's
judged me guilty because of the cursed diary, I can't protest. I can't defend myself. I must admit my guilt and criticize myself. Heaven and earth
have been turned upside down. In this world there is no justice! No
right and wrong!*

After Old Song left, I thought the whole thing over. I just couldn't
understand why Gao would want to report me. There was nothing really counterrevolutionary in my diary. In fact, it started as a revolutionary hero's diary and toward the end all I said was I felt there was
no future for us here and I wished I could leave. Even these feelings I
did not spell out—I used a bunch of metaphors to suggest them. The
truth was, out of the numerous unorthodox thoughts that swarmed my
head and demanded expression from me in those days, about 10 percent of the least dangerous were ones I picked to deal with in my diary.

The only possibility was that Gao planned to eliminate a rival for
going to college. She knew I was popular with the poor peasants here.
If this was true, I ought to pity her, not hate her. For she was even more
foolish than me. She should have tried to attack Yuan, who was popular with Zhao's trusted fellows. Whether that would help her, of course,
was another matter. How could she fail to see that nowadays the poor
peasants here had turned into "clay Buddhas crossing a river who could
not even save themselves"?

Only a few months before, a "gigantic counterrevolutionary incident" broke out in Hulin county. Overnight, almost every house in the
region was searched and who knows how many poor peasants were
implicated. In our village, some fifteen were arrested. My friend Huar
and her mother, Ji Daniang, were among them. Their crime was sticking needles into Chairman Mao's face and body. In fact, they did this
unintentionally, for in those days Chairman Mao's pictures were all over
the newspapers the villagers had always used for wallpaper. So after
the women sewed, if they stuck the needles in the wall at the wrong
places, poor peasants became active counterrevolutionaries and were
shut up in the cow shed for months.

After Huar's arrest, occasionally I saw her from a distance. Neither of us dared speak to the other. Eyeing me, she was on the verge of tears. The poor girl! "Three-tenths like a person, seven-tenths like a ghost." Her face, hands, and clothes were extremely dirty and her hair was a big pancake, filled with lice. As a punishment, the "criminals" were not allowed to wash themselves or comb their hair when they were detained.

Now it seemed my turn had come. Cow shed, interrogation, lice . . . Of course I was worried. Proletarian dictatorship was not something one would want to meddle with. Even a three-year-old kid knew this. But the truth was, this time I was not half as afraid as last time when I made a slip of the pen and that mistake was seized by Zhao.

Yan! What can you do to me? Make me a counterrevolutionary and have me executed? So what? Save me the trouble of committing suicide! "A dead pig is not afraid of boiling water." This saying has a lot of truth in it. Besides, you haven't cornered me yet. It may not be as easy as you think. I promise you I'll play the eel and the fox, the hedgehog and the skunk. After I play all the tricks, what have I got to lose anyway? Nothing! But you've got something to lose in this game. I'll make you lose face in a village where you are the number-one leader. And Gao, she'll have to stand trial in the eyes of everybody. It won't be comfortable! Just wait and see.

Could Yan guess what I was thinking? Or did he worry that my diary might pollute the minds of other educated youths as it did Old Song's? I did not know. All I knew was that he planned the mass rally to criticize me; then he postponed it. Then he made more preparations; then he postponed it again. Finally after nearly a month he called me to his home and told me that because my thinking had serious problems, I was no longer fit to be the head of the pig farm. Therefore the leaders had decided: I should turn the pig farm over to Fang and begin to work with a tractor crew. In the future I should try harder to learn from the poor peasants and reform myself.

So that was it! All he did was strip me of a position that was so insignificant it wasn't even official. Looking back on it, I am convinced that this mishap was really a blessing in disguise. For suddenly I realized I had "enemies" who were trying to destroy me, and my instinctive reaction was to defend myself. While I tried to predict what my opponents might do next so I could outmaneuver them, I forgot I'd wanted to kill myself. Suicide was out of the question under such circumstances. I did not want people to think I was afraid or felt guilty. In fact, I felt I was wronged and that took my mind off the terrible thought of wronging others at the beginning of the Cultural Revolution. I felt better being attacked than attacking myself, as long as the damage they did to me was yet controllable.

The incident shook me up. It damaged me and unnerved me. No doubt about it. As a result, I did not dare write down a single word in that book ever after. My diary stopped on the day before Old Song's visit: April 30, 1972. Henceforth, whenever I had an unexpected visitor or someone called my name, my heart would skip a beat and the muscles of my scalp would tighten. I always expected the worst. I was constantly on the lookout for sudden blows and disasters. The last thing I wanted was to be caught off-guard again. Of course, I lost sleep and had nightmares.

Aside from my diary, letters could be incriminating too, if they fell into the wrong hands. So I made sure to burn all of them on the very day I received them. That was what my parents told me to do. I didn't feel funny about it then, but I do feel funny now. Their letters were so impeccably revolutionary that even with a magnifying glass, one could not find anything wrong in them. Yet at the end of each letter, they would write in big characters and underline them: AFTER YOU READ THIS LETTER, BURN IT IMMEDIATELY! VERY IMPORTANT!

The letters I burned in the passageway outside our room. Sometimes when I was doing this, I had company. Other educated youths burned their letters too. On such occasions, we never talked to one another. Just pretended that others did not exist. Each person turned her face to a corner where a small fire was burning. Added paper to it one piece at a time. Stirred the ashes with an iron poker to make sure no trace of any characters was left behind. The scene often made me think we were burning paper money in front of graves. Solemn faces, ghostly fires. And gray butterflies danced in a small whirlwind. Who were the dead? Why did we offer sacrifices to them? I did not know.

22

My First Love, a Big Mistake?

After I turned over all the keys and account books to Fang, I heaved a sigh of relief. For four years I had worked so hard on the pig farm trying to reform the world and reform myself. In the end I reaped the same punishment Chen got—Chen, a man I had originally come to combat. What an irony! But now I was glad all this was behind me.

I reported for duty to tractor number ten. Old Sui was the head of its crew. Li and Zhou were *shifu* (master workers). Xiang and I were assistants.

Old Sui was a veteran who had fought in the Korean War. To me, he did not look like a hero at all. He was a short and thin man in his late thirties. When he was at work, he seemed listless. Then I heard others say that he had a reputation of falling asleep as soon as his hands touched the operating levers. When his assistants woke him up, he would let them take over, find a place at the end of the field, and sleep there for hours.

Li and Zhou had both been Old Sui's assistants. Then they became *shifu*. They were both very kind to Xiang and me. Li was the one who knew our tractor thoroughly. Actually he knew the tractor much better than Old Sui. If there was a problem and we could not figure out what it was, we would go and find him. Sometimes he could tell us what was wrong by merely listening to it. It was a pleasure working with him. He was smart and dexterous. I always learned a lot from him. Yet sometimes I felt uncomfortable when I was with him. He was extremely cautious. Personal things, he bottled up completely. Other things, he did not want to talk about either. But all this was understandable. Although he was of the same age as us, he was not an educated youth. He was a *mangliu*—part of the unplanned influx of workers—who came from Sichuan province during the famine. Moreover, people said that his father was a landlord.

Zhou, our other *shifu*, was an educated youth from Beijing. In 1968 he had played Xiao Jiye. At that time, we chose him because he impressed us as warmhearted and enthusiastic, just like the hero himself. After that, the young people from the cities gradually ran out of songs and dances to perform and no one was in the mood to stage a new play. We all went our separate ways. I became so involved with the pig farm, I hardly ever thought of him.

Now we met again. Plenty of time to talk. Throughout summer, our job was to cultivate the soybean and corn fields. Each day was long. The sun was bright. Under white canvas awnings, the wind was nice and cool. Our tractor drove through the young crops. Black soil turned up. Weeds went down. I had the illusion of sailing on a boundless green ocean, endless waves rolling up in the wake of our boat.

Secretly I was rather curious about Zhou. I wanted to know, for example, why people said that his father had rather serious historical problems. But that question was too sensitive. I could not bring it up. In the meantime I suspected that since Zhou had read my diary he was curious about me too. But the diary, of course, he could not bring that up either. So we talked about other things.

I don't remember exactly what I told him about myself in that summer. Probably it had something to do with Aunty, Switzerland, and the big yard. In return he told me that there were six of them in his family. His father worked in a crane factory. His mother was a housewife. He was the oldest child. His three sisters were much younger and still in elementary and middle schools.

From our chat, I also found out that before he left Beijing, his family of six had only one room that was not very big. It was assigned to them by his father's work unit in the fifties. At that time, Zhou was the only child and he was small. So it was all right. Later when more children were born, the room became very crowded. So they built a small shack in front of it. The shack took away the yard and the sunshine in the room, but it gave them more space. Their neighbors did the same. Henceforth, by day the shack was their kitchen and at night it was Zhou's bedroom, until he left Beijing.

Zhou's father was a fourth-grade worker. He made fifty-four yuan a month. Of course the money was not enough to support a family of six. Thus the entire family spent numerous evenings making matchboxes for a nearby factory. (In China, a matchbox consisted of the box holding the matches, and its two-sided case.) First Zhou's family had to paste each part up separately, let them dry, then insert the box into the case. Everything was done by hand. And that was only one matchbox made.

Later when I visited his family in Beijing, I tried this myself. For an entire evening, all we made were some two hundred matchboxes. For each one hundred, the factory would pay them eight cents. So for an entire evening, all we made was less than twenty cents. In the end I was so frustrated that I thought I'd rather starve to death than do this. Even so, Zhou said, sometimes the factory had no work for them. Many other workers' families were equally poor. They also needed the money.

Hearing this, I did not know what to say. Suddenly I remembered that when I was small, in summer each day Mother would give me five cents to buy popsicles. I took this for granted. I thought it was no big deal. My classmates had money to buy popsicles too. Only after I talked to Zhou did I realize what a luxury it was. For Zhou's family, five cents meant sixty-three matchboxes. A soda that cost fifteen cents was equal to almost two hundred matchboxes. Zhou and I, we grew up in the same city. Yet it seemed that we had lived in two different worlds.

Perhaps Zhou became sympathetic with me too, after he heard what my childhood was like. Or maybe he was just good-natured and it wasn't just me he was willing to help? Later as the weather grew colder, we had to work in two twelve-hour shifts to plow the land before it froze, to get it ready for spring sowing. This meant we had to eat our meals in the fields. Sometimes the food carried to us was not enough. When this happened, he let Xiang and me eat first. Sometimes the weather suddenly changed and we did not bring enough clothes, so he always gave up his jacket for us. He also had a good sense of humor. Seeing that we were exhausted, he would crack a joke or two to cheer us up. When we worked on the night shift, which was especially hard, he sometimes sent us back after midnight while he worked alone until dawn.

I really enjoyed working with Zhou. After all, he was so handsome. Since he played Xiao Jiye, he had grown leaner and yet stronger. At the age of twenty-four, he looked wonderful even in that bulky black jeans uniform. In those years, tractor drivers were called "greasy rats." Zhou was a greasy rat too. Yet somehow he was different from others. He was only slightly taller than an average man and his thick, black hair just a tiny bit longer. Under it, his eyebrows were black and straight. When he frowned, his eyes were still smiling and sparkling at you. I couldn't take my eyes off him, that is, of course, when nobody was watching me. Each time our eyes met, my heartbeat quickened.

Then it was November. One afternoon Zhou and I were assigned to plow a corn field that had just been harvested. Later the wind grew bone-piercing cold and freezing rain began to fall. The ground turned into mud. Mixed with stalks and roots, the mud clogged our plows. Whenever this happened, Zhou grabbed a poker and his greasy cotton-padded jacket and jumped out to prize the mud chunks off the plows. The job he gave me, in the meantime, was to raise, lower, and turn the plows from the cabin. After a while his jacket was wet through and his slacks and shoes were soaked. Seeing that his lips had lost color and his teeth were chattering, I argued with him, saying we ought to take turns to do this. But Zhou said I should do what he said since he was *shifu*, besides "Two drowned rats are no better than one." Thus saying he smiled and we continued to plow the corn field. But the next day, he was sick.

Old Sui said that Zhou had a fever. The fever did not go away for three days. In those three days, I could not think of anything else but Zhou's illness. I wondered how serious it was and whether he had gotten the right medicine. (Over the years Chen had taught me a great deal about medicine, Western as well as traditional. When the kids in our village got sick, their parents sometimes took them to see me instead of the barefoot doctor. I gave them advice, as well as medicine, which included shots of antibiotics. Looking back on it, I think we were really lucky that nothing went wrong. What if someone had died from those shots? But on the other hand, someone might have died of the illnesses too. Who knows?)

When Zhou was sick, I wanted to see him and give him some medicine. But I did not dare go to his dormitory room, which he shared with nine other men. I was afraid of rumors. Rumors, at that time, were flying all over the sky like the snow that had just begun to fall.

By 1972, the leaders in the Great Northern Wilderness finally realized that the best way to make the educated youths take roots was to allow them to fall in love, get married, and have children. For after that, it would be almost impossible for them to return to the cities. So overnight the red light changed into a green one. After the leaders gave tacit consent, some educated youths quietly paired up. Others were resisting the change.

By this time, most of us were already in our early or mid-twenties. The biological clocks in us were ticking. Convention added pressure on us. "When a man grows up, he ought to take a wife. When a maiden is of age, she should marry." At Cold Spring rumors mushroomed three times a day, providing tasty, juicy topics for gossip. The parties concerned invariably denied that they were in love. Some were just shy. Others were telling the truth. Nobody knew which was which.

So just as I was sitting there thinking of Zhou and hoping that I would run into him at the dining hall during the next meal, my three friends Fang, Liya, and Song showed up. When they told me to confess if I had fallen in love with someone, I was very embarrassed. Then I found out that they were talking about Wen and me. Obviously somebody had created another rumor.

Secretly I heaved a sigh of relief and said, "No way! We were friends, but definitely not that kind of friends!"

I tried my best to explain that Wen and I were just schoolmates who had borrowed books from each other. Sometimes we also talked, but the topics were never personal. No matter what I said, my friends continued to look at me in a very weird way.

If I could not even convince my bosom friends, how could I convince others in the village? Here people believed that a good marriage was between a couple whose families were well matched in social and economic status. To many of them, Wen and I were just like that. Our parents were all professors. We were both from 101 . . . But I believed that such a well-matched couple would bore each other to death. When they looked at each other, it was as if they were looking at themselves in a mirror. The idea was not mine, though. I got it from a Russian novel.

If I were to have a boyfriend, I'd much prefer him to be very different from me. But of course I don't want to have a boyfriend, because I don't want to jump into the trap: get married and have kids, settle down here, and be a slave for the rest of my life . . . Therefore the "if" does not mean anything.

Despite the decision, that evening I was at Old Sui's home. After I chatted with him and his wife, Jiang, for a long time and had their four kids crawl all over me, I finally screwed up enough courage to ask Jiang if she could please bring some medicine to Zhou for me. Hearing this, she narrowed her eyes and looked at me with a small smile, as if she were trying to figure out something. I was thoroughly embarrassed. At last she said something.

"All right. Xiang has asked me to send him medicine too. I might as well take yours. The two of you are both very good to your *shifu*. Aren't you?"

So I gave her the medicine and fled. That night, I kept wondering whose medicine Zhou was going to take. When he recovered, the answer seemed clear. He deliberately avoided me. He was talking with Xiang. The two of them looked very happy together.

By this time the ground was frozen. All six tractors stayed put in the village. Days were short. No more night shifts. In the garage all crew members worked together on repairs and maintenances. I took this opportunity to learn from Li about the tractor. While I did this, somehow I was acutely aware of Zhou's presence. I did not look at him. Yet I saw him. I did not listen to him. Yet all I heard was his voice. Then the idea dawned on me: maybe I should somehow let him know that the gossip about Wen and me was groundless. In a fortnight the idea became irresistible. So I told Zhou.

From then on, Zhou and I became inseparable. That is, our hearts were inseparable. In reality, we hardly had any opportunity to be together. By day, in front of so many eyes, all we could do was to exchange a few quick glances. We did not dare talk, even less touch hands. In the evenings, we had no place to go. In the dormitories there was no privacy. The dining hall was out of the question. Other places such as our tractor or the garage had no fire. When the temperature dropped to thirty, forty degrees below zero, we were freezing in each other's arms in less than twenty minutes. Then we had to run back to the dormitories to embrace the fire walls.

When I was back in the dorm, my thoughts were still with Zhou. So I knitted woolen socks for him. I would have knitted a woolen sweater for him, but I did not have enough money to buy the yarn. Before that, my hands had never touched a needle. Nor did I know how to use a sewing machine. All these skills I learned from Jiang, at Old Sui's home. Jiang watched me with a knowing smile when I mended Zhou's clothes for him. Her smile always made me blush. But I was grateful to her anyway.

As for Zhou, he made a sickle for me. For the handle he used Huangyang wood, which was both lightweight and sturdy. It was the best material available in this region. With tools that he borrowed from the carpenter he cut the wood, shaped it, designed the length, the curve, and the grip size especially for me. The blade was made by a renowned blacksmith who lived more than twenty miles away. It took Zhou a whole day to get there and come back.

Later when I used this sickle to cut soybeans in the snow, it made a world of difference from the ones I had used before. Perhaps only people who've cut soybeans for eight or nine consecutive hours, and know the pain this endlessly repeated motion causes in backs and arms, could understand why I was so touched and why I treasured this gift of his so much.

So this was how Zhou and I expressed our love for each other. Woolen socks and a sickle. No roses. No serenades. Yet I had no complaints, for we were much luckier than young people from real peasant families in this region. According to the local custom that was abolished in the fifties but came back in the early seventies, a man's family must give betrothal gifts to the parents of his future wife. Usually this would amount to some two thousand yuan, a very large sum at the time. This practice drove a young man in a nearby village crazy.

I heard the story from Huar, who had been released from the cow shed in the fall. This man was in love with a woman in his village. But because his family was poor, he was unable to raise the sum her family had demanded. So they gave him a period of time, to make the money or borrow it. He tried, but when the time was up he was still short. Thus her family married her to someone else who could pay. This broke his heart. Subsequently he lost his mind. When I heard this story I felt so sad, because by then I was in love with Zhou. I knew how the young man might have felt and wondered about the young woman as well.

Compared with such a tragedy, Zhou and I were fortunate. Yet our relationship had problems almost from the start. The first problem was his father's history. If it was too hard to talk about earlier, we must face it now. In the seventies, one's family background was of such importance that often it alone decided the person's fate.

Zhou told me that his father had been an officer in the Nationalist army before 1949. He was originally trained as a radio technician in a civilian school. Shortly after he graduated, the Japanese came. So he joined the army because he hated the invaders and wanted to drive them out of China. Hearing this, I felt that his father did pretty much the same thing my father did. Only my father joined the Communist army and his father the Nationalist one.

During the war, Zhou said, his father and the radio communication crew he led were stationed in Guizhou and Yunnan in southwest China. There he fell in love with a young woman who was of a different race. She was a Bai. Not a Han. Nevertheless they got married. She left her hometown and went with her husband to many places in China. Because of the ongoing wars, everything was hard. But she made their home comfortable through her diligence, frugality, and love. One year after they were married, they had a son. The child died at the age of five from a wound after a firecracker exploded in his hand. His death nearly broke his mother's heart, and it was then that Zhou came into this world.

Later I learned from Zhou that his father had a chance to join the Communist army in 1949. By then radio technicians were badly needed. So his father was offered a position comparable to his old one, but he turned it down. When I heard this, I was appalled. I responded instinctively.

"Your father is really a big reactionary!"

Zhou turned pale. Gazing at me, he opened his mouth to say something but no word came out. Then he shut his mouth and turned his head away. After a very long and awkward silence, he explained the situation to me: if his father accepted the offer, he would have to fight against the remaining Nationalist troops in the south. He did not feel he could do it. As a result, he lost everything: his career, social status, money, friends . . .

"Otherwise he would have been a revolutionary cadre too." After a while, Zhou said this with a sigh. Did he feel his father had made a mistake? Did he hate him for that? I did! Partly because of the education I had received in the past twenty-one years, I thought all Nationalists were villains and criminals. There was nothing wrong in killing them. But more important to me was what he did to Zhou. It was all his fault that Zhou's life was so hard ever since he was born. Everything was messed up.

But was it really his fault? Years later I came to change my opinion about Zhou's father. He turned down the offer because he had loyalty and feelings. Thus he would rather give up his rank and career than turn around and kill people who had been his comrades yesterday. Or maybe he did not know that by turning the offer down he would lose his career once and for all? He thought, as a good technician he could find jobs elsewhere. He was wrong. In the field of radio communication, after 1949 who dared hire someone like him who had serious historical problems? What if he wanted to use the radio to contact Taiwan and do espionage? So in the fifties, he went as far as Inner Mongolia trying to find a professional job. Failing that, eventually he returned to Beijing, his hometown, and became a worker who made a living by "selling his physical strength."

Aside from his father, our future was another topic on which we could not reach any agreement. In my opinion, it was simple. The best solution for us was to commit suicide together. Cut our wrists, take poison, walk out of the village in a blizzard . . . Any way he preferred would be fine for me. I did not suggest this on the spur of the moment. I had thought the whole thing through.

Right now, Zhou and I are both young and healthy. Our love is pure and passionate. It has nothing to do with money or any other worldly concerns. It is beautiful. Almost perfect. From here, it could only go downhill. Especially in a world like this, which is filled with injustice, cruelty, deceit, and mistrust. In such a world, after thirty or forty years of hard labor and misery, what are we going to get in the end? We still have to die. Only by then perhaps our love has died a long time ago.

When Zhou heard my argument, he thought about it for a while. Then he shook his head and said: "No, I can't do this. If I die, my mother cannot live. I can't break her heart and kill her like that."

Hearing this, I was a little disappointed. But I couldn't blame him. My idea was definitely out of the ordinary. I knew it. And unlike me, Zhou was a normal, sensible person. Perhaps that was why when my three female friends heard my confession, they spoke almost simultaneously.

"You two are not the same type of person at all!"

"You have nothing in common!"

"This is a big mistake!"

I know Zhou and I are different. I love him because he is different! While I grew up in comfort and privileges, he was born in poverty, grew up in discrimination. Life has been so unfair to him! Unlike me who is guilty, he has done nothing wrong. Simply because he was born from the wrong parents, despite all the good qualities he has and all the efforts he has made, he has been left out and looked down on. No opportunities. No future. Not even much sympathy from others. Is he angry? I am!

So maybe I loved Zhou because I imagined there was a rebel in him, despite the problems I had with his father's history. Yet when I tried to find that rebel, I did not see a trace of it. All Zhou wanted after we became lovers was to marry and settle down. I knew I'd like to marry him, but settling down in the Great Northern Wilderness was probably the last thing in the world I wanted to do. I tried to explain this to Zhou. He could not understand.

"Look at the poor and lower-middle peasants here. If they can live like this, why can't we? Everybody is a human being. With two eyes and one nose. Didn't you hear the local people say a person can enjoy all kinds of comforts as well as endure all kinds of hardships?"

Seeing that he hadn't convinced me, he tried a different approach. Quoting Chairman Mao and the newspaper editorials, he told me taking roots in the countryside was the right thing for an educated youth to do. That really irritated me! Gazing at him intently, I could not tell if he was sincere or merely using such propaganda to hook me. In one case he would be a simpleton—just a *shun min* (submissive subject)—and in the other a hypocrite.

He is not a hypocrite. No, I don't think so. But is it possible that he is so naive that he let himself be brainwashed by such propaganda? Maybe he is just more realistic? In his mind, if the leaders have declared that they will never let us go back, then we ought to think about how to settle down here. Why trouble ourselves with something impossible?

Anyway it seems that my friends are right. He and I are indeed different. I am a rebel at heart. He is not. He is a shun min. Obey the authority. Kowtow to power. Believe the lies wholeheartedly. Submit himself to maltreatment. Be patient and cheerful under oppression and exploitation. Dignity? Maybe he can live without it. I can't! Without dignity or any possibility to assert my free will, I'd rather die!

But this was rather unfair to Zhou. I had such thoughts because what he said upset me. I could understand that for him perhaps life in the Great Northern Wilderness was not so bad, since his childhood in Beijing was even more difficult. Now at least he could support himself as well as send ten yuan each month back to Beijing to help his family. He was quite happy with what he got. But I was not.

Come to think of it, perhaps in China there have always been two types of people. The majority obey the authority under normal circumstances, because survival is the most important thing for them. Only a small group of people, often those who are privileged, can afford to raise questions, challenge and defy authority. My father used to belong to this group. I belong to this group too, maybe? I can't help it that I am who I am, even though I know such an attitude can only get me into more trouble.

"In Rome, do as the Romans do." Why couldn't I live as peasants did and as Zhou hoped to? I was not lazy. I could eat bitter—endure hardship. But when I looked at Old Sui, Jiang, and their four kids, the word Yes died in my throat. If Zhou and I settle down, we will be just like them. Jiang is my example. Zhou will be another Old Sui in fourteen years. The thought made me shudder.

In fact, I was awfully grateful for Old Sui and Jiang, who were so kind to us. Seeing that Zhou and I had no place to go, they invited us to dinner almost every other night that winter so that afterwards we could stay and chat. Of course, in that situation, nobody had privacy. Zhou and Old Sui would sit on one end of the *kang,* Jiang and I on the other. The kids crawled back and forth, up and down. But at least we could watch each other, while being watched by Old Sui and Jiang.

Did we remind them of what they used to be fourteen years before? At that time, I heard, Jiang was one of the prettiest and liveliest young women in this village. Several young men were in love with her. But in the end she married Old Sui. No betrothal gifts and matchmakers. It was her decision as well as his. So they were equal, at least by then. Both were state employees. Both were young, industrious, and frugal.

Then there was the famine and Jiang lost her iron rice bowl. She became a "stinking dependent." Old Sui still had the privilege to fall asleep at work. He did so, I concluded later, not because he was lazy or shameless. With four kids and little money, he had so much to do at home: carry water from the well, cut firewood, make hay, stack up stalks, grow vegetables in a garden plot, feed their own pigs, remove the manure from the sty and the ash from the *kang,* pick up soybeans, and dig potatoes from the fields already harvested, keep the storage shacks in good repair . . .

Bogged down and worn out by the work, sometimes Old Sui vented his frustration on Jiang, calling her names or accusing her of loving someone else. This Zhou and I saw with our own eyes. Others said he also beat his wife. We didn't see that. But the worst was yet to come. Next spring, Old Sui was diagnosed as having cancer. The subsequent treatment at Mishan City some one hundred miles away was long and painful. Despite free health service, the travel alone made the family run into debt.

While Old Sui was in the hospital fighting for his life, Zhou and I tried our best to help Jiang, who was terribly worried and overwhelmed by the work. Now she had to take care of the four kids by herself. Meanwhile she continued to work in the fields, for that was the only way she got paid. In fact, she herself was sick too. She had rheumatoid arthritis, gynecological diseases, and a severe back problem. But since "dependents" had no health insurance, she could not afford to take sick leave, see a doctor, or buy medicine.

When she came back from the fields, she had to cook, wash dishes, wash and mend clothes, repair shoes . . . She was so busy that she often forgot to comb her hair or wash her face. Seeing Jiang and other "stinking dependents," I saw myself in the future. Educated youths? As long as we were women, the state might dump us just as it did Jiang and others. Such a prospect frightened me. I did not want to jump into such a pit! So how could I tell Zhou I would marry him? I had made a big mistake coming to the Great Northern Wilderness. At this juncture, if I erred again, I knew that would seal my fate. Afterwards no one could help me anymore.

On the other hand, it pained my heart to see Zhou suffer. Since he became my boyfriend, all I gave him was frustration and heartache. As a result, he lost weight as well as his sense of humor. Sometimes he tried to smile, but his eyes were so sad. When I saw them, I wanted to cry.

Because of his father's historical problem and his own experience in the past, Zhou was a lot more sensitive than I. He probably knew that some people were gossiping about him in the village. At first they refused to believe and later some of them did not seem to like the fact that Zhou and I were lovers. They called him Julien, the hero of *The Red and the Black,* Stendhal's masterpiece.

That is really unfair! Zhou is no Julien. He knows my family has declined and hit rock bottom; my parents have neither power nor money. He became my boyfriend only after I told him that. But what he knows, others don't. He is too proud to explain. They won't believe him anyway. So now they are waiting to see him get ditched and then laugh at him.

Why are these people so vicious? Zhou hasn't offended any of them. Maybe for them, Zhou belongs to a lower caste by birth, and he should know his place? And according to that theory, once I marry Zhou, I should know my place too. I am no longer the daughter of an old revolutionary, but the daughter-in-law of a Nationalist officer and my children are the grandchildren of . . .

My first love opened my eyes. It made me see traps in the ground, webs in the sky, poison in sweet chitchat, daggers in hearts. At night, I spent a lot of time rereading Cao Xueqin's *Dream of the Red Mansion.* I began to understand why in the novel when Lin Meimei and Baoyu are in love they cry, fall sick, go mad, and die. The two of them love each other deeply. All they wish is to be together the rest of their lives. Despite the wish, there is not a single thing they can do. Everything they do backfires. Every word they say wounds the other in the heart. Tradition and politics. Hypocrisy and jealousy. Lovers' blood and tears. This is China, traditional as well as contemporary. People are caught in situations where the will is so strong that it can melt metal, but there is absolutely no way. Love is impossible! Life is impossible!

Like the heroine in the novel, by the summer of 1973 I found that unless I would lie, I had run out of things to say to Zhou to cheer him up. So one evening I said to him:

"Zhou. I cannot marry you. Our love is a mistake! You ought to marry Xiang. I know she wants to marry you."

"No! I don't love her at all! I love you! How can you say such a thing?"

Not knowing what to say, I began to cry. Once I started, I couldn't stop. I felt that between heaven and earth there was nothing but sadness! Boundless sadness! My heart sank to the bottom of a bitter ocean. *Shang xin* literally means hurt heart. This is the Chinese word for sadness. *Shang xin* was what I felt. My heart was wounded. It was bleeding. Zhou tried to console me. He couldn't. After a while, he held me in his arms and we cried together. So many bitter tears had been dammed up in us, when they burst the dikes, nothing could stop them. Before that I had never cried as hysterically as that; nor did I afterwards. As for Zhou, that was the only time I saw him cry.

That evening I reflected about our situation and talked to myself:

—*Do you love him?*

—*Of course I do!*

—*You shouldn't love him, if you won't marry him.*

—*But I can't help it. He can't help it either. We just fell in love with each other.*

—*Then why won't you marry him? After all, this is new China. No more arranged marriages. Unlike the lovers in the novel, you two can be together for the rest of your lives, that is, if you change your mind and say Yes. Then instead of hurting him, you can make him happy.*

—*Can I? I mean, if I'm miserable, can I still make him happy?*

—*Who knows? Maybe.*

—*All right. If I am willing to die with him, I guess I can try to live for him. Sacrifice myself to make his dream come true. Well, for me it's hardly a sacrifice, as I'm already done for. Also we do love each other. But why on earth is our love so bitter, so difficult? Love should be as sweet as honey . . .*

With such thoughts churning in my head, I decided to write a letter to my parents. In this letter, no more slogans and lies. I told them I wanted to leave this place for good. And I asked them if there was a way they might help me. If not, fine. I told them I was in love with Zhou and I would marry him. We would take roots here.

This letter was very short and abrupt. In it I made no attempt to explain. Either my parents would understand or they would not. I just wanted to find out about my destiny. Thus sending out such a letter was like playing Russian roulette. I had pulled the trigger. I waited for the blast.

The blast came eleven days later. It was a letter from Father. In it, he said that both he and Mother were surprised by some of the things I said in my letter. But in his opinion, I made the right decision to take roots in the countryside. Educated youths should . . . As for my marriage, he said that he and Mother would respect my choice. The decision was entirely up to me. Yet he wondered why I was in such a hurry. At the age of twenty-two, I might want to wait another year or two.

So they would not understand. I knew it! I knew it all the time! Yet I had been unwilling to believe there was no hope. Now I could no longer doubt.

I did not tell Zhou when I wrote this letter to my parents. Now I decided to tell him about it. I thought I would do so that evening. But when evening came, I felt sick. I had lost my appetite and ate nothing during the day. Once I came back from work and lay down, I did not feel like getting up again. So I thought I might as well tell him the next day. The rest of my life had been determined. One or two days was no big deal.

The next day, however, before I had a chance to tell Zhou that I would marry him, a telegram arrived. It was from Father. It was very short. Five Chinese characters read: "Mother Badly Ill, Return Quickly."

I received the telegram from Yan. As political instructor, he was always the first to read everybody's telegrams. So I asked him if I would be allowed to take a home leave, which was overdue in my case. But he said no; the regiment had just issued a notice that said because the wheat harvest was about to begin, unless an educated youth's parent was critically ill, she or he would not be allowed to go home.

So that night, I had no other choice but to write my parents another letter. But it turned out that they didn't need it. Three days later (before my second letter could possibly reach them), another telegram came from Father. This time it read, "Mother Critically Ill, Return Quickly."

Now Yan said the leaders would consider my request. The word he used was *yan jiu*. Everybody in China knew that *yan jiu* could take days, months, and in some cases even years. But what could I do? I could only wait and wonder what my parents were up to. Was Mother really ill? That possibility could not be ruled out. Yet it was also possible that my parents had figured out a way to help me.

Fearing the worst and hoping for the best, I almost hated Father for giving me no clue in the telegrams. But of course I couldn't blame him for that. In those days, everybody knew that telegrams were "public secrets."

Two more days passed. I went to see Yan again. This time he told me that the leaders had decided to let me have a home leave. Hearing this, secretly I was overjoyed. But at that moment, another telegram arrived. When Yan read it, I noticed a sudden change in his countenance. After a moment's silence, he let me read the telegram. It was from Father again. This time it said: "Mother Died. Return Quickly."

Soon everybody in the village heard about my misfortune. People came to offer their condolences. I was awfully embarrassed. For I did not know if I deserved such condolences or not. Nor did I know if I should cry or laugh. Of course, I couldn't laugh. And I was unable to cry. I would feel very bad, if it turned out that I was cheating these people who were so kind to me. I would feel even worse though, if I was not cheating them. The best solution, I decided, was to run away from all this. So I began to pack. Fang, Liya, and Old Song helped me.

That night Zhou walked with me to the nearest train station. It was ten miles away. We had to walk through a swamp. The wind was very strong. The tall grass stooped and then it struggled to stand up. Wolves were howling in the distance. A crescent moon sailed through mountains of clouds. The world around us was dim at one moment, bright the next.

The wind is howling *hsiao-hsiao;*
the water of Yi River is cold.
The hero, once departed, will never come back.

Five years had passed. The girl who had dreamed of being a hero was no more. A young woman who had her name was running away from a battle that had become meaningless to her. The dream died. She felt empty inside. Would the moon be dim or bright for her tomorrow night and the night after at a different place? When would she and her lover be under the same moon again?

Before the train left, Zhou told me that I should try my best to convince my parents so that they would help me find a way to leave this place. But as this was very difficult, he would wait for me here for three years. In that period of time, if I felt I couldn't do it, I could always come back and he would marry me. He did not care what kind of punishment the leaders might want to impose on me. When the train began to move, he pressed a ten yuan note into my hand and told me to take good care of myself. Then he turned to walk back, another ten miles through the swamp, this time all by himself.

Sitting alone in a dark, empty train, watching the moon fly, I thought of the five years I had spent on the Great Northern Wilderness. From seventeen to twenty-two, these were the best years in my life. Tons of sweat. Buckets of tears. I felt cheated. I was angry. Yet in the meantime, I also felt guilty as if I were a deserter. I had jumped off a sinking ship, leaving my friends and my lover behind. And the poor peasants who had been so kind to me, I had left them behind too.

The day I die, I will probably feel like this, should my soul continue to exist. Come with a naked body. Depart with two empty hands. Everything I've cared about and invested in during my lifetime I leave behind. Love, friendship, ambitions, guilt, hatred. All kinds of relationships turned to rainbows and clouds of yesterday. This life is done for. The next is yet unknown. The loss is devastating. The uncertainty is overwhelming. Yet at this moment, I am quite free.

23

What Have I Lost? What Have I Gained?

When I got home, Mother rushed out to meet me. Her face was still yellow and swollen. But at that moment it was lit up by joy, overflowing with love. She looked like a mother who welcomes home her dear little girl, lost in an enchanted forest for three days. Seeing Mother like that, I was moved as well as relieved. Then Father told me what had happened on their end.

According to Father, the message I was trying to send in my short letter went straight past him, even though in our family he had been known as the more sensitive parent. Taking it for an ordinary letter, he promptly wrote back, using the same old official language I'd come to hate. Mother, on the other hand, was disturbed. She kept thinking about my letter. And then one day she knew I was in trouble. Big trouble.

So she said to Father, "Listen! Rae is in trouble! You know what a stubborn child she is. Before this, she never complained about the Great Northern Wilderness. Instead, she kept telling us she was doing just fine. Proud as she is, she'd never go back on her word and ask us for help, if things hadn't gone terribly wrong for her! She needs our help! She is desperate! She wrote us this letter as a last resort!"

That made a lot of sense to Father. Suddenly he was very worried too. So they took immediate action. The telegrams were all Mother's ideas. Father merely carried them out. The third time he went to the local post office, all the workers stopped what they were doing. They came out from behind the counter, shook Father's hands, and offered him condolences. That caught him by surprise and he was terribly embarrassed too.

By that time, my parents' cadre school had been at the county seat of Ji for over a year. In such a small town, everybody knew everybody. And because Mother went to the post office all the time to mail letters and parcels to her three children, people there knew her very well. After that, Mother no longer dared set foot in the place. She said she did not want to scare those kindhearted postal workers and make them think they had seen a ghost in broad daylight.

Although both Father and I thought Mother went a bit too far by writing that third telegram, I was really touched. Mother! Who would have thought she was the only person who understood me at the most difficult and crucial moment in my life? That made me think I'd been unfair to her in the past. For didn't I conclude that she could only echo Father's opinions and the two of us could never talk and see eye to eye? I was truly glad to find that I had been wrong.

Therefore things were not as bad as I had feared, and less good than I had hoped. My parents called me back because they were worried about me. But neither of them had the vaguest idea how in the future they might transfer my *hukou* back from the Great Northern Wilderness.

"Just forget the *hukou* for now!" Father said. "If your mother and I have things to eat, you won't starve. Your biggest problem is not *hukou,* but your age! You are twenty-two years old, but you haven't even finished junior middle school. Time is running out for you. If you don't start getting some kind of education immediately, soon it will be too late!"

"But the good thing is," he continued, "nowadays neither of us has much to do. We are not allowed to leave. We are not interested in making furniture or raising hens as some people here are. From now on, we'll teach you English. Two professors. One student. Who ever heard of such a ratio? Our success is almost guaranteed, that is, if you can concentrate on your studies."

Mother and I were not entirely convinced. But we went along with the plan, because we had no better alternatives. Thus in the next two and a half years I followed a rather rigorous schedule: get up at six, jog for half an hour, memorize and review vocabulary for one hour. After breakfast, work on grammar and texts with Father for three hours. In the afternoons, go over conversation and exercises with Mother for another three hours. In the evenings, either practice calligraphy or listen to a special program by Voice of America called "900 Sentences," which was not jammed in that part of the country.

My favorite activity was our daily walk at dusk. After supper we usually walked on the remains of an ancient city wall, which might date back to the Three Kingdoms period (A.D. 220–280). At that time Ji was the stronghold of Yuan Shao, the most powerful warlord in China. The city wall must have been tall and thick, the moat around it deep and formidable. But the warlord was defeated by his opponent Cao Cao and died spitting blood. Since then, the city wall had fallen into ruin and the moat was flattened. Now on both sides of the wall winter wheat grew, thin and short because of constant drought.

This place, my parents discovered, was ideal for people to talk. At home they did not dare to. Even with windows closed and doors shut, the walls had ears. That is, they thought the neighbors were eavesdropping on them. Some became my parents' enemies at the beginning of the Cultural Revolution. Espionage was these people's specialty anyway. World-class espionage.

But my parents were no fools. Thus they discovered the city wall, on which they could say things as loud as they liked. Usually the wall was deserted. In case someone came, they could see the person from the top of the wall long before he or she was within earshot. The moment I got there, I poured out what had been on my mind these couple of years.

"You know what? The campaign of educated youths going to the countryside has become a tremendous waste and unprecedented human tragedy! Nevertheless I did learn a few things from it, things the leaders may not have anticipated. For example, now I agree with Chairman Mao that class struggle continues to exist in China under socialist conditions—but not between landlords and poor peasants or capitalists and workers. It goes on between Communist Party officials and the ordinary Chinese people! The officials at all levels abuse their power. The corrupt ones as well as those who are not so corrupt yet. As for the Party, it has been blocking information and creating lies. By doing so, it made us into idiots and clowns! But now I can see it in its true light and I have lost faith in it! Over the years it has been purging those who are honest, intelligent, and dare take responsibility. Those who survive the incessant inner struggles are the mediocre and cowardly ones. As a result, you see nowadays more and more officials curry favors with their superiors and care nothing about the people! They are all hypocrites! . . ."

"Stop!" Mother said under her breath. "Your thoughts are very dangerous! How come you talk like a counterrevolutionary?"

I shut up. I had anticipated that my parents would be upset or furious. After all, they were both Communist Party members for many years. I wasn't trying to provoke them though. I just wanted to let them know what my reeducation in the countryside had taught me.

Father, on the other hand, remained calm and silent. A trace of smile in his eyes? That could be just my imagination. It was not until several days later when Father and I walked by ourselves on the city wall that he told me he agreed with much of what I had said the other day. In fact, even before 1949 in the liberated areas the Party leaders had already begun to abuse their power and the struggle within the Party was ruthless. If the problem then was like cancer incubating in the body of the Party, now the disease was full-blown.

As if to prove his point, he told me a story. It was about his first love. Later the story kept me wondering: if its outcome had been different, someone else would have been born in my place. What would she (or he) have been like? Would Father have liked that child better than me?

In 1942, when Father was a student at Furen University, he fell head over heels in love with a young woman whose name at first he did not want to reveal. Later I found it out anyway. (I will call her Lilac, which is not her real name.) At that time she was a college student too. Her father was a bank manager.

Their love met with disapproval from Father's grandfather, who thought Lilac's family was not wealthy enough. But the young lovers paid no attention to him. Soon they left Beijing. A few months later, they were together again at Jinchaji, a Communist base for guerrilla war against the Japanese invasion.

There they studied together at Huabei Lianda. They got engaged. The leaders and their fellow students congratulated them. When their wedding date drew near, however, Father was transferred to Yan'an and Lilac back to Beijing to do underground work. After that, the lovers lost touch. For three years, Father knew nothing about his fiancée's whereabouts. But the decision of the Party and the requirements of revolutionary work came before personal concerns, and so Father asked no questions.

At last in 1946 Father had a chance to go back to Beijing as a member of the Communist delegation to a peace talk. Soon he met an old friend who told him that she had attended a wedding where the bride's behavior was weird. At one moment she was laughing, and the next, crying. Throughout the entire ceremony, she was like that. The guests were made so uncomfortable that they left. The friend thought the bride was probably mentally ill.

By and by, Father realized that this weird bride was none other than Lilac, his fiancée. Agony filled his heart. Questions bombarded his mind. For days he could neither eat nor sleep. At last, he decided that he must see her, even though this meant he had to violate some rules for underground work.

And soon they met. Lilac told Father that the man she married was a high-ranking underground leader. At first she worked as his assistant. Then she was assigned the task of taking care of him as well. Eventually she was persuaded to marry him. The arguments the leaders used on her stressed the requirements of revolutionary work and the hope of the Party organization. As a Party member she should place the Party's cause above personal feelings. So after a while, she gave in. But afterwards no matter how hard she tried, she just could not make herself love her husband, who was a much older and rougher man. So she had been miserable ever since and her husband had no peace of mind, knowing that Lilac was unable to forget Father. Finally Lilac asked Father to forgive her and he did. After that, he never saw her again, even though later they lived in the same city and he knew exactly where she was.

"So you knew how false and selfish some of the leaders were! You knew it even in the forties, Father! Yet you kept telling me the Party was always right and I must do whatever it asked me to do! Why? Why didn't you tell me what you knew? Instead you let me grope in the dark, bump into walls, be scared to death, and make terrible, terrible mistakes!"

"Because I did not want you to get into trouble! Do you know what the famous artist Zheng Banqiao once said? 'It is a blessing to be dull-witted.' This is especially true today! On the other hand, of course, I did not want you to get *me* into trouble either. If I had told you I was disillusioned about this revolution a long time ago, and I thought with all our good intentions, relentless efforts, and tremendous sacrifice we only managed to build a gigantic prison as strong as cast-iron, and also I felt maybe I made a mistake by joining the revolution, because the proletarian dictatorship was worse than the corrupt rule of the Nationalist government . . . If I had said all this to you back in the sixties when you were a fanatic Red Guard, how would you have responded? Would you have reported me and condemned me? Or if you didn't, on the other hand, how would you have felt? I did not want to put you into such a dilemma!"

He was right. I had to admit it. In 1967, without his confession, my mind was already in a turmoil. If he had told me all this, I might have become another Zhang Heihei. In fact, even in 1973 there were things Father and I could talk about, but we would not discuss them in front of Mother. Mother belonged to a generation that came of age in the fifties. For many of them, the Nationalist Party was corrupt to the core and the Communist Party was the savior of China. Many of them were the so-called Three-Door Cadres—they went from home door to school door, then to the doors of government organizations. Thanks to their privileged positions and limited scope, the harsh reality in China did not seem to strike them as hard. Or maybe they thought and felt that way because of fear, which had been driven home by the anti-Rightist campaign and the Cultural Revolution. Thus they not only obeyed authority, they identified themselves with it. There was a big generation gap between them and us.

Between Father and me, for some reason, there was no generation gap. So we could talk rather freely. Sometimes the subjects grew quite personal. Once I was shocked to hear Father say that marrying Mother was a big mistake he made. He realized this soon after he made the proposal. His personality and Mother's were incompatible. But he married her anyway, out of a sense of honor and despair, thinking he'd never be able to find the woman of his dreams. Afterwards, he said, he was quite unhappy and wanted to have a divorce. But he decided against it, mainly for the sake of us. It was also for Mother, he said, for he knew she loved him still and did not want a divorce. In China, divorce always did more harm to women than men.

Though shocked at first, I knew what Father said was true. I could see the huge differences between him and Mother. Father's talk reminded me of the stormy years, when I was a little girl. The frightful, loud quarrels that erupted in the middle of the night. I woke up. I heard them yell in the next room.

"I can't stand this anymore! Let's have a divorce!"

"All right! Divorce! Divorce! Go ahead! I can't stand this either!"

So I was the result of a mistake Father had made many years ago. Then I became the shackle that held him in a loveless marriage. No wonder he used to get mad at me, beat me with a ruler on the palm, say I was a bad girl . . . After thirteen years, he finally apologized and I forgave him. My childhood wasn't so bad after all. Whether my parents loved each other or not, they both loved us. Then there was my dear old Aunty! She was my safe haven when a storm hit home. And there was Nainai too. What else could I ask?

So after I came back from the Great Northern Wilderness, I discovered that Father was quite different from what I had imagined. Our relationship changed. In the past five years I had grown up and Father realized this. So he began to treat me as an adult who was his equal. We became good friends. This was very rare in China. I enjoyed our talk in the evenings, on that dilapidated city wall. Watching the setting sun, I could feel his unspeakable loneliness in my own heart. I realized that he too was vulnerable, while in the past his prestige and authority had oppressed me.

My relation with Mother, on the other hand, was still stuck in difficulties, despite the excellent new start. This distressed me, for now I knew for sure Mother loved me. She was not the evil stepmother I had imagined. In fact, she'd do anything she could to help me succeed. Then why did we quarrel so frequently? Over such trifles as a mispronounced word or a wrong preposition, a dish that was too salty or a chicken I bought that was a bad bargain . . . Anything could trigger a row. Mother was a keg of gunpowder; I was a land mine. Neither of us seemed to have much control over our explosive temper.

Over the years I have been trying to figure this out. I know why I was so irritable, but I am not sure about Mother. For one thing, she was in poor health: menopause, high blood pressure, brittle bones, weak ankles, sleepless nights . . . Mother never complained about these. She endured the pain, and we did not know exactly what illnesses she had. The county seat of Ji did not have a real hospital. It only had a clinic. Two or three brick bungalows. Empty rooms. No lab, no X-ray or any other modern equipment.

Aside from poor health, Mother was in a bad mood. Unlike Father, Mother was ambitious and competitive. In the past, because of Father's glorious history as well as her own Party membership, superb education, and hard work, she was considered successful. Moreover, in the sixties, I was at 101 and Lian did well in elementary school, and she had been envied by other parents. But look at our family now: Mother and Father were stuck at cadre school. Their three children all faced uncertain futures. Among us, none was in the army; none could get into college. Failing that, we could not even find a job in a factory. If my brothers were still young, I certainly had failed her and vice versa, for in the seventies parents were supposed to help their children find back doors to those sought-after places. Mother was worried and ashamed, while Father was quite indifferent to what others might say about us.

As for me, I was equally worried and ashamed. In the past, I was a good student at 101, but that was seven years ago. Now I found it hard to concentrate on my studies, even though I wanted desperately to excel so as to prove to the world that I was no inferior, actually I was better, than those who had a chance to go to college.

Among the many distractions, the biggest one was probably the fact that I was still in love with Zhou. Even though I recognized that as long as the situation in China did not change, our love was hopeless. We would never be able to marry and live together. So what I should do was uproot my love for him, but the mere thought of it sent pangs through my body. I would burst into tears and lose sleep.

At night, I kept dreaming of him. It was strange that those dreams were so colorful, and they were filled with joy. No wonder people say that dreams are the exact opposite of reality. Under a violet sky, millions of gold flowers stretched to as far as the eye could see. Zhou and I were running and laughing, hand in hand. We were out of breath. But we did not want to stop. The wind began to blow. It gave us wings. We flew up. The world receded from us. Millions of stars revolved around us. The moon was round. It began to shine. I was so happy, I felt dizzy . . .

When I woke up, it was to darkness and I was alone. Zhou's caressing touches and warmth were a thousand miles away. The world around me was so empty, so cold. But the world around him was even colder. Though in his letters he never mentioned the difficulties he faced, how could I fail to see them? It was all my fault that he was having such a hard time.

Hukou was another thought that oppressed me day and night. Without it, I was an illegal resident in my native country. I had no right to work or go to school. No right to eat, wear clothes, or live at any place, even just as a visitor. So sometimes I really doubted the use of learning English at home, while my *hukou* was lost in the Great Northern Wilderness.

The children of others at this cadre school were probably thinking along the same line. So out of the twenty-odd young people who came back from the countryside to study foreign languages with their parents in the wake of Nixon's visit and China's restored membership in the United Nations, only two kept it up a few months later. I was one. The other was a man. After four years' study at home college, his English was excellent.

Mother was worried about my *hukou* too, because she was more practical than Father. At first, the two of us tried to persuade Father he should do something to get my *hukou* back. But each time we told him that, he would frown, shake his head, and say he had no idea how he might be able to do so. Besides, he would say, he believed the situation would change or else the country would perish; sooner or later a person who had proficiency in a particular field would find employment and be valued . . . It sounded fantastic, like a tale out of the *Arabian Nights*. But we'd better not count on it.

So after a while Mother and I gave up on him. We decided to take things into our own hands. But we did not know how to proceed either. One thing seemed clear though: we needed to find a back door. We had to find a person who was willing to help us. In addition, he must have the power to do so. We began to make inquiries. Meanwhile we made sure that our neighbors did not know what we were up to, fearing their efforts to "sabotage" our project.

A few months later we got a clue. Third Aunt said that she had a colleague who was from this area. His father was a retired county magistrate. This old man was not a Communist, however, or a Nationalist. He was a so-called Democratic Personage. At first, this did not sound very promising. But Mother said she'd give it a try anyway. "Doctor a dead horse as if it were still alive." So she prepared gifts, took the bus, and visited the old man at home.

At dusk, she came back utterly exhausted yet exuberant. Dropping into an armchair to massage her swollen legs, she told us that the old man was exactly the one we'd been looking for. He knew almost everybody in the local government, through work as well as family ties. Relatives, friends, old superiors and subordinates up and down and all over. As a "local snake," he had more power here than a fierce dragon from above.

A local snake? Later I visited the old man and found that he was actually very kind. It was not for our gifts that he helped us. He was sympathetic to us. But others were less decent, officials who had to stamp my return documents with the many seals they controlled. Even with the old man's help, Mother had to grease their palms and beg them for mercy. When her health deteriorated, I took over and Mother became my adviser.

Thus during the two years when I studied at home college, I actually had a double major. I took courses on dealing with officials and also studied English. By the time I got all the seals fixed on my documents, I had become a pretty good backdoor dealer.

Now I faced the ultimate test. I had to go back to Cold Spring to get my *hukou* back from Yan, who had been threatening all kinds of punishment since I failed to report back. I was confident that I could handle him. Instead of fear and anger, now I had knowledge that led to power. My knowledge boiled down to a few points.

To deal with officials, one must be patient and observant. In addition, one must be diplomatic and persuasive. But the most important thing is to remember that these officials are human beings, not gods. They may look intimidating, but they all have their soft spots and weaknesses. So one must deal with each of them accordingly. Use reason and appeal to move the honest ones. Back it up with connections, for even the honest officials did not want to offend their superiors and colleagues. As for the dishonest ones, bombard them with cannons and hand grenades. They would surrender. (In the seventies, people in China called cigarettes cannons and bottles of *baijiu* hand grenades. These were the most common gifts used to bribe officials.)

Thus I set off with the best quality "weapons" available to me at the time: Big China brand cigarettes and Maotai brand *baijiu.* I got them from a relative who had recently been released from Qincheng Prison. Though not formally rehabilitated, he got back some of the privileges, including the one to shop at some exclusive stores in Beijing.

When I arrived at the village, I decided that I had to treat Yan as a dishonest official. Otherwise he'd put on airs, give me lectures, and my mission was bound to fail. To put my best foot forward, I would give him the cigarettes. The brand was well known in China. In fact, it was a status symbol at the time, for only a small group of very high-level officials had access to it. I was quite sure that Yan had never tried such cigarettes before. So how could he resist the temptation? He could enjoy them or use them to impress others. If it was necessary, he could use them as gifts too.

That evening, I visited Yan at home. After some greetings, I took out two cartons of Big China cigarettes and put them on the *kang.* "These are some little gifts from my native place. Please accept them." With a smile, I pushed them toward him.

For a split second, he hesitated. I could see it. Then he put on his usual stern expression of a number-one leader and spoke.

"What are you doing? I can't accept these. Take them back!"

Of course, I couldn't take them back. Yet I couldn't insist that he accept them either. It was a very awkward moment. I tried to relax the atmosphere by giving the kids some candy, which was all right.

Just then, I heard someone knocking on the outer door. It turned out to be a group of educated youths. I was flustered. I felt like a thief who was seized with my hand in someone's pocket. I broke into a sweat and felt my cheeks burning. My mind went blank.

The educated youths came in and sat down. Yan smiled and exchanged greetings with them, as if nothing had happened. I managed some greetings too. Then I stole a glance down at the cigarettes, my worst nightmare. They were gone! Covered up by Yan with a quilt. Thank heaven! Thank earth! I'm saved! Soon I stood up, smiled, and bade them good night.

After that, everything was smooth sailing. Yan not only gave me all the green lights I needed for the return of my *hukou*, he even reimbursed me for the train tickets, including the ones I bought two years before. I was elated. I was triumphant. I knew that my *hukou* would go to Shijiazhuang, the capital city of Hebei province, as soon as I returned. For my parents were finally given jobs there. Next, we would fight our way back to Beijing, with cannons and hand grenades or whatever. With Father's *guanxi* and Mother's advice, with my own diligence and newly acquired insight, I could deal with officials big and small, up and down. A master key was in my mind. Henceforth anywhere I wanted to go, I could find a back door, open it, and get in. I would be fish in water in Chinese society.

Then I remembered Yuan, whom I had despised. *Now am I any better than her? Look at me! In order to achieve my goal, I am willing to do all sorts of despicable things: cry, smile, pretend to be naive or frank or angry or delighted, give honeyed words, use bribery . . . If I had known that someday I could become as base as this, I might as well have done what Yuan did and go straight back to Beijing. When I acquired this cursed knowledge about officials and congratulated myself, did I know what I lost? I lost my purity and the* zhiqi *Aunty taught me. Moral principles and dignity, I have given them all up. I'm changed beyond recognition. Once I reach this point, I can never go back. If this is the price I have to pay for getting on in the world, maybe it's not worth it. Yet if the society is a huge dye vat, can I or anybody come out of it as a piece of white cloth?*

Half a month later, I was ready to leave Cold Spring for good. Suddenly I found I was attached to it. I spent hours walking around, trying to remember everything. My friends did not share this sentiment of mine. They hated this place. Old Song was still as determined as before about not having a boyfriend. Liya, on the other hand, fell in love with a Shanghai youth. So she had a boyfriend for a couple of years. After he went to college, they broke up.

Fang sometimes joined me in my walks. She asked me to advise her if she should marry a peasant in a suburb of Shanghai called Chongming. This was her parents' idea. It was to help her go back. Yet Chongming was not Shanghai itself. And Fang hated to marry a total stranger. So we talked and talked, as I tried to figure out which was the lesser evil: stay here or marry the stranger. Finally I said to Fang that in my opinion she should marry the stranger, since she had declared she'd never love anybody here. And that was what she did.

After that Fang's *hukou* was transferred to Chongming where by and by she became a worker in a textile factory. In the eighties, she wrote me letters saying that since she was stuck in such a marriage and such a job, her only hope in this life was that someday her son would be happy and successful. When I read this, I blamed myself for making a wrong decision for my best friend. I had not anticipated that three and a half years later all educated youths would be allowed to return to their native cities. Fang might have been able to find a better job and a husband she could love in Shanghai.

As for my boyfriend, Zhou, what could he say except that he was glad for me? Maybe he was sincere; maybe not. It didn't matter. The love we had for each other didn't matter either. "Situations are always stronger than people's will." Our situations had decided that our love was no more than what the local people call "a lie flower." Blooming for a while. Then blown away by the wind, struck down by the rain. No fruit would grow out of it.

In fact the love of most educated youths at Cold Spring turned out that way. In 1979, when the educated youths went back in throngs, lovers said farewell, shed tears, and then went separate ways. Even those who came from the same cities broke up by and by. Some went on to college. Others became workers, shop attendants, or unemployed youths. In the village, we had been equal. In cities, we were not.

Zhou married Xiang a year after I left Cold Spring. Later when the majority of educated youths returned to the cities, they chose to stay. That finally convinced me that Zhou was sincere when he said taking roots in the countryside was, in his opinion, the right thing for an educated youth to do. By and by I lost touch with him, that is, after he told me that Xiang was not comfortable about our friendship. We stopped writing letters to each other.

Before I left Cold Spring, I felt uneasy seeing Jiang and Old Sui. They knew so much about what happened between Zhou and me. In the past, they had tried very hard to bring us together. Yet their efforts backfired. Their life was a painful eye-opener. How could I possibly tell them that? Furthermore, the plight of the family distressed me. Old Sui was not cured; yet the hospital released him, for there was little else they could do. When I visited him at home, he seemed resigned to his fate. Yet he worried about the four kids. Once he asked me, "What will happen to them when I die and Jiang remarries?" What could I say to answer that question?

Huar and her parents, Old Ji and Ji Daniang, gave me a farewell dinner. It had a happy start. But in the end when Huar said good-bye, tears welled up from her eyes. She cried for a long time, venting her anger and frustration. I had no words to comfort her. Any words from me would be hypocritical. I was leaving. She had to stay. Her talent was wasted. Her dream was shattered. In the past I had helped put that dream into her head. It was my dream too. I wanted to cry with her, but I did not dare, for fear that my tears would be crocodile tears.

In China, things were so unfair. (And they still are.) City people exploited the rural population, deprived them of almost all opportunities, and these people were not even grateful to the peasants! They took their privileged positions for granted; the positions were guaranteed by the *hukou* system. They truly believed they were superior to the peasants by birth. My generation was probably the only one that might know better because we had been peasants ourselves. Yet in recent years I have seen my peers forget what they had learned, when they blame the crimes and the lack of space in the cities on the peasants. I hope I will never forget what I was at Cold Spring and how I felt back then.

24

Epilogue

A week later, I was back home. My parents welcomed me as if I were a victorious Napoleon. Mother was so proud of me that she made me promise: in the future I would help my brothers out the same way. I agreed. Then we moved to Shijiazhuang, where I resumed my studies.

In December, my parents went back to Beijing to celebrate New Year with Lian, Yue, and Aunty. I stayed behind "to look after the house." By that time, of course, nothing in our house was worth a burglar's trouble. I said that because I wanted to save my parents the train fare. Meanwhile I would use the time to study on my own. The years I spent in the countryside made me believe that heaven would reward only those who behaved themselves. So I tried to behave myself and hoped that by so doing my parents would soon have good news for me. For Mother had said before she left that on this trip she would explore possibilities for all of us to go back to Beijing.

Ten days later, I received a telegram from Father. As before, it was very brief. It said, "Mother Died. Return Quickly." I was sure that Mother had discovered something and now she needed my help: a connection, a back door, some kind of opportunity . . . She is amazing! She is a genius! All right, Mother. I'm coming. Let's work on it!

I rushed back to Beijing, ready for action. But Mother was not there. Father told me that Mother had had a heart attack. She had died on the way to a hospital the day before. It was January 7, 1976. For a while, I could not believe the news. But Aunty and Father were both crying. Lian and Yue were crying too. Confused as I was, I had to believe his words.

Before long, I saw Mother in the hospital mortuary. I touched her face and her hand. She was cold and hard, like a rock. Her face was no longer swollen, but her eyes were closed forever. She would never see or hear us. I started to cry too.

The next several days, we wore black armbands to mourn for her. People in the streets looked at us and thought we were wearing them for Premier Zhou Enlai, who had died the day after my mother. That week, numerous people in Beijing shed tears for the premier. When we cried, people took it for granted that we were crying for him too. Poor Mother! While she was alive, her life was disrupted, her health destroyed, and her career went down the drain because of a so-called great revolution. When she died, even her death was overshadowed by that of a "beloved premier."

But that was not the worst. Half a month later Father began to talk about an old friend of his, a woman he got to know in 1948 after he and Lilac parted. She had been divorced a number of years ago. One month later, he married her. This shocked everybody but me. Knowing Father's frustration over the years and the fact that he could not love Mother, I could not blame him. Yet I did. The fact that he remarried only a month and a half after Mother died hurt me deeply.

How could he be so heartless? Are all men as heartless as this? After all, Mother loved him for twenty-seven years. She gave him three children and made all the sacrifices she could for him. In the end, what did she get in return? Nothing!

Suddenly I felt so sorry for Mother that I cried, alone, there in Shijiazhuang in our new home, which had been full of hope only a short while before. After Mother died and Father remarried, he moved to Tianjin. The house became empty and desolate, especially when the power went out. Sitting in front of a lone candle that was shedding waxen tears, I could not concentrate on my studies. My thoughts went back to Ji county, the Great Northern Wilderness, and my childhood in Beijing.

Father did not understand the letter I sent back asking for help and Mother did. That tells me who truly cared about me and who did not! Then there were the telegrams. Mother was the one who made them up. The peasants at Cold Spring would never do such a thing. They believed in the power of curses. The messages, they would say, were ominous—and they caused Mother to die.

What about Mother herself? Might she in any way credit such time-honored beliefs? Maybe not, since she was well educated and she said she was a materialist. Yet she was also a Chinese. In the past when I said that Lian would die before he reached the age of five, she trembled and her face turned white. I remember this vividly, because I was frightened by the sudden change in her. That shows perhaps she did believe in such things, even though she'd never admit it. Yet she sent out the telegrams to rescue me from the Great Northern Wilderness, while she was in such poor health. All because she was my mother and she loved me!

I want to tell her I love her too. But it's too late! In the past when she was alive, I did not even know I loved her. Nor did I ever try to talk to her so she and I might become friends as Father and I did. Mother was very lonely too. I knew it. Now come to think of it, didn't I secretly take pleasure in the fact that she and Father were estranged? When I came back to live with them, maybe I had made things even more difficult for her and that was why she quarreled with me constantly?

Now I want to tell her I am sorry. But she is gone. If I go to the ends of the world, I can't bring her back! In the past, I never held her hands, much less hugged or kissed her. Yet I took her for granted, assuming she'd always be there to help me out. When I first heard she was dead, wasn't I angry at her? As if I felt she had let me down. I can't believe I was so selfish! I was as heartless as Father, while Mother endured all the pain and never complained. She struggled for the survival of our family, until she literally dropped dead . . .

Mother's death hit Aunty even harder, a fact I had not anticipated. Their relationship in the past was ambivalent. On Aunty's side, there was the old grudge against my maternal grandparents who had tried to replace her with a Shanghai nurse. Later this grudge became a prejudice against almost everybody from Shanghai. As for Mother, she had been jealous of Aunty because of the love Lian, Yue, and I had for her, which we did not hesitate to display. So the two had been rivals for many years. Yet throughout the years they had also fought side by side to hold our family together. When Mother was alive, Aunty thrived on the secret rivalry. When Mother died, she began to crumble from the inside.

I could feel the change in her from one month to the next because of the mysterious tie between the two of us. Somehow the fighting spirit and confidence that had propped her up in the past several decades had dissipated. Without them, Aunty was weak and vulnerable. She needed support. I was the only one she could lean on. Lian and Yue were both too young. Father was in a different world, enjoying his belated and prolonged honeymoon. I had to get back to Beijing as quickly as possible. If I got there on time, I might be able to catch her in her fall and tide her over. I must save her! I could not afford to lose her as I did Mother! This time I knew danger was imminent. I was desperate. Day and night my heart was burning like a joss stick.

By then I had started working at a pharmaceutical factory in Shijiazhuang. I could no longer let Father support me, after he remarried. The factory I worked in was relatively modern, designed by the Soviet experts in the fifties. In 1976, although it employed seven thousand workers, it was still making good profit. The workers here wore white robes and sat in front of control panels. The workshops were sunny, with large windows and high ceilings. Thus in many ways, this factory was every Chinese worker's dream. Once I got in (through a back door, otherwise the factory would reject me because I was a woman), I lost no time negotiating a deal with a veteran who worked in Beijing.

This veteran's wife and children were peasants in Hebei province. For several years he had tried in vain to move their *hukou* into the capital. Failing that, he finally agreed to exchange positions with me. But before I could take over his Beijing *hukou*, of course I had to meet his numerous conditions. It took me two years to work the whole thing out.

In June 1978 I finally went through all the formalities and came back to Beijing as a legal, permanent resident. I moved into Aunty's house. But she was not there to welcome me. I was too late. Aunty had died earlier that year.

At first what she got was just a cold. A fortnight later it became pneumonia. She was hospitalized. I rushed back to Beijing to take care of her, for the situation in the hospital was chaotic. Patients who had no connections were neglected by doctors. Nurses declared they were too busy to take care of the critically ill so their family members had to live there and do part of the job, which turned out to be everything except giving injections.

Thus for a month, Lian and I took turns to look after Aunty in the hospital. Twelve hours at a stretch. One worked by day and the other at night. Yue was too small. Father was not available. There was no one else to relieve us. So Lian and I kept it up. The night shift was especially hard; we had to sleep on a concrete floor next to Aunty's bed, sharing a ward twenty feet by nine feet with two other patients and their family members. By day, despite our exhaustion and worries, we had to put on smiling faces to make friends among doctors and nurses.

This experience, trying as it was, finally brought Lian and me together. Around Aunty's sickbed, for the first time in my life, I felt I could love and trust Lian. In this huge world, among billions of people, I realized, there were things only the two of us could share, such as our love for Aunty and our memory of Mother. Our relationship was special. We were "from the same womb."

Besides, in those days we were like two soldiers fighting back to back, trying to fend off death, which had already cast dark shadows around our dear old Aunty. If one of us should collapse, the battle was lost. It was a matter of life and death! So much was at stake! This awareness finally put an end to the feud we had kept up for more than two decades.

When Aunty's condition was somewhat stabilized, she would not let me stay. The reason was the upcoming entrance examination for college, which had been suspended since 1966. Now the Cultural Revolution was over, anyone who wanted to take it could do so and the competition was expected to be fair. But in my case, I had to take this examination in Shijiazhuang where my *hukou* belonged. Staying in Beijing with Aunty, I would miss the opportunity.

"Rae! Go! Go! Don't you worry about me! I won't die. I have not brought up your children for you yet. I can't die before that! But now I want you to go and take that exam. Come back to Beijing as a college student! You hear me?"

She fixed her large, sunken eyes on me. In those eyes the love was unfathomable and the hope was feverish. I could not resist them. I did not want to put anxiety and disappointment in them. So I left. I left one day before the examination began.

On that day, snow was falling heavily all the way from Beijing to Shijiazhuang. Everywhere I looked, it was white. The sky, the fields, the villages, the roads . . . It was a bad omen, as if the whole world was in mourning. I had a very sick feeling in my heart. I should have trusted my instinct and turned back, because it did not cheat me. After I left, Aunty's illness took a sharp turn for the worse. A few days later, she died.

Then it turned out that I did well in the entrance examination. But I decided that I would not go to college. Father was very upset when he heard about this. He took an overnight train to Shijiazhuang to "bring me to reason."

"You know if you go to college, you will become a cadre after you graduate. Your future is guaranteed! The government will assign you a job, which is going to be much better than the one you have now. In the past, I thought you really wanted to go to college. You were deprived of the opportunity because of the Cultural Revolution. Now I hear from Li, my old friend, who was in charge of college enrollment in this province, that according to your score, you can go to any university in Hebei, even some in Beijing. But you say you are not interested in going to any. Why? Do you know there are many young people who'd do anything to be in your shoes?"

Of course, I knew that. Many of my fellow workers took the same examination and failed. So at first they envied me. Then some of them told me I was a fool. These were my friends who thought I was making a big mistake. Behind my back others said I was weird. They did not like me and I knew it. But I did not care.

After Aunty and Mother died, many things that would have mattered in the past did not matter to me anymore, including success or failure in the eyes of others. The world was a desert. I was a grain of sand, drifting along. The ones who would be proud or ashamed of me were all gone. So why should I bother to go to a university and study what I had already learned? Four more years of my life wasted, in exchange for a college diploma—for a piece of paper. It did not make sense to me.

So I did not go to college. Instead I returned to Beijing and lived in Aunty's house. I lived there alone. Lian and Yue had both moved out after Aunty died. Yet I was not alone. The house was filled with Aunty's memory. Her spirit was with me all the time.

On the wall hung an old coat. Aunty bought it after she came back from Switzerland. She had been wearing it every winter since then. Twenty-two years. The blue cotton cloth on the outside was almost black; grease shone on the sleeves; the fur on the inside was worn off along the edges. I hugged it to me, and the familiar smell of Aunty brought tears into my eyes. Once upon a time, I had stolen money from these pockets and expected she would say I was a bad girl, as my parents had done. But she continued to love me and trust me. By so doing, she saved me and I would be indebted to her ever after.

In a drawer, among rusty needles and tangled threads, I found a silver thimble that had been part of Aunty's dowry. It was shaped like a big ring, and she wore it around her middle finger when she sewed. More than fifty years. Millions of stitches. The needles had poked some of the holes into horizontal slots. It was a witness, telling me how in widowhood she had struggled to support herself and bring up her two children. After she lost both of them, she gave her love to us, especially to me. But in 1968, I went away too.

After that, for nearly ten years Aunty had waited for me to return to this house. When I thought of how happy we would have been to live once again under the same roof, tears streamed down my face. Aunty was weeping with me. I could hear her cry in the wind. Lured by such a dream, I left her in the hospital and went to Shijiazhuang to take the exam. Henceforth endless remorse would gnaw my heart, as it did Aunty's in the olden days.

In the fifties, Aunty's desire to help her son took her, an illiterate old woman who had never left Beijing, to Switzerland. In five years she made the money, but her son had died. When she was back in this house, she must have felt the same emptiness I did. Why were the efforts we made always futile? As a matter of fact, they were worse than futile. In her case, they deprived her of the chance to be with her son in his last years and in mine the opportunity to pull Aunty through or at least to be with her when she left the world.

Fate! That was her fate; this was mine! Fate was cruel. It played vicious jokes on us. Sweet dreams. Bitter ironies. The harder we struggled, the more remorse we reaped. Yet throughout Aunty's life, she had never given up hope. Nor did she ever stop loving and caring about people.

"Rae! Go! Go! Don't you worry about me! I won't die! I have not brought up your children for you yet. I can't die before that! But now I want you to go and take that exam. Come back to Beijing as a college student! . . . "

Even when she was dying, she was still hoping, for me, for herself, and for the children she was destined not to see.

Thinking of Aunty, I knew somehow I had to go on. She brought me up. I was her own daughter. I would continue to hope and strive, even though now I knew that hopes often led to broken hearts. By and by, I began to think about going to graduate school. The next year I took the entrance examination. I was accepted by the graduate school of the Chinese Academy of Social Sciences. This time, I did not need to use any *guanxi* or go through a back door. The competition was fair indeed.

In the next two years, I majored in journalism. Our department was situated in the big yard of the *People's Daily,* number-one official newspaper in China. Our teachers, however, were Americans and Canadians, something unthinkable only a couple of years before. Through them, information about the outside world trickled in. I became very curious. Yet I would not have left China in 1981, had Deng Xiaoping not shut down Democracy Wall in Beijing, arrested Wei Jingsheng and other political dissidents, and banned private publications, including a magazine named *Today* where Lian and his friends published their poems. (Lian continued to write poetry and has been a poet ever since.)

Earlier, I had hoped to become an investigative reporter and poke through some lies, especially those told by the Party and government, which in the past had drowned out different voices and led us to make terrible mistakes. When the political climate changed for the worse in 1980, however, it dawned on me that as a reporter in the future I would not be able to remain silent as others might. My choice would be either to lie for the Party or to tell the truth and pay a high price for it.

To tell the truth and pay a high price? Humph! Zhang Zhixin, whose story became known in 1979, did that and so she was imprisoned, divorced, raped, and had her vocal cords cut before she was executed in public. Yet who would have heard her challenge of the Cultural Revolution if some leaders had not decided to publicize her story? I do not want to pay such a high price. Nor do I want to wait any longer. The Cultural Revolution has cost me twelve years. I am not young anymore. Who knows how many more years I'll have to wait until there is freedom of press in China. I'd better get on with my own life.

I still loved China. Yet I had long since stopped dreaming that I was a hero who could lead the Chinese people to freedom and liberation. I knew that I had neither great vision nor extraordinary courage. I was just an ordinary woman. I liked to read good books. I wanted to see the world with my own eyes. "Read ten thousand books. Travel ten thousand miles." In the spring of 1981, suddenly this seemed possible, for the lucky ones among us, at least. A friend of mine had just departed for England. My classmates were talking about graduate schools in the United States. A few had sent out applications.

I did not think I deserved such good luck. Yet each night when I woke up at three o'clock and lay in the dark, I saw the idea hanging on the horizon like a dream, beyond an ever so slightly lifted bamboo curtain. Contemplating it, I became wide awake. I felt my energy surge up and my heartbeat quicken.

The opportunity, vague as it is now, might dissipate like the morning mist and before you realize it, the gate of the country is closed once again. I have to do something before it is too late! Just give it a try. If heaven says my fate is to stay, I will not be heartbroken. "The planning lies with people, and heaven will decide the outcome." In the past, Father used to quote this saying to cool Mother down, while the latter was going all out to help me. I didn't like to hear it then. Now it makes sense to me.

Thus thinking, I biked to Beijing Library where I found a few brochures. I selected three universities, for three was a lucky number: University of Massachusetts on the East Coast for comparative literature, University of California at Los Angeles on the West Coast for English literature, and a university in Kansas for sociology. Despite the fact that I knew next to nothing about these universities, I sent out my applications. In the meantime, I was not entertaining much hope, since I had neither money nor connections outside of China.

Then just as I had anticipated, I received a letter from Kansas a few weeks later, saying they could not give me any financial support. Too bad. That shipwrecked my dream of becoming a sociologist in the middle of the United States. Later that month in the reading room of our journalist department, which had dozens of Chinese and foreign magazines, I ran across an article in *Newsweek* or *Time*. The article reported that a serial killer was at large in Los Angeles and his victims were all women of my age. That was a shocker. The news reminded me of what the Chinese media had been telling us over the years: America was a place filled with violence, crimes, lunatics, and moral degradation. I wondered if some of this propaganda might be true after all. "Better keep out of harm's way. For don't people say that one can't buy remedy for regret?" I decided that I was not going to California either.

This decision left me without an option. To make things worse, soon some leaders began to worry about a brain drain in China and that caused the policy on Chinese students studying abroad to change almost overnight. As a result, the graduate school I attended refused to give me transcripts or anything to help my application. Without these and the scores of graduate entrance exams such as the TOEFL and GRE, for such tests were not yet available in China, all I had in the end were two recommendation letters from my teachers and a paper I wrote on *Jane Eyre*.

Of course no graduate school in America or anywhere in the world would accept me with such an application, even less give me financial support. Yet since I had gone this far and dreamed so much about the idea, I was not going to quit without a last-ditch struggle. So I sat down and wrote a long letter to the school in Massachusetts, recounting my experiences in the Cultural Revolution and hoping my words would explain why I had longed so much for an opportunity to study abroad.

Heaven was merciful after all. The letter fell into the hands of a few very warmhearted professors, who in their turn brought it to the attention of an extremely supportive dean. Before long I heard the good news: I was accepted by the University of Massachusetts as a graduate student in comparative literature, and the dean had created a teaching assistantship in the East Asian Studies department so that I could work to support myself.

This was like a dream come true. When I heard of what happened at UMass, I was moved. But the dream was still a mountain away from being materialized. I knew if in two months I could not get permission from various officials and obtain a passport, my dream of studying in America would vanish like so many soap bubbles. Moreover, I was aware that under the present circumstances, it would be extremely difficult to get approval from the officials. In order to do so, I definitely had to use *guanxi,* knock on back doors, put on a smiling face, beg people to intercede for me up and down and all around . . . I loathed such acts! Yet in the summer of 1981, these acts filled my life. Day and night I biked all over Beijing like an ant in a hot wok. Two male students in my department were doing the same. We traded information and felt some sort of comradeship growing among us.

By early September I finally got what I wanted. The applications of the other two, however, fell through. Then, of course, they were very angry at the officials. They were angry at me too. They accused me of backdoor dealings. What could I say to defend myself? I was indeed guilty of such a charge. Nevertheless, the hint that perhaps I liked backdoor dealings made me feel funny. In my case, I thought, if the situation were normal and the policy reasonable, I would not need to degrade myself by going through back doors. My request (like theirs) was entirely legitimate. The trouble was, after the Cultural Revolution although some front doors opened, more often than not, without *guanxi,* legitimate requests ran up against stone walls.

Thus I knew that as long as I was in China, I could not quit backdoor dealings. In each case, somehow I had to do it. For instance, when Second Uncle came back from the salt farm, he had no work unit. He asked me if I could help him get into a research institute that wanted him. There was a problem: its quota of new employees for the year had been filled. I could help him. I knew it. And I felt that he deserved a decent work unit, after what he had gone through in the past twenty-two years. He was my uncle after all. Nainai had said I would help him. She was right and I did so. Yet my conscience bothered me.

Does the end really justify the means? I wonder if such questions troubled Mother in the past when she tried to help me. Throughout her life, she believed in the Party and its doctrines. At the same time, she loved her daughter. She knew if she did not help me out, nobody would. I would be stuck in the Great Northern Wilderness. Something might happen to me . . . Yet perhaps she was uncomfortable about what she did. So in those days she only talked to me about strategies and tactics. She never let me know if she had a moral dilemma.

Now as I was leaving the country, I could quit backdoor dealings at last. I was relieved, for I feared if I went on like this, someday I would get addicted to the practice and lose my sense of right and wrong all together. I was glad that henceforth I would be competing with others fair and square. If I won, I would feel happy rather than guilty. If I lost, I would double my effort. No complaints. I knew that in the United States competitions were very tough and there was no iron rice bowl. Moreover this time I would be alone, and not as I had been thirty years ago when I left China in Aunty's arms with Father by my side.

When I boarded the airplane that would take me across the ocean to the new world, I had only fifty dollars in my pocket (and even that was borrowed money). Yet I knew I was not poor. For I had a heritage. I was carrying it with me. It consisted of Aunty's *zhiqi*, Nainai's wisdom eye, Mother's energy and ingenuity, Father's broad-mindedness, the education I received from the peasants . . . These were the materials that over the years made up the core of me. In the future they would endure while other aspects of me changed with the outside world. Through wind and rain, from graduate studies to college teaching, no matter where I went and what I did, as long as I was in touch with this core, I knew who I was and what I wanted. I might be lonely. Or feel frustrated. But I was not lost.

As for the memory of the Cultural Revolution, the dreams and nightmares, I carry them too. I don't think I will ever forget them as long as I live. I don't think I should forget them either, despite the pain and shame they constantly cause me. Using Lu Xun's metaphor, I and my peers are the ones who ate spiders. Long before we did, my parents and their peers had eaten spiders too. The spiders tasted bad. They were poisonous. Nevertheless, in my case, they became a bitter medicine. The

Chinese say, "Bitter medicine cures illnesses." The spiders I ate made my head cooler and my eyes brighter. Because of them, I cherish freedom and value human dignity. I have become more tolerant of different opinions. Lies, big and small, cannot easily hypnotize me. And I believe as a human being, Chinese or American, I have responsibilities beyond ones to make a living for my son and myself. Part of these is to make the lessons we learned with such tremendous sacrifice known and remembered by people in the world, including the younger generations in China.

Compositor:	Integrated Composition Systems
Text:	10/13 Sabon
Display:	Sabon
Printer:	BookCrafters
Binder:	BookCrafters